National Institute of
Economic and Social Research
Economic Policy Papers I

DEMAND MANAGEMENT

National Institute of
Economic and Social Research
Conferences on Economic Policy

STEERING COMMITTEE

National Institute of
Economic and Social Research
Economic Policy Papers 1

DEMAND MANAGEMENT

Edited by
MICHAEL POSNER

HEB
Heinemann Educational Books · London

Heinemann Educational Books Ltd

LONDON EDINBURGH MELBOURNE AUCKLAND TORONTO
HONG KONG SINGAPORE KUALA LUMPUR NEW DEHLI
NAIROBI JOHANNESBURG LUSAKA IBADAN
KINGSTON

Hardback ISBN 0 435 84600 0
Paperback ISBN 0 435 84601 9

First published 1978

Published by Heinemann Educational Books Ltd
48 Charles Street, London W1X 8AH
Printed by Richard Clay (The Chaucer Press) Ltd
Bungay, Suffolk

Foreword

This volume presents the papers – together with a report of the discussion – given at the first of a new series of conferences on Economic Policy. The format was inspired by the Brookings Panel Conferences in the United States, and the papers on Economic Activity in which their proceedings are published. The proposed series of conferences will take as their subjects the important economic policy issues of the next decade: the second topic will be 'De-industrialisation'. They will be working conferences, limited to 25–35 people, and all the papers, including those of discussants, will be on the table before the conference begins. In this way the conference time can be devoted to an intensive interchange of views. The papers, with a report of the proceedings, will be published quickly.

The choice of subjects, contributors and participants is guided by a Standing Advisory Panel. We hope to ensure that all important views on the various subjects receive expression. We shall seek agreement, and where that fails, fair statement of disagreement. In this way we hope to increase the contribution of economists and other social scientists to the national welfare.

If it is to succeed, this programme needs resources, and our first thanks are to the Nuffield Foundation for the generous grant which has enabled us to launch the series. My colleague Frank Blackaby is in general charge of the series. For the opening conference, Michael Posner of Cambridge University agreed to take full responsibility for deciding the rules of the game, and for editing the papers and proceedings; we are most grateful to him and also to Robin Matthews, who as Chairman was able to steer the discussion so admirably because he had done a great deal of preparatory work. We are also very grateful to the authors of the papers – and particularly to the authors of the first round of papers; the cost of those papers, in both human and computing time, far exceeded the amount we were able to pay. We were fortunate in being able to hold the first conference in Birkbeck College.

G. D. N. Worswick
London, January 1978

Contents

Foreword by *G. D. N. Worswick* v
Notes on Contributors x
Introduction by *M. V. Posner* 1

PART I Demand Management in Britain 1964–81 7

1 Simulations with the Cambridge Economic Policy Group Model by *T. F. Cripps, M. J. Fetherston and W. A. H. Godley* 9

Introduction 9
Policy Assessment of the Three Episodes 9
Policy Simulations 15
Notes on Tables of Results 33

2 A Monetarist Viewpoint by *David Laidler* 35

Introduction 35
Monetarist Analysis of an Open Economy 37
A Model of the United Kingdom, 1954–70 44
The Policy Problems of 1964, 1970 and 1977 51
Appendix: Data 1952–77 65

3 Stabilisation Policy in Britain 1964–81 by *R. J. Ball and T. Burns* 66

Introduction 66
Simulation Analysis 67
Policy Simulation of the Three Episodes 73
Analysis of Recommended Policies 84
Conclusion 97

4 Demand Management in Britain 1964–81 by *M. J. C. Surrey and P. A. Ormerod* 101

Introduction 101
The National Institute Model 102

Episode 1: September 1964–September 1969 104
Episode 2: July 1970–July 1975 111
Episode 3: Early 1977–December 1981 118
Conclusions 124

PART II Assessment of the Model Builders 127

5 The Main Issues by *M. V. Posner* 129
Episode 1 129
Episode 2 132
Episode 3 135

6 A Statistician's View by *A. J. Boreham* 139
Introduction 139
Episode 1: 1964 140
Differences between 1964 at the Time and with Hindsight 142
Episode 2: 1970 145
Differences between 1970 at the Time and with Hindsight 147

7 Comparisons of the Four Econometric Models by *M. H. Peston* 151
Introduction 151
Size of the Models 151
Limitations of the Models 154
Theory behind the Models 155
Prices, Wages and Money 159
Conclusion 165

8 Fiscal Policy and Crowding Out by *M. J. Artis* 167
Introduction 167
Fiscal Stance in the Policy Simulations 167
Effectiveness of Fiscal Policy 173
The Assignment Rule 173
Crowding Out 174

9 Monetary Policy by *C. A. E. Goodhart* 180
Introduction 180
Model Structure and the Role of Money 180

The Transmission Mechanism 182
External Effects 183
Policy Proposals 185
Monetary Operations 188

10 Counter-Inflationary Policies by *Ralph Turvey* 191
Introduction 191
The Wage–Price Spiral 191
Collective Agreements 194
Social Justice and Relativities 195
Implications for Policy 196

11 The Balance of Payments by *John Williamson* 200
Introduction 200
Balance of Payments Constraint 200
Devaluation or Import Controls 204
The Level of Competitiveness 204

PART III Report of the Discussion 209

12 The Search for Common Ground by *M. V. Posner* 211
Introduction 211
The Underlying Economic Issues 213
The Historical Episodes 226

List of Participants 236
Index 237

Notes on Contributors

M. J. Artis is Professor of Economics at the University of Manchester

R. J. Ball is Director of the London Business School

A. J. Boreham is Deputy Director, Central Statistical Office

T. Burns is a Senior Lecturer at the London Business School

T. F. Cripps is a Senior Research Officer at the Department of Applied Economics, University of Cambridge

M. J. Fetherston is a Research Officer at the Department of Applied Economics, University of Cambridge

W. A. H. Godley is Director of the Department of Applied Economics, University of Cambridge

C. A. E. Goodhart is on the staff of the Bank of England

David Laidler is Professor of Economics at the University of Western Ontario

P. A. Ormerod is a Research Officer at the National Institute of Economic and Social Research

M. H. Peston is Professor of Economics at Queen Mary College, University of London

M. J. C. Surrey is a Senior Research Officer at the National Institute of Economic and Social Research and Editor of the *National Institute Economic Review*

R. Turvey is Economic Adviser to the International Labour Office, Geneva

J. Williamson is Professor of Economics at the University of Warwick

Editor:

M. V. Posner is a Fellow at Pembroke College, a Reader in Economics in the University of Cambridge

Introduction

by M. V. Posner

This book reports the results of a conference held in December 1977, the object of which was to provide the best informed views on a major policy issue, that of demand management. Exponents of the main schools: the Cambridge Economic Policy Group, the London Business School, the National Institute of Economic and Social Research and Professor Laidler (representing a version of the 'monetarist' position) were invited to develop their ideas in terms of what policies they would adopt in certain real economic situations. Part I contains the papers of these 'first-round' authors. A second-round of authors were then invited to assess the models and policy measures outlined under various instrument headings in an attempt to find common ground. Their papers are grouped in Part II. A report of the discussion, rearranged to emphasise the main analytical and policy strands of thought, is contained in Part III.

Readers may find it useful to look first at this introduction, at Chapter 5 on the main issues and then at the report of the discussion in Part III before studying the papers in Part I. The report of the discussion may help to give the flavour of some of the points at issue. The wide range of papers in Part II can be used to elucidate particular problems.

'Rules of the Game'

The authors in Part I were asked to address themselves to three episodes. Episode 1 started in September 1964; episode 2 in July 1970 and episode 3 in the course of 1977. In each episode the authors were invited to look forward for a period of about five years, implying that episode 1 would end in September 1969, episode 2 would end in the mid-summer of 1975 and the final episode, referring to 'the present', would run to the end of 1981.

The data base on which the simulations are performed is essentially that of the 1976 Blue Book, and generally the official series available by the end of 1976. Participants made available to each other, and to those second-round authors who seemed chiefly concerned, print-outs of any data used which diverged from those generally available.

Each author was free either to use his existing model without alteration, or to amend the behavioural equations to reflect the ways in which the economy in the past behaved differently from 'today'. This has raised deep and complicated questions about residuals, which are discussed in all the papers.

An initial problem arises from the apparent need for the 'de-policisation of the past'. The National Institute provided all authors with a check list of the major government policies introduced over the whole period from 1964 to the present day, and participants were asked either implicitly to accept these policies or to substitute some alternative (including of course inaction). The London Business School paper makes the most explicit attempt to carry out this task, which is in fact formidable. But all the papers implicitly tackle it in one way or another, and readers should be reminded that there is no unambiguous way to do the job: it requires a theory, and a model, to remove from the historical record of the past the effect of any given policy measure. Indeed, it might have been possible, although rather arid, to build a whole conference around the alternative methods available for 'de-policisation'.

Within each of the three five-year periods, authors were free to vary policy as many times as was necessary. But we envisaged that even those who leaned most favourably towards 'fine tuning' would prefer to concentrate on setting their policy instruments in the first two years, filling in subsequent years rather more roughly. Different authors have taken different stands on this matter, but as far as I can see all of them are consistent with the Rules of the Game that we laid down.

I made it clear to all first-round authors that the conference and most readers would attach as much importance to the prose as to the tables, but that nevertheless there was a certain minimum set of quantitative answers which could reasonably be expected. I did, however, negotiate a rather looser version of this minimum set with David Laidler, on the grounds that he was not a 'model proprietor' in the same sense as the other authors.

One minor difficulty about episode 3 is that the papers in Part I were composed on the basis of provisional data for only the first quarter of 1977. The figures for 'year 1977' therefore are substantially forecasts rather than facts. That is an unavoidable consequence of playing the forecasting game, a point we ask readers to bear in mind.

Three Caveats

On these ground rules, there are three important ways in which our results might be misread in a way unfair to our authors and unfair to successive ministers who were in charge of economic policy over the last fifteen years.

First, there is the question of the 'political practicality' of the policy recommendations which participants have put forward. No general precise guidance has been offered to authors on this point. But we all agreed implicitly that we needed to weigh carefully the political practicality as well as the economic plausibility of the recommendations and calculated outcomes. This is a matter taken up explicitly in the National Institute's comments on the timing of a suggested 1964 devaluation. For instance, I myself believe that as a matter of fact there is no way in which Mr Heath's government could have attempted to use an incomes policy to control the wages explosion in 1970 unless he had abandoned the Industrial Relations Bill, which was a central point of the Conservative election manifesto of 1970. This sort of issue poses severe problems for economic historians concerned to examine counter-factual hypotheses. But with some exceptions, I hope that the policy recommendations made throughout these papers could have been carried out by (admittedly unusually wise and powerful) Chancellors of either main political party.

The second caveat concerns the problem of hindsight. The background against which the first-round authors have composed their simulations is the established economic history of the last fifteen years. Neither the 'authorities' nor any economic commentator could have forecast the timing of the breakup of the Bretton Woods system, the timing and extent of the collapse of money illusion, the simultaneity of the 1973 boom and the OPEC price rise, and the disarray of OECD governments in face of the OPEC surplus. To an extent, therefore, we are playing the role of gods, and cannot abuse our temporary dwelling in Olympus by presuming to criticise the mere mortals who held the responsibility of government during these years. This book is *not* to be read as a series of essays on how clever we would have been if left to run the country without political interference over the last fifteen years. Rather it is a collective attempt by economists to discover whether a set of even half-way plausible policies could have been adopted which would have made the past a little better. Of course, those amongst us with a public record of recommendations during the period may be able to say 'I told you so' where they find their recommendations to have stood the test of time, outside events, and sophisticated analysis; but we all must be wary of seeming to suggest that because we were right once or twice it follows that we have been right throughout.

Finally, a remark about uncertainty. In endowing our authors with foresight, we have also inevitably removed from their minds the systematic uncertainty about events, and about the extent to which the path of the economy will correspond to the forecasts produced by their models. Episodes 1 and 2 of history are incurably marred by this property of our method, but the full horrors of uncertainty still characterise completely episode 3. Those readers who wish to preserve something like the full flavour of economic policy making as it really is will relish the discussion of episode 3 more than the discussion of the first two episodes.

The Second-Round Papers

The four first-round papers were all finished in the late summer of 1977, and made available in one form or another to the authors in Part II in August. In turn, the authors in Part II completed their papers by late October or early November, with the exception of my own paper which I deliberately held up until I had seen all save one of the others. Some overlap has occurred, but it is for the most part slight, as there was an explicit division of labour agreed between us early in the exercise. Thus second-round authors are not to be criticised for failing to comment upon or argue about issues which lie outside their own sphere of responsibility. Essentially, their task was divided by policy instruments (fiscal, monetary, exchange rate, and so on), with some general papers on model comparison (Peston), the difference between historical statistics and those available at the time policy was made (Boreham), and a general round-up paper by myself.

Conduct of the Conference

Frank Blackaby, to whom credit for conceiving this form of conference is due, introduced a sub-title – 'Demand management: the search for common ground'. This was the spirit in which we approached the conference. The papers in Part I have a degree of predictability about policy recommendations, and about the beauteous forecasts built on those prescriptions. Only from David Laidler do we have thoroughly unexpected features, and that is no doubt partly due to the fact that he is a new member of Computa Nostra – without all those soldiers with whom the other Mafia Dons are equipped, and without the embarrassment of past forecasting experience or a past record to defend.

My slight disappointment about the predictability is tempered by my recollection that the convergence of policy recommendations is only one, and possibly the most superficial of the ways in which common ground might be found. The other technical levels at which convergence is likely are those of the specification of behavioural equations in the models, and of model construction and analysis. In a naive way, of which I am myself guilty, many outsiders feel that it should be possible to specify equations in which the right-hand side contains terms that will capture all the effects which any of our participants wishes to suggest are important. Provided that estimation methods can be agreed, this would give everyone's 'theory' a fair run, and provide a common model against which to judge policy prescriptions.

The naïvety of this approach arises partly, no doubt, from its ignorance of econometric problems of estimation and specification; but it also stems I think from the much simpler point that many (far too many!) of the parameters in most of the models in front of us are imposed rather than estimated. This is a matter which was discussed at the conference and is reported in Part III. The main way in which common ground may be sought, it seems to me, is not in technical questions of model construction but in detailed discussion and interpretation of the historical events and policy recommendations pertaining to the episodes we are analysing. Even Keynesians like myself should not wish to deny the important influence of monetary events in 1972–4, and the discussion of the 'transmission mechanism' in that period should also bring an element of desirable concreteness into the analysis of the monetarists. Similarly, the effect of incomes policy on damping inflationary expectations in the period 1975–8 may not be quantifiable, but is surely something which we need to consider, whatever our theoretical preconceptions, in our analysis of the course of events in the next two or three years. I believe that economists have done their profession and the country somewhat of a disservice in recent years by stressing their differences and, while I do not want to turn out a completely bland dish for our readers, I do not see why some of the more indigestible vegetables should not be chopped up and combined in the way they presumably used in Macedonia.

PART I

Demand Management in Britain 1964–81

1 Simulations with the Cambridge Economic Policy Group Model

by T. F. Cripps, M. J. Fetherston and W. A. H. Godley*

Introduction

This paper is in two parts: the first is concerned with a general analysis of economic policy during the periods covered by the simulations, and with how past policy could have been improved. The second part describes in detail the methods used to generate simulations of alternative policies for each period, and discusses the results so obtained.

Policy Assessment of the Three Episodes

The Cambridge Economic Policy Group (CEPG) at the Department of Applied Economics has now carried out six annual assessments of economic policy in the medium term, as part of a project financed by the Social Science Research Council. Each of these assessments has contained analysis and criticism of recent economic policy, as well as projections of developments over several years. In the course of these assessments, and in other publications, CEPG has often been critical of the past conduct of policy and have proposed principles according to which economic policy should be conducted in future, and by implication should have been conducted in the past.

These criticisms have developed as part of the process of building a model to consider medium-term problems of resource availability and use, and in particular as a result of the need to consider explicitly the macroeconomic conditions – for example productive potential and trade performance – necessary for satisfactory economic performance

* The authors wish to acknowledge the benefit of numerous discussions with K. J. Coutts.

in the medium term. The principal features of these criticisms have consistently been that conventional *short*-term economic management, with a time horizon of no more (and often rather less) than eighteen months, is an inappropriate basis for policy, and that a key factor in medium-term performance must be the contribution of net exports of goods and services to the growth of demand and output, and of course to the balance of payments. The most recent statement of CEPG views on principles of economic management is contained in [1], pp. 5–6.

The main sections of this paper comprise, in accordance with the 'rules of the game', simulations which embody the results of what appear as the best macroeconomic strategies during various episodes. This introductory section compares these policies and their outcomes with what actually happened and draws inferences about the main mistakes which seem to have been made.

Episode 1: September 1964–September 1969

In 1964 the fiscal stance was too slack, the pressure of demand being very high with the balance of payments moving into substantial deficit. The fact that 1962 and 1963 had been relatively good years for the current balance may have encouraged policy-makers to believe that the weak balance of payments of 1964 was *solely* the result of over-rapid expansion of domestic demand, and that there was no necessary incompatibility between the current level of export competitiveness and the future achievement of internal and external balance. Although in 1964 a tighter fiscal stance would probably have achieved external balance without unacceptably high unemployment, the major strategic error was the failure to implement at that time the devaluation which, with hindsight, was inevitable.

It is now clear that devaluation improves trade performance only with long lags – to be measured in years rather than months – and also that there have been persistent adverse trends in British producers' share of world and home markets. So simultaneous achievement of external and internal balance in the second half of the 1960s required that action should be taken well in advance.

The best way of achieving a satisfactory growth rate in this period whilst preventing further decline in trade performance would therefore have been to devalue in September 1964 (that is as soon as possible under the 'rules') and then maintain the resulting improvement in competitiveness by further small devaluations as and when necessary. Incomes policy, although it is not satisfactory as a permanent instrument for controlling inflation, should also have been introduced on a temporary basis in September 1964 in order to prevent the benefits of devaluation from being eroded by subsequent wage inflation. A fairly tight but temporary incomes policy could, in the circumstances of 1964–5 when the catalogue of past economic failure was not so long, probably have been used to depress wage settlements and thus provide time for devaluation to generate improved exports and faster growth. An early incomes policy, progressively and quite speedily relaxed during a period of reasonable growth of real earnings, should have made it possible to avoid the build-up of inflationary pressure which brought about the wage explosion of 1970–1.

If a devaluation strategy had been adopted immediately, then the actual fiscal stance of the years 1965 and 1966 would have been about right overall: of course with devaluation in late 1964 faster growth would have occurred during this period. In 1967, however, the actual fiscal stance was probably too lax, mainly due to a sharp rise in public expenditure, despite the famous cuts in July 1966. There were, however, reductions in public expenditure in the years after the devaluation in November 1967. A strategy of early devaluation would have provided conditions for more stable growth and should have been accompanied by a steady expansion of public expenditure, and thus also of the burden of taxation, avoiding any need for severe restraint in the 1968–9 period.

On this strategy the cumulative current balance over the years 1965–9 could have been about £1 billion better, total output and consumption could have been 5 per cent higher at the end of the period, and unemployment well under half a million. The simulation shows inflation a little higher than actually occurred *within this period*, but without any stored-up inflationary tension which in the event produced a wage explosion in 1970–1.

Episode 2: July 1970–July 1975

The incoming Conservative government in mid-1970 inherited a fiscal stance which was unnecessarily tight: GDP was growing at less than the rate of growth of productive potential and the balance of payments was moving rapidly into substantial surplus. On a full-employment basis, however, the balance of payments would have looked much less healthy. The Government did nothing to maintain the improvement in competitiveness in home and world markets which had been brought about by the 1967 devaluation. Instead it presided over the complete erosion of this improvement by mid-1972, due to accelerating wage inflation combined with an absurdly high exchange rate for sterling negotiated in the Smithsonian agreement of December 1971. The rather weak fiscal expansion undertaken from 1970–2 did not stop the rise in unemployment. In mid-1972 the exchange rate was allowed to fall and float; the Government adopted fiscal and monetary policies of unprecedented laxity in the hope that with a floating pound fast growth need no longer be sacrificed to the balance of payments. But earlier policies had aggravated Britain's weak competitive position so that rapid consumption-led expansion of demand generated massive increases in imports of manufactured goods. As stated earlier, devaluation takes time to work, and indeed its initial effects on the trade balance may be perverse. Satisfactory trade performance is in no way guaranteed by a floating exchange rate, especially if combined with fast growth of domestic demand.

Even if the oil crisis had never occurred it seems unlikely that devaluation would have been adequate as the sole instrument of trade policy during this period, given the very large deterioration in our trade performance which had by then taken place. By the early 1970s the trends in trade performance – particularly the propensity to import – had become so adverse that repeated effective devaluations would probably have been necessary to sustain internal and external balance, and these would most probably have generated unacceptably high rates of inflation. In 1970–1 money wages rose sharply as trade unions (particularly in the public sector) bargained to regain ground lost during previous years of tight restraint; any substantial effective devaluation in this period would have squeezed real wages and generated still higher wage inflation. After 1972 the commodity boom and the oil crisis made the trading position worse and intensified inflationary pressure. With hindsight it is clear that devaluation would have been an entirely inappropriate and inadequate instrument for coping with the adverse effects of these developments. If undertaken early enough and on a sufficient scale to sustain a high level of employment through to 1975, most probably it would have had unacceptable implications for inflation and for real wages. This would have been the case even in the absence of the threshold scheme which increased inflation in 1974–5 and the introduction of which was the other principal error of policy in this period.

Accordingly the Government should have followed a 'neutral' policy on competitiveness by depreciating sterling to an extent sufficient to prevent any erosion of the 1969 level of competitiveness, together with rather more positive fiscal expansion in the first two years of the period. But the partial abandonment of control over the financial system following the inception of Competition and Credit Control in 1971, which created unstable conditions in asset markets in 1972–3, should not have occurred. Fiscal policy should not have been relaxed suddenly in 1972. Instead, from 1973 onwards the Government should have introduced restrictions on imports of manufactures to soften the impact of the commodity boom and subsequent world recession – a consequence of the failure of other countries to introduce expansionary fiscal policies. In this way Britain could have avoided the worst effects of terms of trade deterioration and world recession on domestic income and employment. Although a sharp rise in the inflation rate was unavoidable in 1974–5 because of the great increase in import prices, in the absence of the threshold scheme this would probably have been far less serious than what actually happened, even without tight formal controls over pay and prices. Despite the stimulus to demand provided by import restrictions, it seems likely that the increase in the inflation rate in 1974–5 would still have required a substantial rise in the public sector financial deficit, not so much to generate expansion of domestic demand as to offset the deflationary effects of the rise in the private sector's financial surplus associated with the faster inflation rate. Provided growth and full employment had been maintained through 1974 and 1975, the rate of inflation should not have reached such a high peak as actually occurred and should have fallen off quite quickly in 1975.

The performance of the economy in the simulation for this period, by all of the main criteria, is enormously superior to what actually happened. The growth of output is sustained at just over 3 per cent (ending up in 1975 about 9 per cent higher than was actually achieved), unemployment is brought below half a million after 1972, and the current balance, though by design in deficit to the extent of about £1½ billion on average in 1974 and 1975, is about £4 billion better over the period as a whole. Inflation in 1975 is 8 per cent better than actually occurred.

Episode 3: Early 1977 – December 1981

A detailed assessment of alternative strategies for the period from now into the 1980s was recently published by CEPG [1]. It is argued there that 'the fashion for fiscal and monetary restriction, including cuts in public expenditure, taken up by governments of other industrial countries, the IMF and most commentators has been the cause of continuing world recession.... The Government should now prepare to reflate the economy and restrict imports as soon as they start to rise too fast. On this basis it should immediately reduce income tax and taxes on consumption by £2 billion or more.' Instead the Government is committed to a restrictive fiscal stance under the terms of the IMF Letter of Intent which imposes unconditional targets for the public sector borrowing requirement. Perversely therefore, any failure of the world economy to expand as expected will require further cuts in public expenditure or increases in tax rates to offset the lower-than-expected level of tax revenues.

The CEPG Review considered three strategies – conventional policies, devaluation, and restriction of imports. 'Conventional policies' were defined as maintaining constant competitiveness by varying the exchange rate, whilst using fiscal policy to meet year-by-year targets for the basic balance of payments. This strategy implies a continuation of industrial stagnation with unemployment rising to over one and a half million in 1981 and inflation continuing in double figures. A strategy of devaluation to generate a satisfactory growth of GDP and employment up to 1981 would, because of the length of time lags involved, require immediate devaluation on a scale which seems unfeasible if only because of the large further compression of real wages which would be required. Only our preferred strategy of import restriction produces sufficiently rapid growth with no initial compression of real wages.

The indications are that the strategy actually being pursued is even more conservative since it involves continuation of restrictive fiscal policies with the nominal exchange rate over the next two or three years being held constant or even allowed to rise. Discussion of the implications of this strategy was an unfortunate omission from the Review, although it has since been analysed by Godley[5]. In the short run it is likely to produce some superficially attractive results – moderation in the rate of inflation and rapid improvement in the current balance of payments as continuing domestic recession coincides with the build-up of North Sea oil production. Yet all the while the competitive position of British industry is being allowed to deteriorate further, and unemployment will continue to rise, probably to over two million by 1981. Looking further ahead, the prospect is even more dismal: 'While the prospect of a decade's industrial decay together with steadily rising unemployment is in itself an unacceptable one, if, as we should at present assume, income from the North Sea then declines it is the prospects for the *succeeding* period which are more truly alarming. For we could then find ourselves deprived simultaneously of our (so to speak) unearned income and also of our earning power; the blood transfusion would be cut off while the haemorrhage was still increasing.' (Godley, [5])

Policy Simulations

Simulation of the Past

The methodology of simulations of different policies for the future is relatively straightforward and CEPG's own approach has been described in the Economic Policy Review. The following paragraphs discuss the construction of simulations for the past.

Treatment of residuals. Although participants have been afforded complete freedom to amend main behavioural equations to reflect different past behaviour, we have chosen to rely on the current explicit version of our model and have therefore decided in principle against amendment of past residuals. The only exceptions to this rule are made in the case of certain 'semi-endogenous' policy variables. These variables represent policy instruments which are normally, in part at least, responsive, and where the exogenous policy element is incorporated in the residual of an equation for the variable in question. Different assumptions about policies in force have thus been represented partly by changes in values of fully exogenous instruments and partly via amendment of residuals of semi-endogenous instruments. The only adjustments of the latter type are those made to reflect the effect of incomes policies on the timing and coverage of wage settlements, and the effect of 'Competition and Credit Control' on growth of the money supply.

Where the model does not fit the past well, simulations may generate odd-looking results as a consequence of residuals in one or more key behavioural relationships (for example those which determine money earnings, private expenditure and exports). Rather than fudge the results we have decided to present them as they stand, together with the values of residuals which generated them.

Specification of time periods. The two past periods are each defined as five years starting from a mid-year month. Since the CEPG model is an annual one the specification of the timing of the policy changes and their results can only be approximate. Allowing for time lags in policy implementation which would confront even the wisest of policy-makers, we have made only very small changes to the actual outcomes in the initial half-years, 1964 and 1970, with the main revisions to policy instruments beginning in the subsequent year. Similarly we can only present a view of each terminal year as a whole. The future period 1977–81 is more straightforward as it is defined to cover full calendar years.

Political constraints. Rather than indulge in political speculation about, for example, the extent to which the 1964–6 Labour government was constrained by its small majority, or the possible effects of different policies by the 1970–4 Conservative administration on the February 1974 election result (and its timing), we have simply put forward our view of the best strategy in each period: the results must then be judged according to the reader's own notions of political practicality. We have accepted certain policies, notably acceptance of the CAP following accession to the EEC, which might be judged disadvantageous on strictly macroeconomic grounds.

Changes in past policy. Simulations of past periods incorporate a number of changes to policy which can conveniently be grouped under four headings: (a) fiscal; (b) monetary; (c) trade; (d) incomes. In constructing simulations we have first removed past policy variations in each of these areas, and then investigated the results of alternative strategies. Attention has been concentrated on the design of appropriate combinations of fiscal and trade policies to secure internal and external balance. The methods used to define 'neutral' past policies are discussed in this section in general terms and are described in detail in the notes to Tables 1.1 and 1.6.

(a) *Fiscal policy.* In its analysis of future policy prospects, CEPG has usually taken planned public expenditure on goods and services as given, accepting that these plans are determined by criteria distinct from questions of overall fiscal balance; the given set of expenditure plans implies a particular burden of taxation in order to achieve any desired fiscal stance. But it is undeniable that changes in public expenditure have in the past been used as a fiscal instrument in conjunction with, or even as a substitute for, manipulation of tax rates, and that this has resulted in some sharp year-to-year fluctuations in real public expenditure – such as 1969, when post-devaluation cuts secured real reductions in both current and capital expenditure.

It is our view that public expenditure authorisations *should* be 'neutral' in the sense of not being used, in general, as a short-run fiscal instrument. Without undertaking a detailed investigation of what the outturn of public expenditure would have been had authorisations been made solely according to longer-run criteria, we have defined neutral policy simply by smoothing the recorded growth rates of relevant variables – public service employment, other current expenditure and fixed investment – over each simulation period.

Neutral tax policy has been defined as a constant effective rate of direct tax on property income and a constant marginal rate of direct tax on income from employment. Discretionary changes in fiscal policy are introduced as a package consisting of changes in the value of income tax allowances, the amount of tax levied on property income, and the rate of sales tax on income-elastic consumption.

The fiscal stance adopted in simulations may be compared with the actual historical stance in past periods by comparing estimates of what the public sector financial deficit would be at (a) simulated, (b) actual tax rates and expenditure authorisations if the economy were growing along a full-employment path with a satisfactory external payments position; in each case they are calculated by correcting tax receipts and transfers for deviations of income and expenditure from levels consistent with external and internal balance. Estimates of the full-employment balance are presented in the discussion of the results of the simulations.

(b) *Monetary policy*. Neutral monetary policy is defined by constant values of the exogenous variables which are assumed to be under the control of the authorities – an index of credit conditions which influences private expenditure and the money supply, and the ratio of sterling bank lending to the public sector to the change in total money supply. It is also assumed that discretionary changes in hire purchase regulations are not made.

These assumptions imply that the money supply is allowed to expand to meet demand, given nominal income and short-term interest rates. This determines the amount of finance for the public sector borrowing requirement provided by the banking sector; the remainder must be financed either externally or through sales of securities. The margin between long- and short-term interest rates is assumed to move to the level at which the authorities can sell enough securities to finance the rest of the borrowing requirement, given the balance for official financing. Bank rate/minimum lending rate is assumed to be determined by Eurodollar interest rates and by the United Kingdom inflation rate.

This definition of neutral policy does not correspond to the traditional approach of maintaining stable yields in the gilt-edged market: some degree of fluctuation in interest rates is possible. While the assumption of neutral monetary policy is maintained throughout the simulations, it is recognised that short-term discretionary changes in monetary policy might be useful in certain circumstances. We have chosen not to use them, partly because the short-term nature of such policy changes is not well represented in an annual mode. A full account of CEPG views on the role of monetary policy is given in Cripps and Fetherston [3].

(c) *Trade policy.* Neutral trade policy is defined as a constant level of export competitiveness, maintained by appropriate variation of the exchange rate, together with the absence of general restrictive measures on imports. Each of the simulations involves some departure from this neutral benchmark in order to achieve certain policy targets.

(d) *Incomes policy.* Neutral policy under this heading is defined as no policy: the level of wage settlements, together with their timing and coverage in a given year, is assumed to be determined under free collective bargaining to secure exogenous target annual increases in the real post-tax value of settlements. A full explanation of this section of the CEPG model is given in Coutts *et al.* [2] with further details in Fetherston [4].

Episode 1: September 1964–September 1969

Assumptions. The period 1963–4 was one of fast growth and a deteriorating balance of payments following the introduction of expansionary fiscal policies. GDP grew by 3½ per cent between 1962 and 1963 and 6 per cent between 1963 and 1964, with the current balance moving from a surplus of £131 million to a deficit of £355 million, and the basic balance deteriorating by over £600 million to a deficit of £758 million. Export competitiveness deteriorated by over 6 per cent between 1960 and 1964, despite the rate of inflation never exceeding 3½ per cent in any year during that period, so that there were grounds for concern that sterling was becoming increasingly over-valued.

The major strategic issue of policy in this period concerns the magnitude and timing of devaluation to remedy this worsening competitive position. As explained earlier, it is our view that an early devaluation accompanied by incomes policy would have provided the best chance in this period of securing a sustained improvement in Britain's trading performance. Accordingly Tables 1.1 and 1.2 show the results of a simulation in which the exchange rate is adjusted so as to give a step improvement in export competitiveness of 7.7 per cent in 1965, maintained throughout the period, sufficient to achieve a £200 million surplus on the basic balance of payments by 1969.

The initial devaluation in 1965 is accompanied by an incomes policy which is assumed to have a similar effect on the level of wage settlements as the actual policy introduced in 1966. Thereafter the real post-tax value of wage settlements is assumed to increase at 2 per cent per annum, such that by 1971 it is equal to the actual past level. The actual 1971 value was the result of two years of substantial wage settlements which may be viewed as the catching-up period after

Table 1.1 Policy simulation 1964–9

	1964	1965	1966	1967	1968	1969
£m. 1970 factor cost						
Consumers' expenditure	22945	23214	24486	23966	25866	26556
Public current expenditure	7561	7687	7794	8007	8123	8226
Public fixed investment	3001	3115	3233	3356	3484	3616
Private fixed investment	4012	4109	4244	4041	4519	5075
Stockbuilding	767	527	829	−282	557	1241
Exports of goods and services	7683	8212	8833	9127	10055	10726
Total final expenditure	45970	46865	49420	48215	52605	55440
Imports of:						
food, drink and tobacco	2047	2008	2058	2129	2047	2028
materials and fuels	1929	1953	2061	1945	2228	2366
manufactures	2788	2830	3272	3187	4147	4750
services	1720	1763	1673	1727	1762	1841
Imports of goods and services	8484	8554	9064	8988	10184	10984
GDP at factor cost	37486	38311	40356	39228	42421	44456
£m. current prices						
Balance of trade on goods and services	−576	−332	−200	227	107	−63
Current balance	−355	7	40	493	211	312
Basic balance	−758	−299	−332	61	−4	200
Balance for official financing	−695	98	−180	1166	−615	619
End-year money supply	12453	13481	14578	15431	17565	19031
Financial surpluses:						
public sector	−987	−1079	−820	−1472	−1106	148
private sector	632	1086	860	1965	1317	163
overseas sector	355	−7	−40	−493	−211	−312
PSBR	972	1433	813	1694	1251	−286

Note: (see over).

Note to Table 1.1

Adjustments to policy variables (A – Actual; S – Simulation)

Fiscal policy

Constant annual growth rates for public expenditure, 1964–9:

Planned public service employment	:	1.6%
Other current expenditure	:	2.0%
Fixed investment	:	3.8%

		1964	1965	1966	1967	1968	1969
Effective rate of tax	A	0.2839	0.2854	0.2711	0.3352	0.3173	0.3174
on property income	S	0.2839	0.29	0.30	0.30	0.30	0.30
Marginal tax rate on	A	0.260	0.280	0.280	0.285	0.285	0.300
employment income	S	0.260	0.260	0.260	0.260	0.260	0.260
Average value of	A	0.0848	0.0924	0.0897	0.0973	0.0898	0.1036
income tax allowances	S	0.0838	0.0861	0.0878	0.0907	0.0937	0.0969
Monetary policy							
Index of credit	A	1.0	1.7	2.6	1.3	2.0	2.6
restrictions	S	1.0	1.7	1.7	1.7	1.7	1.7
Ratio of bank lending to public	A	−0.26	0.64	0.56	0.49	0.17	−0.45
sector to change in M3	S	−0.26	0.30	0.30	0.30	0.30	0.30
Net increase in consumer hire	A	137	83	−112	−17	23	−31
purchase debt (£m.)	S	137	50	50	50	50	50
Trade policy							
Rates of protective import duty:							
Semi-finished	A	0.059	0.097	0.082			
manufactures	S	0.051	0.049	0.047			
Finished	A	0.096	0.170	0.141			
manufactures	S	0.080	0.075	0.070			
Export	A	1.1410	1.1460	1.1627	1.1473	1.0445	1.0630
competitiveness[a]	S	1.1410	1.0534	1.0534	1.0534	1.0534	1.0534
Incomes policy							
Real post-tax value	A	1.149	1.150	1.083	1.134	1.129	1.134
of wage settlements	S	1.149	1.100	1.122	1.144	1.166	1.190
Proportion of manual workers settling	A	0.8345	0.8318	0.5140	0.8179	0.8054	0.6631
in the year[b]	S			0.800			0.810
Mean date of	A	0.541	0.462	0.795	0.500	0.441	0.521
settlement	S			0.500			
Time since last settlement for manual	A	1.187	1.272	1.283	1.552	1.439	1.206
workers settling in the year[b]	S				1.390	1.299	

[a] *1.0732 in 1970: the figures in the results tables are rebased on 1970 actual = 100. The values shown are obtained by manipulation of the exchange rate.*

[b] *Endogenous variables where the adjustment is made to the residual in the years shown: the adjustment is such that the modified value would be generated if the explanatory variables maintained their actual values.*

several years of fairly tight restraint; the assumption in the simulation is therefore that the effects of the hypothetical 1965 policy on settlements are only temporary, and that the catching-up process is spread over several years.

The notes accompanying Table 1.1 specify the changes made to variables in the model to implement the devaluation and incomes policy and the assumption otherwise of a neutral stance. The latter involves:

(i) smooth growth rates of public expenditure over the period;
(ii) constant rates of direct tax on property income (from 1966) and employment income;
(iii) stable credit conditions and financing of the public sector borrowing requirement through the banking system;
(iv) removal of the effects of the 1966 wage freeze on the timing and coverage of settlements in 1966 and subsequent years, and of the dip in coverage of settlements prior to the 1970 wage explosion; also adjustments of the real value of settlements to represent introduction of an incomes policy in late 1964, with subsequent relaxation;
(v) removal of the effect of the import surcharge on rates of protective import duty.

Income tax allowances are revalorised to the extent of 75 per cent of the inflation rate over the period.

Table 1.2 Policy simulation, 1964–9

	1964	1965	1966	1967	1968	1969
Percentage change						
GDP deflator	2.5	3.8	2.8	5.7	4.6	4.3
Consumption deflator	3.3	4.8	2.5	6.1	3.8	6.8
Average pre-tax money earnings	7.0	5.4	4.4	11.1	8.3	9.6
Average post-tax real earnings	2.9	0.2	1.6	3.9	3.8	2.0
Indices, 1970 = 100						
Exchange rate	117.4	108.0	107.2	103.1	99.0	97.1
Terms of trade	97.1	95.6	96.3	97.5	98.6	97.9
Export competitiveness	99.6	91.9	91.9	91.9	91.9	91.9
Unemployment (thousands)	403	380	247	647	528	333
Bank rate (%)	5.2	6.5	6.0	8.1	7.7	8.3
Yield on long-term debt (%)	6.1	8.4	6.8	12.0	8.5	8.8

Results. In the simulation GDP growth averages 3.4 per cent per annum over the period, a rate slightly in excess of the rate of growth of productive potential, and also of the actual average growth rate of 2.6 per cent. The average level of unemployment thus tends to fall over the period. The improvement in export competitiveness in 1965 necessary to achieve the terminal-year balance of payments target is 7.7 per cent, which requires an initial nominal devaluation of 8 per cent in 1965, followed by a sequence of small nominal devaluations, amounting to a further 10 per cent, which serve to offset inflation in Britain relative to other countries.

Table 1.3 Average annual growth rates, 1964–9 (percentages)

	Actual	Simulation
Consumers' expenditure	2.2	3.0
Public current expenditure	1.8	1.7
Public fixed investment	3.8	3.8
Private fixed investment	3.2	4.8
Exports	6.1	6.9
Imports	4.1	5.3
GDP	2.6	3.4
Consumer prices	4.0	4.8
Average post-tax real earnings	1.4	2.3

Table 1.3 summarises average growth rates over the period for components of final demand, inflation and average earnings. With growth of public expenditure virtually unaltered, faster growth of GDP in the simulation is reflected mainly in faster growth of consumption and private investment. Earlier devaluation improves the growth of exports over the period, but not by as much as the increase in imports generated by faster GDP growth. The balance of payments target for 1969 is slightly smaller than the historical outcome, which for the current account was a surplus of £460 million compared with £312 million in the simulation. This conceals the fact that over the period as a whole balance of payments performance is very much improved, with a cumulative current surplus over the period 1965–9 of £1063 million in the simulation as compared with an historical cumulative *deficit* of £35 million. Corresponding improvements are evident for the basic balance

and the balance for official financing, although the 1967 performance is partly spurious, as explained below.

The simulation performs less well as far as inflation is concerned *in the period shown*, with the average rate of increase of consumer prices about 0.8 per cent per annum higher in the simulation than actually occurred. The early devaluation in the simulation produces a higher share of profits at the expense of wages as well as consistently inferior terms of trade; in addition the restraining effects on money wages of the hypothetical incomes policy had worn off by the end of the period although the actual incomes policy was still enforcing considerable restraint at that time. But simulation of the succeeding two years (not shown in Tables 1.1 and 1.2) shows inflation considerably lower than what actually happened.

Table 1.4 The full employment budget balance, 1964–9[a]

	1964	1965	1966	1967	1968	1969
Actual[b]						
£ billion	1.4	1.1	1.3	1.8	1.2	−0.5
% of GDP at factor cost	5.1	3.7	4.0	5.2	3.3	−1.3
Simulation[c]						
£ billion	1.4	1.3	1.4	1.4	1.5	0.0
% of GDP at factor cost	5.0	4.2	4.2	3.8	3.9	0.1

[a] *The full employment balances are computed on the basis of steady growth of GDP at rates sufficient to maintain unemployment at an average level of 600,000 and of a zero balance of payments in each year. These hypothetical outcomes are achieved by the device of exogenous adjustments to private consumption and exports. For further explanation of the basis of this procedure, see Ward* [6].

[b] *Assuming actual tax rates and public expenditure.*

[c] *Assuming the tax rates and levels of public expenditure of the policy simulation.*

Examination of simulation results for individual years, particularly 1967 and 1968, reveals some surprising fluctuations. As may be seen from Table 1.4, the fiscal stance adopted in the simulation, measured by the full employment budget balance, is one of gradual tightening over the period 1965–8, mainly achieved by income tax allowances which are only partly revalorised to take account of inflation. This fiscal position is associated with reasonably smooth growth of real post-tax earnings, which reaches nearly 4 per cent in 1967 and 1968. Yet in the simulation GDP falls by 2.8 per cent in 1967 and then rises by no less than 8.1 per cent in 1968. This results from the fact that the CEPG model does not explain 1967 at all well; the key residuals nearly all go in the same direction, as shown in Table 1.5.

Table 1.5 shows in each column the effect, measured at 1970 factor cost, of changes in residuals between successive years on the value of each variable, given the values of explanatory variables (that is before allowing for any consequential multiplier effects). In addition there are movements of 2.6 per cent and −2.3 per cent in the residual of the equation for standard earnings.

Table 1.5 Changes in residuals

	1966–7	1967–8
Consumers' expenditure	−374	441
Private investment	−107	283
Stockbuilding	−212	−50
Exports	−244	153
Total	−937	827
% of total final expenditure	−1.9	1.6

We do not seriously suggest that the outcome in 1967 under the recommended strategy would have been the one shown. But in line with our policy of not tampering with residuals no attempt has been made to fudge them so as to produce a more plausible predicted outcome. It may be argued that what actually happened was associated with low confidence resulting from the failure of the Government's pre-devaluation policies – and therefore would not have occurred if our recommended strategy had been adopted. However, such 'confidence' effects are not represented in the model.

Allowing the abnormal residuals to stand has a number of consequences for the results of the simulation. Despite low exports, the balance of payments in 1967 is considerably improved by the depressed state of domestic demand, which also magnifies the size of the public sector borrowing requirement. The combination of these factors with our assumption of 'neutral' monetary policy drastically increases the size of that part of the public sector borrowing requirement which must be financed through sales of securities, and drives up the long-term interest rate to 12 per cent. The size of this predicted rise in the long interest rate reflects what is probably a weakness in the model – that no allowance is made for the fact that external capital inflows may increase demand for British government securities. In the model external capital inflows reduce the amount of official external finance for the borrowing requirement and force a rise in long-term interest rates which would not necessarily occur to the same extent in reality. Correction of this fault would help to damp the anomalous fluctuation predicted for 1967 but would not materially affect our conclusions about the conduct of policy.

Episode 2: July 1970–July 1975

Assumptions. The background to this period is very different from that of the first period. Although GDP grew by 4 per cent in 1968, the period 1968–70 was characterised by fiscal and monetary restriction, rising unemployment and a steadily improving balance-of-payments position. The restrictive policies were aimed principally at ensuring success for the 1967 devaluation, which in terms of its effects on competitiveness was still proving effective in 1970 – nearly 8 per cent better than in 1966. Accelerating wage inflation from 1969 onwards, however, undermined this improvement, which was completely eliminated by 1972.

The major issue in this period is still that of finding policies to combat the continuing decline in Britain's competitive position and share of world markets, a problem exacerbated by the rapidly increasing penetration of the domestic market by foreign manufacturers. With hindsight these policies must also contend with the problem of the effects of the oil crisis and world recession on domestic employment and inflation in 1974 and 1975.

As explained in the first section, it seems highly doubtful that devaluation would have succeeded in sustaining internal and external balance without generating unacceptable rates of inflation. Instead our view is that the Government should have introduced import controls during the period in order to sustain domestic income and employment whilst protecting the balance of payments position.

Tables 1.6 and 1.7 therefore show the results of a simulation in which the 1969 level of export competitiveness is maintained throughout the period by appropriate variation in the exchange rate. Quantitative restrictions on imports of manufactures are introduced over the period 1973–5 in order to stabilise the volume of such imports and restrict the level of unemployment in 1975 to 450,000, and discretionary fiscal policy is used to meet targets for the basic balance of payments in each year. No formal incomes policy is assumed to be in force, and it is assumed that import restrictions do not provoke retaliation. If they did, then it would be necessary either to introduce tougher restrictions or to adopt less ambitious targets.

Table 1.6 Policy simulation, 1970–5

	1970	1971	1972	1973	1974	1975
£m. 1970 factor cost						
Consumers' expenditure	26086	26988	27877	27681	28575	30322
Public current	8452	8687	8915	9113	9329	9578
Public fixed investment	3714	3840	3971	4106	4245	4389
Private fixed investment	4824	5136	5742	6013	5522	6023
Stockbuilding	431	110	447	956	725	192
Exports[a]	10865	11860	12527	14116	14667	13705
Total final expenditure	54372	56620	59478	61985	63062	64209
Imports of:						
food, drink and tobacco	2047	2047	2088	2088	2027	2006
materials and fuels	2307	2328	2372	2451	2347	2198
manufactures	4569	5195	6203	6651	6692	6424
services	1961	2073	2347	2573	2581	2561
Total imports[a]	10884	11644	13010	13763	13648	13189
GDP at factor cost	43487	44976	46468	48223	49414	51020
£m. current prices						
Balance of trade[a]	391	623	−11	88	−2156	−1774
Current balance	750	961	328	1000	−1322	−1527
Basic balance	559	700	−200	800	−500	−1000
Balance[b]	1382	3467	−284	2123	1169	−2078
End-year money supply	18590	21086	24445	27364	31756	40055
Financial surpluses:						
public sector	680	−958	−1559	−769	−3129	−6783
private sector	70	1919	1888	1710	1731	5256
overseas sector	−750	−961	−328	−941	1397	1527
PSBR	12	2017	1881	2003	4176	8828

[a] *Of goods and services.*
[b] *For official financing.*

Note to Table 1.6
Adjustments to policy variables (A – Actual; S – Simulation)

Fiscal policy

Constant annual growth rates for public expenditure, 1970–5:

Planned public service employment : 2.2%
Other current expenditure : 3.3%
Fixed investment : 3.4%

		1970	1971	1972	1973	1974	1975
Effective rate of	A	0.3179	0.3196	0.2954	0.2676	0.3107	0.2775
tax on property income	S	0.3179	0.3179	0.3179	0.3179	0.3179	0.3179
Marginal tax rate	A	0.325	0.325	0.345	0.350	0.375	0.405
on employment income	S	0.325	0.325	0.325	0.325	0.325	0.325
Average value of	A	0.1318	0.1481	0.2058	0.2311	0.2947	0.3823
income tax allowances	S	0.1323	0.1580	0.1859	0.1853	0.2216	0.2863
Monetary policy							
Index of credit restriction	A	2.7	1.3	0.0	0.0	1.7	1.0
	S	2.7	1.7	1.7	1.7	1.7	1.7
Ratio of bank lending to public	A	0.75	0.81	−0.10	0.20	0.08	1.36
sector to change in M3	S	0.75	0.25	0.25	0.25	0.25	0.25
End-year money supply	A	18565	20954	26184	33478	37698	40569
(£m.)	S			25589	29916	32089	
Net increase in consumer	A	43	191	253	183	−66	57
hire purchase debt (£m.)	S	43	100	100	100	100	100
Trade policy							
Export competitiveness[a]	A	1.0732	1.1442	1.1779	1.0898	1.0070	1.0474
	S	1.0630	1.0630	1.0630	1.0630	1.0630	1.0630
Degree of restriction on imports of finished	A				1.00	1.00	1.00
manufactures	S				0.90	0.70	0.54
Incomes policy							
Real post-tax value	A	1.177	1.237	1.266	1.272	1.224	1.358
of wage settlements	S	1.177	1.198	1.219	1.240	1.262	1.284
Proportion of manual workers	A	1.1102	0.8280	0.8366	0.8524	1.3186	1.2311
settling in the year[b]	S					0.9	1.0
Value of cost-of-	A	0.0	0.0	0.0	0.0	0.066	0.075
living supplements	S					0.0	0.0
Ratio of non-manual to manual average	A	1.374	1.306	1.290	1.250	1.232	1.173
earnings	S	1.374	1.306	1.290	1.270	1.260	1.250

Notes: as for Table 1.1.

Table 1.7 Policy simulation, 1970–5

	1970	1971	1972	1973	1974	1975
Percentage change						
GDP deflator	8.0	9.0	8.0	8.8	15.3	19.9
Consumption deflator	6.7	6.9	7.7	12.0	14.8	15.5
Average pre-tax money earnings	12.8	9.3	8.8	13.4	22.6	19.2
Average post-tax real earnings	4.1	3.6	2.2	−0.8	6.4	4.4
Indices, 1970 = 100						
Exchange rate	98.9	93.1	88.7	86.5	90.5	83.2
Terms of trade	99.8	99.0	99.8	94.2	81.5	86.2
Export competitiveness	99.0	99.0	99.0	99.0	99.0	99.0
Unemployment (thousands)	602	687	703	535	419	450
Bank rate/MLR (%)	7.3	5.5	5.0	9.5	11.2	6.6
Yield on long-term debt (%)	9.5	11.2	7.5	11.4	14.6	10.1

The notes accompanying Tables 1.6 and 1.7 give details of the changes made to variables in the model to implement these policies and the assumption otherwise of a neutral stance. The latter involves:

(i) smooth growth rates of public expenditure over the period;
(ii) constant rates of direct tax on employment income and property income;
(iii) stable credit conditions and financing of the public sector borrowing requirement through the banking system, including the removal of the impact of the 1971 Competition and Credit Control regime on the growth of the money supply from 1972–4;
(iv) removal of the effects of the 1972–4 incomes policies on the level of wage settlements and the acceleration of the decline in the relativity between non-manual and manual earnings, and removal of the effects of the threshold scheme on the level and coverage of wage settlements in 1974 and 1975. In the absence of formal incomes policy it is assumed that wage bargaining results in annual increases of $1\frac{3}{4}$ per cent in the real post-tax value of settlements.

It is assumed that the Government carries out its commitment to abolish SET.

Results. The balance of payments targets in the simulation are chosen so as to maintain a sound external position in advance of the strains imposed by the oil crisis, whilst not prejudicing GDP growth. It turns out that with the introduction of import restrictions from 1973 onwards a much improved 1974 balance of payments is feasible as compared with the actual large deficit, whilst in the next year protection permits a higher level of output and unemployment for roughly the same balance of payments outcome.

Table 1.8 Average annual growth rates, 1970–5 (percentages)

	Actual	Simulation
Consumers' expenditure	1.8	3.1
Public current expenditure	3.0	2.5
Public fixed investment	2.7	3.4
Private fixed investment	2.0	4.5
Exports	4.8	4.8
Imports	4.5	3.9
GDP	1.6	3.2
Consumer prices	12.9	11.3
Average post-tax real earnings	2.6	3.2

As in the first period, faster growth of GDP is reflected in faster growth of real post-tax earnings, real consumption and real private investment. Within the total figure for imports, imports of manufactures grow on average by 7 per cent per annum compared with the historical figure of 9.2 per cent – with the 1975 level below that of 1973 in each case. In the simulation total imports of manufactures are about 23 per cent lower than would be expected at the same level of demand in the absence of restrictions. Exports fall sharply in 1975 under the influence of the world recession. The improved performance on inflation compared with actual experience occurs almost entirely in the last year of the period, and is in part attributable to the removal of the threshold scheme.

Table 1.9 indicates the fiscal stance adopted over the period. Comparing the simulation with actual, the stance is slacker in 1971 and 1972, considerably tighter in 1973 and 1974, but slackening again fairly sharply in 1975. The change in the fiscal stance in 1975 is the necessary counterpart, in terms of sustaining real demand, of the very sharp rise in the private sector financial surplus in that year.

Over the period 1970–3, the changes in timing of fiscal policy compared with what actually occurred, together with a policy of maintaining competitiveness, permit considerable improvements in

Table 1.9 The full employment budget balance, 1970–5[a].

	1970	1971	1972	1973	1974	1975
Actual[b]						
£ billion	−1.0	−0.4	0.8	2.3	3.8	5.2
% of GDP at factor cost	−2.3	−0.7	1.4	3.6	5.0	5.2
Simulation[c]						
£ billion	−1.0	0.6	1.1	0.4	2.6	6.6
% of GDP at factor cost	−2.2	1.1	2.0	0.6	3.5	7.3

[a] *As for Table 1.4 except that external balance is defined for 1974 as a deficit on the basic balance of £2500 million and for 1975 as a deficit of £1000 million.*
[b] *Assuming actual tax rates and public expenditure.*
[c] *Assuming the tax rates and levels of public expenditure of the policy simulation.*

balance of payments performance, most notably in 1973 (when imports of manufactures are assumed to be restricted by only 5 per cent). GDP growth in 1973 is almost entirely export-led, with exports rising by nearly 13 per cent and tight fiscal policy inducing a slight fall in consumption. Subsequently real consumption resumes fairly rapid growth.

The simulation produces a sharp rise in long-term interest rates in 1971 – this is again associated with the flaw in the model discussed on page 25.

Episode 3: Early 1977–December 1981

Assumptions. CEPG have recently published projections of alternative strategies covering the period up to 1985 [1], and we do not wish to alter the main conclusions of that analysis. Tables 1.10 and 1.11 therefore reproduce the results of the import restriction strategy (No. 3) in [1], with one change, namely that a 12-month rule for the frequency of wage settlements is enforced. (In the Review projection a gradually increasing frequency of settlements was inadvertently assumed.)

The principal assumptions underlying this projection are:

(i) growth of the volume of world trade of 8 per cent in 1977 and 9 per cent per annum thereafter, with world prices of manufactures, oil and primary commodities all rising at 5 per cent per annum in foreign currency (a weighted average of the currencies of Britain's main competitors);

Table 1.10 Policy simulation, 1977–81

	1976	1977	1978	1979	1980	1981
£m. 1970 factor cost						
Consumers' expenditure	28667	29508	30449	32269	34212	36283
Public current	10157	10125	10068	10137	10250	10414
Public fixed investment	4164	3714	3747	3956	4372	4830
Private fixed investment	4938	5185	5834	6091	6515	7097
Stockbuilding	−693	−23	976	1273	1321	1473
Exports[a]	14593	15968	17653	18887	20288	21765
Total final expenditure	61826	64476	68727	72613	76957	81863
Imports of:						
food, drink and tobacco	2088	2073	2075	2078	2080	2083
materials and fuels	2122	2032	2191	2268	2316	2423
manufactures	7713	8429	9708	10688	12300	13905
services	2464	2742	2859	2976	3097	3229
Total imports[a]	14387	15276	16833	18010	19793	21639
GDP at factor cost	47439	49201	51893	54603	57164	60223
£m. current prices						
Balance of trade[a]	−1774	−17	1576	2969	3639	3967
Current balance	−1448	−99	554	1181	591	−783
Basic balance	−1826	−548	−581	0	0	0
Balance[b]	−3529	−986	−277	1639	1628	817
End-year money supply	45869	53469	62283	74695	87974	102000
Financial surpluses:						
public sector	−8856	−10267	−7295	−7473	−8701	−9059
private sector	7408	10168	7849	8654	9291	8276
overseas sector	1448	99	−554	−1181	−591	783
PSBR	10200	11199	8060	9204	10756	11335

[a] *Of goods and services.*
[b] *For official financing.*

(ii) public expenditure plans as announced by February 1977 up to 1978–9 and as expected up to 1981, except that additional public investment is assumed for 1978 up to a level in 1981 16 per cent higher than in 1976;

(iii) the general structure of taxation as at January 1977, adjusted for future inflation, but allowing for future changes already announced by that date;

(iv) targets on the basic balance of payments expressed in foreign currency, of the equivalent at 1976 exchange rates of deficits of £500 million in 1977 and 1978 and zero in later years;

Table 1.11 Policy simulation, 1977–81

	1976	1977	1978	1979	1980	1981
Percentage change						
GDP deflator	14.0	12.8	12.0	13.8	13.1	11.2
Consumption deflator	15.5	11.3	11.7	11.7	11.3	10.0
Average pre-tax money earnings	14.8	11.5	14.5	17.2	14.7	13.2
Average post-tax real earnings	−2.4	1.0	0.9	5.7	3.9	3.5
Indices, 1970 = 100						
Exchange rate	62.1	56.7	53.4	49.7	46.7	44.4
Terms of trade	90.1	91.9	94.4	96.0	98.2	99.6
Export competitivenesss	92.2	89.5	89.5	89.5	89.5	89.5
Unemployment (thousands)	1274	1364	1350	1300	1250	1200
MLR (%)	11.7	10.3	10.1	11.0	10.4	9.4
Yield on long-term debt (%)	14.0	13.8	11.9	13.3	12.7	11.2

(v) discretionary changes in income tax allowances and in VAT such as to ensure that the targets for the basic balance of payments are achieved in each year;

(vi) increases of the real post-tax value of wage settlements of 3 per cent in 1978, 2 per cent in 1978 and 1 per cent per annum thereafter, together with enforcement of a 12-month rule for the frequency of settlements;

(vii) movements in the exchange rate so as to maintain the January 1977 level of export competitiveness throughout the period;

(viii) restrictions on imports of manufactures by non-tariff methods from 1978 onwards, calculated so as to meet unemployment targets in each year falling to 1.2 million in 1981. As in period 2, it is assumed that these restrictions are not followed by retaliatory measures by other countries.

Results. A full discussion of the projected results of the recommended strategy is given in [1]. The main conclusions are that with the build-up in North Sea oil production and the projected increase in the labour force, together with planned slow growth of public service employment, quite rapid GDP growth by historical standards will be necessary for a sustained period to effect even a very gradual reduction in unemployment. The current position is one of continuing recession and prospective substantial improvement in the balance of payments,

Table 1.12 The full employment budget balance, 1976–81[a]

	1976	1977	1978	1979	1980	1981
£ billion	3.6	3.5	−0.6	−1.3	−1.1	−1.5
% of GDP at factor cost	3.1	2.6	−0.4	−0.7	−0.5	−0.6

[a] *As for Table 1.4 except that external balance is defined for 1976 as a deficit on the basic balance of £750 million. The 1976 figures are based on actual tax rates and public expenditure, whilst those for 1977–81 are based on the figures assumed in the simulation.*

which indicates considerable scope for fiscal relaxation. (On current policies the full-employment budget balance in 1977 is estimated to be roughly zero.) The degree of restriction of imports of manufactures which is necessary to sustain GDP growth whilst balance of payments targets are met rises from just over 2 per cent in 1978 to 15 per cent in 1981. With this stimulus to demand, and the inflation rate stabilising at about 10 per cent, the public sector deficit on a full employment basis is able to move into modest surplus from 1978 onwards despite a very large fiscal relaxation.

Notes on Tables of Results

Volume series for expenditure on gross domestic product are defined in the CEPG model as at 1970 factor cost, and are reproduced as such. Conversion of the results to 1970 market prices would not produce results strictly comparable with *Blue Book* series, since the latter are based on a much more detailed breakdown of indirect taxes by category of expenditure. Real domestic expenditures exclusive of the North Sea and public services are defined inclusive of the 'relative price effect' after allowing for differing incidence of net sales taxes on components of expenditure, and the consumption deflator is defined on the basis consistent with this procedure. (For a fuller explanation, see Fetherston [4].) GDP is defined on a compromise basis, with the discrepancy between compromise and expenditure estimates allocated to stockbuilding. The discrepancy between compromise and income estimates is allocated to private income, so that the whole of the *Blue Book* 'residual error' between expenditure and income is allocated to the private financial surplus. The money supply is defined as end-year M3 (seasonally unadjusted).

Earnings series are derived from *Blue Book* income data. The three series expressed as indices to base 1970 = 100 are measured relative to the 1970 actual value in Table 1.7. The exchange rate series is based on the official index published in Economic Trends prior to its revision in March 1977. Export competitiveness is defined as a ratio of domestic wholesale prices to competitors' export prices expressed in sterling. Unemployment is the average of monthly figures of wholly unemployed excluding school-leavers and adult students. Interest rates are expressed as the average of monthly figures: the yield on long-term debt is the yield on War Loan.

References

[1] Cambridge Economic Policy Group, *Economic Policy Review No. 3*, March 1977, chapter 1.

[2] Coutts, K. J., Tarling, R. J. and Wilkinson, S. F., 'Wage bargaining and the inflation process', chapter 2 of Cambridge Economic Policy Group, *Economic Policy Review No. 2*, March 1976.

[3] Cripps, T. F. and Fetherston, M. J., 'The role of monetary policy in economic management', chapter 4 of Cambridge Economic Policy Group, *Economic Policy Review No. 3*, March 1977.

[4] Fetherston, M. J., *Technical Manual on the CEPG Model*, Department of Applied Economics, University of Cambridge, mimeo, 2nd Edition, May 1977.

[5] Godley, W. A. H., 'North Sea oil and economic strategy: the dangers of going for the soft option', in *The British Economy, Trends and Prospects*, Vickers da Costa & Co. Ltd, April 1977.

[6] Ward, T. S., 'The public sector financial balance', chapter 7 of Cambridge Economic Policy Group, *Economic Policy Review No. 2*, March 1976.

2 A Monetarist Viewpoint

by David Laidler*

Introduction

This paper takes a monetarist approach to the policy problems of 1964, 1970, and 1977, and so is likely to differ significantly from others presented. It would be as well to be clear from the outset what the main characteristics of this approach are, so as to minimise the chance that the analysis will be criticized for having failed to achieve what it did not set out to achieve. Of course I do not mean to rule out as illegitimate any disagreement about what macroeconomic analysis ought to be trying to accomplish, or about the most fruitful way of achieving an agreed set of goals.

To begin with, monetarism is a *macroeconomic* doctrine. It deals with the behaviour of the general level of prices, of aggregate output and employment, and the overall balance of payments. When applied empirically it attempts to explain the behaviour of these aggregates directly. This approach contrasts with that taken in orthodox post-Keynesian macroeconomics, where typically the behaviour of components of aggregate variables is first modelled as a basis for building up that of the aggregates themselves. Monetarists operate at a relatively high level of time aggregation as well. Annual, and even cycle average, data are what they have typically set out to explain, rather than the quarterly and monthly data that are so often used in large-scale econometric models. In its present state of development

* I am grateful to the University of Western Ontario, the Reserve Bank of Australia and the Canada Council for supporting the research discussed in this paper. The model is the result of joint work carried on with Mr Patrick O'Shea of the Reserve Bank of Australia. He is to be exonerated of blame that may be attached to the uses to which the model is put in this paper. The model is still under development. It is hoped that a detailed description of it and its characteristics will be forthcoming in a paper written jointly by the author and Mr O'Shea. Peter Jonson, Patrick O'Shea, Michael Parker, Michael Sumner, John Williamson and George Zis have made many useful comments on the work reported here. They are, however, in no way implicated in any errors or omissions.

monetarist analysis cannot go into the same degree of detail as can orthodox macroeconometric models. Although there is no rule of the monetarist game that forbids work being carried out at a more disaggregated level, such work has hardly as yet begun. (However, some recent work using the London Business School model has had a distinctly monetarist character. See, for example, Ball and Burns [2].) Also the Reserve Bank of Australia RBA 76 model, though small by the usual standards of econometric models, nevertheless goes into much more detail than does most monetarist analysis (see Jonson, Moses and Wymer [5]). In part this is for no better reason than that monetarism, in its contemporary form, has developed only relatively recently and that there has not been time for much work of this type to be carried out. It may also stem from the fact that monetarists have not, on the whole, been involved in the day-to-day conduct of policy and hence have not been forced by the nature of their work to attach high priority to disaggregation over either time, economic agents, or economic variables.

However, there is something more fundamental involved here and it would be wrong to gloss over it. Though it is always dangerous to draw sharp distinctions about such matters, monetarists do seem on the whole to take a view of research strategy in economics, and a view of the current state of our quantitative knowledge, that differ from those underlying orthodox post-Keynesian macroeconometrics. They regard the relatively detailed large-scale econometric model, not as a vehicle for research *per se*, but rather as a means of summarising and making deductions from the results of research that is itself best carried out on a piecemeal small-scale basis. Moreover, they are sufficiently dubious about the quantitative accuracy, and even qualitative robustness, of much of our knowledge of the particular relationships that might go into a large-scale model, as to be extremely sceptical of the quantitative results that such models currently yield in simulation exercises. In short, monetarists are much less ambitious in the degree of detail into which they go when explaining and forecasting macroeconomic phenomena.

All this has implications for the way in which demand management policy is viewed. The successful implementation of an activist demand management policy requires accurate quantitative knowledge of the structure of the economy. Pessimism about the quality of such knowledge naturally leads to pessimism about the scope for activist policies; hence the monetarist predilection for simple rules rather than complex rules or discretion, particularly as far as the conduct of monetary policy is concerned. Given that it is seldom if ever the 'right' time immediately to put in place a monetary rule, the predilection for gradualism in the implementation of rules is also explained in these terms. The majority of monetarists would probably agree (if we except those who adhere to a strong form of the rational expectations hypothesis) that, given sufficient quantitative knowledge of the economy, it would be possible to do better in achieving such desirable goals as full employment and price stability with an activist policy than with a simple rule, gradually implemented. It is because they believe adequate quantitative knowledge to be lacking that they take the policy position they do.

The policy prescriptions offered in this paper are broad in outline, and concern monetary factors only; they are applications of the gradualist principle just discussed. Nevertheless, the prescriptions are quantitative in nature, and would have had quantitative results. Moreover the 'rules of the game' ask for predictions concerning the outcome of the policies prescribed. In order to abide at least by the spirit if not the letter of those rules, I have therefore used a small-scale econometric model, which encapsulates a monetarist view of the economy, to provide some quantitative assessment of the consequences of adopting monetarist gradualist policies in two of the three episodes discussed. The model in question is being developed for pedagogic purposes; it is not a forecasting model, nor was it designed as a device to aid in the construction of policy prescriptions. Thus it plays a far less central role in this paper than would be accorded a forecasting model in a more orthodox policy exercise.

Monetarist Analysis of an Open Economy

The monetarist framework in terms of which this paper is written rests on three postulates, each of them empirically testable, at least in principle. (Of course a great deal has recently been written about the characteristics of monetarism. See, for example, Thomas Mayer [9].) First, there exists a well-defined relationship between the aggregate demand for money in the economy and a few key variables. Secondly, the money market adjusts, though not instantaneously, so as to equilibrate the supply and demand for money. Thirdly, a number of the factors influencing both the supply of money and the demand for it have their values determined, in the long run, but not necessarily in the short run, independently of what occurs in the money market.

To be more specific, the demand for money equation determines the demand for real balances as a function of a 'scale' variable – typically permanent real income – and a pair of interrelated opportunity costs variables, the real rate of return on assets other than money and the expected rate of inflation. As to the supply side of the market, the quantity of money is by accounting identity equal to the sum of the domestic assets and the net foreign assets of the banking system. Furthermore, the volume of domestic assets may be controlled by the monetary authorities (which is not to say, of course, that such control can be exercised in a fashion that is independent of the way in which other policy tools are being utilised).

In the long run the economy converges on a 'full employment', or 'natural unemployment rate' level of income at which the real rate of interest is determined by the traditional forces of 'productivity and thrift'. Thus, at least two of the three arguments of the demand for real balances function are exogenous to the money market in the long run. The determination of the expected inflation rate and the price level by which nominal balances are deflated, depend critically upon the exchange rate regime, as does the role played by the net foreign assets of the banking system in determining the supply of nominal money. Under a fixed exchange rate the economy has its price level and inflation rate, and hence its expected inflation rate, determined abroad. The only variable left free to equilibrate the money market is then the value of foreign assets held by the banking system. Therefore, in the long run, under a fixed exchange rate, domestic monetary policy only influences the balance of payments.

With exchange rate flexibility, it is up to the monetary authorities to decide on the extent to which they will permit changes in the banking system's net foreign assets; they can always permit the exchange rate to vary by whatever amount is necessary to clear the foreign exchange market. Under such a regime, the quantity of money becomes exogenous to the money market, and the domestic price level, its rate of change, and hence the expected inflation rate, become the variables whose values are determined, again in the long run, by the interaction of the supply and demand for money.

The propositions set out above concern a long-run equilibrium upon which the economy would only converge if all exogenous variables had their values held constant over time. Neither the balance of payments nor the price level and its rate of change (actual and expected) adjust rapidly enough for it to be reasonable to analyse the actual year-by-year behaviour of the economy as if those variables *alone* adjusted in response to a change in domestic monetary policy. The transmission mechanism that lies between monetary policy and the variables it ultimately affects is complex and drawn out, and involves in principle, no matter what the exchange rate regime, fluctuations in real income and employment (not to mention in interest rates). It may be viewed as having two stages. The first of these involves the efforts of firms and households to rid themselves of excess cash balances (or if we consider monetary contraction, to make good a deficiency in money holdings). Excess money holdings spill over, not only into the purchase of financial assets so driving down interest rates, but also into the purchase of real assets such as consumer durables and indeed into current consumption. In an open economy of course some, and perhaps the majority of the assets and goods in question, might originate abroad so that there is a direct effect on the balance of payments under a fixed exchange rate, or on the exchange rate itself if it is flexible.

The initial *domestic* impact of expansionary monetary policy (and of fiscal policy) is to increase the level of income and employment. It is here that the second stage of the transmission mechanism comes into play. Its key element is the expectations-augmented Phillips curve. The basis of this relationship is the observation that, although each firm is involved in attempting to set a *relative* price for whatever it produces, and although those involved in wage bargaining are seeking to achieve a particular level of *real* wages, wages and prices are in fact stated in money terms. Thus a firm wishing to set a relative price, or those wishing to achieve agreement about a real wage, must form an expectation about the general price level before they can arrive at a money price or a money wage that will achieve their aims. If individual firms respond to an excess demand for their particular output by seeking to increase its relative price, and if in response to an excess demand for a particular class of labour the real wage of that class begins to increase, then a state of general excess demand in the economy will lead to both money wages and prices rising at a rate faster than the expected rate of price inflation.

An expected rate of inflation for the economy as a whole is of course an analytic fiction. Different economic agents hold different expectations about the inflation rate, and with different degrees of confidence. Our lack of understanding of the role that the dispersion of expectations plays in the inflationary process represents a major gap in our knowledge. In the absence of such understanding, it is nevertheless postulated that the economy acts as if all agents held with complete confidence a common expectation about the future course of prices, the expectation in question being formed in a different manner depending upon the nature of the exchange rate regime.

Under a fixed rate, a major influence on domestic expectations is the behaviour of prices ruling in the world economy. Any deviation of domestic from foreign inflation must lead to a structure of relative price levels incompatible with the maintenance of balance of payments equilibrium. Domestic prices therefore must eventually adjust so as to approach and maintain an appropriate level *vis-à-vis* the rest of the world. It is postulated that this fact is recognised in the expectations of agents. Under a flexible exchange rate, on the other hand, the authorities always have the option of permitting deviations in the domestic inflation rate from that ruling abroad to be offset by exchange rate changes. Under these circumstances the behaviour of the world price level must be complemented by that of the exchange rate, or superseded by that of the domestic price level as the principal influence upon expectations of inflation.

Since fiscal policy and money wages behaviour play a central role in orthodox post-Keynesian accounts of the workings of the macroeconomic system, it is worth digressing for a while to discuss their role in the monetarist schema outlined above. Turning first to fiscal policy, I agree that changes in government expenditure on goods and services, or in taxes, do of course have a direct effect on the level of income and employment. (In this I perhaps differ from some monetarists, but it is not a new position. See, for example, Laidler [6].) However, such changes, if they are unaccompanied by variations in the rate of monetary expansion, will lead to variations in the level of output only in the short run, and in the long run to changes in the division of output between the public and private sector. The crucial fact for the monetarist view of the macroeconomic aspects of fiscal policy is that any change in the public sector's borrowing requirement resulting from fiscal policy must be financed. It will influence the rate of DCE to the extent that it is financed by borrowing from the banking system, and set in motion a transmission mechanism like that already described. Thus, although the present framework does not ignore the macro side of fiscal policy, and indeed takes a view of it that is qualitatively similar to that of prevailing orthodoxy, there is an important difference of emphasis between the approaches. Post-Keynesian macroeconomics stresses the direct effects of fiscal actions, particularly on real income and employment and regards the means adopted to finance public sector borrowing as of secondary importance. The alternative framework stresses that the means of finance is crucial to the ultimate effects that fiscal policy is likely to have upon income, employment, prices, and the balance of payments.

Perhaps the sharpest contrast between the two approaches lies in their treatment of money wages. Post-Keynesian macroeconomics sees the money wage rate as the key determinant of the price level, and treats it as an essentially exogenously determined variable, not significantly susceptible to influence by market forces. Money wages play, at most, a subsidiary role in the analysis upon which this paper is based. It is argued that the adjustment of variables to equilibrate the supply and demand for money is the driving force behind economic fluctuations. Money wages are thought of as adjusting with the general price level in order to determine the level of real wages. These in turn are viewed as responding to the usual market forces of supply and demand for labour whose operation may well be vitally influenced by institutional factors. For example a change in the monopoly power of one or more trade unions can lead to an increase in the real wages of their members. To achieve this increase, money wages must, for a while, rise faster than prices whose own rate of increase is, however, determined by the processes discussed earlier. This increase in real wages must either lower real wages elsewhere, or lead to an increase in the economy's equilibrium or 'natural' unemployment rate.

Differences in view about the importance of the behaviour of money wages in the inflationary process naturally lead to differences in view about the effects that can be expected to follow from direct controls on their behaviour. The monetarist view would be that the effects in question will differ depending upon the exchange rate regime, although in either case it would be that controls on money wages, not accompanied by controls on prices, if they are effective at all, influence the behaviour of money and real wages but not that of prices. If wage and price controls are both implemented, then under fixed exchange rates and on the assumption that the world inflation rate is higher than the target rate set at home, to the extent that controls do influence domestic prices in the short run, this will lead to reserve inflow, a step-up in the monetary expansion rate, and hence to demand pressures that must ultimately undermine the controls. Under flexible exchange rates, any tendency that controls induce for domestic prices to fail to keep pace with the rate of monetary expansion must lead to a spillover of excess cash into the balance of payments, downward pressure on the exchange rate, and by that route a rise in the overall domestic price level that will again undermine the operation of controls. Thus, regardless of the exchange rate regime, for the monetarist, wage and price controls are unsatisfactory policy tools in an open economy, unless perhaps controls on prices are accompanied by direct controls on quantities.

I have already asserted that the macro behaviour of the British economy and the policy problems it has generated, from the end of the Korean War onwards, can be understood in terms of the theoretical scheme outlined above. Inherent in the foregoing discussion is a theory of the behaviour of the economy during what would usually be termed the 'stop-go' cycle.

Let us consider the fixed exchange rate case first of all, starting in a state of full equilibrium for the sake of simplicity. The characteristics of such a state would be full (or at least 'natural') employment; balance of payments equilibrium; a rate of domestic inflation compatible with the world inflation rate, and equal to the rate of monetary expansion minus the income elasticity of demand for real balances times the growth rate of real output. If there is an increase in the rate of DCE, perhaps resulting from an increase in public sector borrowing, the rate of change of the supply of nominal money will initially exceed that of the demand for it. Excess cash begins to spill over both into the balance of payments and into expenditure on domestically produced goods and services. In response to the increase in expenditure, output starts to increase, the domestic inflation rate rises above its expected value and there emerges a divergence between domestic and world prices which accentuates the already present tendency of the balance of payments to go into deficit.

If there were no other exogenous changes, the dynamics thus set in motion would eventually lead to a state of affairs in which the higher domestic credit expansion rate was just matched by a perpetual balance of payments deficit, with employment having returned to its natural level and inflation to a rate equal to that ruling abroad. A perpetual balance of payments deficit is, of course, an impossibility. Long before a steady state is reached, a contractionary policy must be set in motion to correct the deficit. In the British case, that would typically be fiscal policy which would lead on to a reduction in the DCE rate. Such a reduction begins to create an excess demand for money, has a direct effect on the balance of payments and puts some downward pressure on output, additional to that being exerted by the direct effects of fiscal policy; pressure which in turn begins to bring the inflation rate down below its expected value, so that there is a further factor working to improve the balance of payments. Again, left to itself, the economy would return in the long run to a full employment steady state with prices rising at the world rate, but with an improved balance of payments position as a result of the lower DCE rate. However, as has been noted, a depressed level of income and employment characterises the economy's short-run behaviour. If monetary and fiscal policies respond to this by becoming expansionary, then there is set in motion an upswing in real activity which marks the first stage of the 'go' phase of a new cycle. The 'go' phase culminates in a balance of payments problem, a new 'stop' phase begins, and so on.

Although the nature of the 'stop-go' cycle under flexible exchange rates has much in common with the fixed exchange rate case, there is one crucial difference. Under fixed rates, an increase in DCE has its initial impact on both the balance of payments and output and in the long run only on the former. Although the domestic inflation rate may vary, it does so relative to an expected inflation rate that is largely determined by what is happening to world prices. However, under flexible rates, pressure on the balance of payments drives the exchange rate down, and has a direct effect on domestic prices that is absent under fixed rates. Under flexible rates, because the behaviour of the exchange rate, and/or of domestic prices, plays a more important role in determining the expected inflation rate, these effects on domestic prices are accentuated as inflation expectations are revised upwards in the light of experience and begin to influence domestic wage and price-setting behaviour, not to mention the subsequent behaviour of the exchange rate. It is a desire to correct a high inflation rate and a falling exchange rate, rather than a balance of payments problem that triggers the 'stop' phase of the cycle under flexible rates, but it is still concern with unemployment that tempts the authorities to take the measures that set the 'go' phase into motion.

The essence of the hypothesis about the causes of the 'stop-go' cycle upon which this paper is built is thus simply stated. The cycle as we have known it for the past thirty years has been caused by fluctuations in the rate of DCE. These fluctuations in turn have been the result of the way in which public sector borrowing has been financed. Typically, at the trough of the cycle, fiscal stimulus has been given to the economy, but insufficient account has been taken of the expansionary effects of the indirect monetary consequences of that stimulus, and *vice versa* at the peak. The overall effect of policy has been to overcorrect recession and boom alike and to produce a repeating cycle in the balance of payments and in economic activity.

It would follow from this diagnosis that if the interconnection of fiscal and monetary policy were recognised, and the effects of monetary fluctuations properly appreciated and avoided in the DCE rate, that would lead to the end of the 'stop-go' cycle. Hence the monetarist prescription that monetary policy be governed by some sort of a rule.

This is *not* to say that adherence to a monetary rule would prevent all significant economic fluctuations. To argue that monetary shocks have been the typical cause of recent economic instability is not to argue that real shocks do not occur. There are many factors other than money that can cause fluctuations in income, employment, prices, and the balance of payments, and in my view (which is not a universal one among monetarists) their consequences are potentially a legitimate target for active fiscal stabilisation policies. The argument for a monetary rule has implications for the way in which the budgetary consequences of fiscal policy should be financed, but it does not imply that discretionary fiscal stabilisation policies should be given up.

(There are other arguments, however, having to do with the way in which the use of fiscal policy for stabilisation purposes might interfere with the achievement of distributive and allocative goals, which do much to weaken the case for deploying it mainly with the achievement of macro stability in view.)

To suggest that a monetary rule be adopted is not to offer a complete policy prescription. First the nature of the rule itself must be specified, and second the manner of its introduction must be considered. There is no presumption that immediate adherence to any particular rule will be stabilising. This will depend on the nature of the exchange rate regime and the behaviour of the world economy, and upon the particular phase of the stop-go cycle at which it is decided to opt for a rule. Before we go on to discuss the policy problems facing the United Kingdom in 1964, 1970, and 1977, we present a highly aggregated econometric model that seeks to quantify and make more concrete the foregoing qualitative analysis, a model which may be used later in the discussion of the policy prescriptions.

A Model of the United Kingdom, 1954–70

The analysis contained in the last section has been relatively informal and qualitative in nature. In this respect it reflects a much criticised characteristic of a good deal of monetarist analysis. Nevertheless, it has proved possible to construct a formal model that encapsulates most of the salient features of that analysis and to quantify that model. It consists of an output function, a price formation function, a balance of payments function, a demand for money function, an expression determining inflation expectations and a money supply identity. For estimation purposes it is cast in log linear terms using log linear approximations to linear relationships where appropriate.

The expenditure function may be set out, in linear terms, as follows. Where H is private sector expenditure plus net exports, G is government expenditure, M_s the supply of money, M_d the quantity of money demanded, P domestic prices, π foreign prices, E the price of foreign currency, A a constant whose significance will be discussed below, T an average tax rate, Y real income Y* permanent income, and the subscripts −1, −2, etc., refer to time lags of one year, two years, etc.:

$$Y = G + H = G + k \cdot \left[\left(\frac{M_s}{M_d} \right)^{\theta}_{-1} \cdot \left(\frac{\pi}{P} AE \right)^{\phi}_{-1} T_{-1}^{-\rho} \right] \cdot Y^* \qquad \text{(i)}$$

If we treat Y* as the trend value of income at a constant growth rate, and G* as the trend value of government expenditure at a constant growth rate, then a log linear approximation to this relationship is given by:

$$y = a_0 + a_1(m_s - m_d)_{-1} + a_2(\pi + e + a - p)_{-1} - a_3 t_{-1} + a_4 g \qquad (1)$$

where lower case letters represent logarithms of the variables of equation (i) with the exceptions of yt and g. These variables represent the difference between the logarithm of actual value of each variable and that of its trend value or, in the case of taxes which were trend free, their mean value. The parameters of equation (1) are related to those of equation (i) in the following way:

$$a_0 = k\log k;\ a_1 = k\theta;\ a_2 = k\phi;\ a_3 = k\rho;\ a_4 = (1 - k) \qquad \text{(ii)}$$

The price formation equation is a standard expectations augmented Phillips curve. Where Δp is the rate of inflation, X the expected rate of inflation, and y is defined as above, it may be written:

$$\Delta P = \beta y_{-1} + X_{-1} \qquad (2)$$

The balance of payments equation determines total currency flow (which is identically equal to the change in official reserves R, minus that in official borrowing overseas L) in the following way:

$$\frac{R}{R_{-1}} - \frac{L}{L_{-1}} = \left(\frac{M_s}{M_d} \right)^{\zeta}_{-1} \cdot \left(\frac{\pi}{P} AE \right)^{\psi}_{-1} \qquad \text{(iii)}$$

A log linear approximation to this expression is given by:

$$\Delta r = \gamma_1(m_s - m_d)_{-1} + \gamma_2(\pi + e + a - b)_{-1} + \gamma_3\Delta l \tag{3}$$

The relationship between the parameters of equations (iii) and (3) will be discussed in a moment.

The demand for money function is cast in constant elasticity terms, and has the demand for real money balances depending upon permanent income, thus:

$$\frac{M}{P} d = dY^{*\delta_1} \tag{iv}$$

or in log linear form, with $\delta_0 = \log d$:

$$m_d = \delta_0 + \delta_1 y^* + p \tag{4}$$

The expected inflation rate is given by the following expression:

$$X = \epsilon_1(\pi + e + a - p) + \epsilon_2\Delta\pi \tag{5}$$

which captures the hypothesis that the domestic price level is expected to move towards a level at which the expression $(\pi + e + a - p)$ takes a value of zero and hence influences neither aggregate demand nor the balance of payments, the pace at which it changes being adjusted as a function of the rate at which the target value of the price level is itself moving. The reader will note that this formulation of expectations is somewhat different to that developed by Cross and Laidler [3] and used by Laidler [8]. It does appear to be the case that as far as Britain is concerned the formulation adopted in this paper is superior. Work is currently in progress to try to ascertain whether this superiority is particular to the British data, or also holds for the data for other countries studied by Cross and Laidler.

Finally, with C being domestic credit, the money supply identity is:

$$M_s = C + (R - L) \tag{v}$$

to the difference of which the following equation is a log linear approximation

$$\Delta m_s = \mu_1\Delta c + \mu_2\Delta r - \mu_3\Delta l \tag{6}$$

where

$$-\mu_3 = (1 - \mu_1 - \mu_2)$$

so that in equation (3):

$$\frac{\mu_3}{\mu_2} = -\gamma_3;\ \gamma_1 = \frac{\mu_2}{\mu_2 + \mu_3}\zeta;\ \gamma_2 = \frac{\mu_2}{\mu_2 + \mu_3}\psi$$

The model to be estimated consists of equations (1)–(6), and it is worthwhile highlighting some of its economic characteristics. Equation (1) says that output varies in response to government expenditure and taxes (monetary disequilibrium) and the ratio of foreign to domestic prices at the going exchange rate. Given that the base year for the domestic and foreign price indices is arbitrarily chosen as 1970, and that the exchange rate is defined as unity in that year, the parameter 'a' may be interpreted as telling us the proportionate amount by which domestic prices would have had to be higher for the balance of payments (*ceteris paribus*) to have had a zero value in that year, or equivalently, the proportion by which the domestic currency was undervalued in that year. Equation (2) is virtually self-explanatory though it might be noted that the variable 'y' is used there as a proxy for excess demand. It is being assumed implicitly that the trend value of output may be taken not only to represent permanent real income, but also the level of output that is compatible with the natural unemployment rate.

It is tempting to identify the first two terms of equation (3) as representing the capital account and the current account of the balance of payments respectively, but this would be an error. Excess cash balances may spill over into the capital account, to be sure, but they may also be spent on imports and on current domestic production diverted from exports. A deviation of international relative price levels from a long-run equilibrium value will influence the balance of trade, but it can also influence the capital account if the existence of disequilibrium is recognised by speculators.

The absence of an interest rate variable from the demand for money function is of course a significant omission. To have made it does, however, enable us considerably to simplify the model by allowing the omission of an equation to determine the interest rate. However, because this model is one in which the community is permitted to be off its demand for money function, to make the demand for real balances depend only upon income *does not* imply that only money matters for the determination of income, employment and prices, as it would in conventional IS-LM analysis. To the extent that variations in the ratio of current to permanent income may be regarded as a proxy for interest rate variations, the formulation of the money market adopted here is compatible with a systematic positive relationship between velocity and the level of interest rates. As to equation (5), its characteristic of having domestic prices expected to converge on a value given by world prices and the exchange rate means that the model as presented is suitable for analysing policy regimes where the exchange rate is treated as a policy variable, but not those which involve a clean float. To deal with the latter case, at least one extra equation determining the exchange rate would have to be added to the model. Finally, it should be noted that though the model contains both fiscal policy variables and the DCE rate, it does not link these two through explicit modelling of government budget constraint. This is for no better reason than that work on the model has not yet progressed to the stage of tackling this problem. The extent to which the results now to be presented are affected by this omission must remain to be seen.

The model was estimated using annual data for the period 1954–70. (The choice of time period was conditioned by the fact that economic growth seemed to follow a rather steady time trend over that period.) Given the role played in the model by trend income and deviations from it, to estimate over this period minimises the chance that difficulty in determining the value of trend income will undermine the estimation process. After 1970, there is a case to be made for the proposition that growth slowed down in the British economy.

The data used are printed in the Appendix and are described there (page 64). It is, however, worthwhile to make the following observations about them. World prices are proxied by a GNP geometrically weighted average of the consumer price indices of sixteen countries. The exchange rate is a similarly weighted average of exchange rates of the relevant currencies. Geometric weights were chosen to permit the multiplication of the price index by the exchange rate index to get a 'world price level in domestic currency' variable. A certain amount of early experiments with trade weights seemed to show that nothing hinged on the choice between them and GNP weights. The money supply variable used is M3. Reserves minus loans is defined as the integral of total currency flow concept of the balance of payments. Data on these variables are taken from Jonson [5] where the reader is warned that changes in this gross variable are probably more accurately measured than its level. Since the difference between M3 and this variable is equal to domestic credit outstanding, the latter variable was generated as a residual and therefore this series does differ from that contained in Bank of England statistics. Government expenditure includes both current and capital items while the tax rate is given by the ratio of direct plus indirect taxes minus cash benefits and subsidies paid to the public (excepting payments and receipts of the National Health Service) to national income. (In deriving the estimates reported in Table 2.1, the level of the tax rate rather than its deviation from its mean was used. This affects the value of the intercept of equation (1), but none of its other parameters.)

The model was estimated using full information maximum likelihood techniques, imposing all within and cross-equation constraints upon parameter values with the exception of the non-linear restriction on the intercept of equation (1). (The program used for estimation was developed by Dr Clifford Wymer.) A certain amount of difficulty was encountered in estimating the structure as specified above, especially as far as equation (1) is concerned. The years after 1967 saw a lower exchange rate, higher taxes, lower government expenditure relative to trend and, after 1968, tight monetary policy as well. Although this did not interfere with the estimation of the fiscal policy parameters α_3 and α_4, it did lead to great difficulty in simultaneously

Table 2.1 Parameter estimates and goodness-of-fit

Parameter	Value	SE	T
α_0	−.296	.049	6.04
α_1	0	Value imposed	
α_2	.066	.055	1.21
α_3	.232	.044	5.58
α_4	.171	.039	4.38
β	1.414	.210	6.72
γ_1	−2.240	.772	2.90
γ_2	2.587	1.027	2.78
δ_0	.880	.157	5.58
δ_1	.405	.035	11.68
ϵ_1	.202	.054	3.78
ϵ_2	.969	.200	4.83
a	.105	.029	3.62
μ_1	.760	.053	14.43
μ_2	.275	.057	4.81

Equation No.	R^2	R^2 in dynamic simulation
1 (with 4 substituted in)	.671	.555
2 (with 5 substituted in)	.573[a]	.993[b]
3 (with 4 substituted in)	.033	.031
6	.729[a]	.995[b]

[a]*On first difference of variable.*
[b]*On* level *of variable.*

getting well-determined estimates of a_1 and a_2. This problem was dealt with by successively constraining each of these parameters to zero. Overall, the more satisfactory results were obtained when a_1 was set equal to zero. It is these results which are presented in Table 2.1 and were used in the simulation exercises described later.

A few comments on these parameter estimates are necessary here. Most importantly, the fact that a_1 takes a zero value implies that, over the period 1954–70, variations in the quantity of money had a negligible effect on domestic output. Rather, the direct impact of monetary policy was overwhelmingly on the balance of payments. That is to say, and admittedly to my surprise, the results support what may be termed an extreme 'global monetarist' interpretation of the behaviour of the United Kingdom economy under the Bretton Woods system. (One implication of this result is that the causative channel running from DCE to domestic output and then through domestic prices to the balance of payments, emphasised in Laidler [7] is unimportant as far as the United Kingdom is concerned.) The second noteworthy (and troubling) point about the estimates is the extremely low value for the income elasticity of demand for money. Here, I would conjecture, the experiment of simplifying the model by not attempting directly to model the influence of the rate of interest on velocity has proved unsuccessful. Interest rates did rise on average over this period, and a downward bias to the measured value of income elasticity would be expected to result from their omission from the demand for money equation. This misspecification of the demand for money function may also have something to do with the model's inability to pick up any influence of money on real output, but this cannot be taken for granted. Another parameter about whose value there were *a priori* expectations is 'a', which appears in no fewer than three equations. The widely held view that the sterling exchange rate was an equilibrium one in the late 1950s would imply that the currency was overvalued by perhaps 7.5 per cent in 1970. It is therefore encouraging that the estimated value of 'a' is well within one standard error of this value.

The value of a_4, the coefficient on government expenditure, in equation (1) should be roughly equal to government expenditure's average share in GDP. It is a bit on the low side but well-determined as is the value of a_3, the coefficient on the tax rate. Thus, there can be no doubt that equation (1) does give support to the view that fiscal policy variables played an important and systematic role in determining the behaviour of output over the period to which this model was fitted. Equation (6) is an approximation to a linear identity, with the parameters μ_2 and μ_1 being estimates of the proportions borne by reserves and domestic credit respectively to the money supply. The former is a little on the high side and the latter on the low side, but not significantly.

Finally, it should be noted that all the parameters of the model are of the right sign and, with the exception of that attached to the relative price level term in the first equation, well within the usual bounds of statistical significance. The goodness-of-fit statistics for the four equations of the model do (with the exception of that for reserves) fall well within acceptable bounds, particularly when it is remembered that these are R^2s for constrained equations so that the possible range for this statistic is $-\infty$ to $+1$ rather than 0 to $+1$. It appears that this model, like many others, does not handle reserve movements very well, but it is notable that the errors made here do not cumulate systematically over time. If they did, this would be a serious matter because the money supply would then also go systematically off track.

In the simulation exercises reported in the next section, data are given for unemployment. These have been generated mechanically from the following regression, fitted to data for 1954–75, of the unemployment rate on y the proportional deviation of output from trend:

$$\underset{}{\mu} = \underset{(8.20)}{1.535} - \underset{(1.63)}{.183y} + \underset{(4.47)}{1.296} \text{ (D 1967 and after)}$$

It may be noted in passing that the intercept of this regression can be interpreted as giving a value for what is often called the 'natural' but is more neutrally termed the 'minimal sustainable' unemployment rate before 1967, and that the addition of the coefficient on the post-1967 dummy yields an estimate of that same variable for subsequent years. (Obviously these estimates are not sophisticated ones, and should not be taken too seriously.)

The Policy Problems of 1964, 1970 and 1977

This section will discuss the policy problems of 1964, 1970 and 1977 in the light of the foregoing analysis, and derive policy prescriptions for those problems. Attempts at predicting the outcome of these prescriptions, in terms of the explicit model of the British economy constructed along lines laid down in the preceding section, will also be described. The analysis confined itself to dealing with questions concerning inflation, real activity and the balance of payments and so does the following discussion. Failure to discuss other policy problems such as income distribution, or the balance between various sectors of the economy, does not imply that they are unimportant but only that I take the view that they may be treated as separate issues.

Episode 1: September 1964–September 1969

The two salient features of the international background against which policy decisions had to be taken in 1964 were the existence of the Bretton Woods system of more or less fixed exchange rates, and the extremely low and stable inflation rate ruling in the world economy. Though the world inflation rate was to rise dramatically later in the decade and although the Bretton Woods system was to collapse under the subsequent stresses, there was no way in which these eventualities could have been foreseen in 1964. Although the world inflation rate did step up by one percentage point after 1965 it was not until 1968 that its acceleration became really apparent. This is important, because it means that, in 1964, there was no incompatibility involved in pursuing price stability while maintaining a fixed exchange rate (which is not to say that a step change in the rate might not have been called for).

It is relatively uncontroversial that the early 1950s saw sterling undervalued, but that by the second half of the decade, equilibrium (in the sense of an exchange rate at which currency flows would be zero on average) had been restored to the foreign exchange market by the marginally faster pace at which British prices had risen in the intervening years (see, for example, Ball and Burns [2]). It is an implication of the economic theory of the preceding section of this paper that under such circumstances an equilibrium exchange rate, and balance of payments equilibrium, can be maintained if the rate of DCE is such as just to match the growth in the demand for money. In the 1950s and 1960s the real growth of the British economy was at about 3.1 per cent per annum, while world prices rose at an average rate of 2.4 per cent between 1960 and 1964. 3.1 per cent per annum is the trend growth rate upon which the variable Y^* used in the model described in the preceding section of this paper was based. Estimates (for example, those of Artis and Lewis [1] which I would regard as more reliable than that presented in Table 2.1) of the real income elasticity of demand for money (broadly defined) suggest that this parameter is unlikely to be less than unity. Thus, to maintain an inflation rate equal to that running abroad, and balance of payments equilibrium at the going exchange rate, after 1960, domestic credit should have grown at about 5.5 per cent of the money supply each year thereafter.

Although DCE had fallen somewhat short of this target in 1960–2 (a 'stop' phase of the cycle) it greatly exceeded the same target in 1963 and 1964. On this diagnosis a golden opportunity had been missed in 1963 to exercise patience and break out of the stop-go cycle once and for all while maintaining the exchange rate. Instead a 'dash for growth' had been undertaken and the monetary consequences ensured that a new government came to power just as the 'go' phase of a new cycle was building up to a balance of payments crisis. This, combined with a domestic inflation rate that was overtaking that ruling in the rest of the world, meant that sterling was becoming overvalued. However, one must not exaggerate the latter problem. On the assumption that the existing exchange rate was 'right' over the average of the 1956–60 period, sterling was overvalued relative to a weighted basket of world currencies by only 2.2 per cent in mid-1964 and was becoming progressively overvalued, again at most, at a rate of 2 per cent per annum. (The exchange rate in question is that on a weighted basket of currencies and not on the US dollar. The calculations given here are based on data presented in the Appendix to this paper.)

One can envisage three broad policy strategies to cope with the state of affairs that ruled in 1964, each involving a different treatment of the exchange rate. It could have been maintained, devalued, or floated. The latter step would have been incompatible with commitments under the Bretton Woods Agreement, and it would only have been necessary if the decision had also been taken to live with the existing inflation rate rather than pay the costs of reducing it. Inflation was then accelerating towards a peak of 4.6 per cent, a level regarded at the time as unreasonably high. For two reasons then, this alternative must be regarded as politically unrealistic.

At the other extreme lies the option actually chosen. It is commonly argued that failure to devalue in 1964 was an error. It is worth considering this view in terms of the evidence so far exhibited. In 1964, to make the existing exchange rate viable in the long run, the domestic price level would have had to be brought back into the same relationship that it, on average, bore to world prices over the period 1956–60. Moreover, it is hard to believe that policy measures undertaken in mid-1964 could have begun to influence the domestic inflation rate to any noticeable degree before mid-1965. Even so, if the only policy problem had been to restore an equilibrium exchange rate by, shall we say 1967, then there was still scope for prices to rise slightly over the intervening period.

Nevertheless, to set in motion at the very peak of the boom policies that would reduce the inflation rate to close to zero would have involved the near certainty of a sharp downturn in real activity. Such a policy might well have been politically possible, but a better one was available: namely, a small devaluation of 5 per cent, say, followed by a gradual tightening up of monetary policy over the following three years, approaching the long-run viable DCE rate of 5.5 per cent over a three-year horizon. The specific policy recommended here, then, is a devaluation of 5 per cent followed by the adoption of a time path for the DCE rate of 9.5 per cent in 1964, and 8.0 per cent, 6.5 per cent, 5.5 per cent and 5.5 per cent in the following years.

In order to carry out what is termed below the 'counter factual simulation' of the consequences of such a policy, values do of course have to be assigned to the other exogenous variables of the model. In this case, all other exogenous variables including those relating to fiscal policy were given their actual values. Thus the simulations tell us what, according to our model, would have happened if only exchange rate policy and monetary policy had been different over the period. The results are given in Table 2.2. Three sets of data are presented dealing in turn with what actually did happen and, according to a dynamic simulation of the model with actual values of all the exogenous variables, what ought to have happened, and finally what would have happened under alternative policies.

Given that all simulations were dynamic ones – that is, that they involved starting off in 1954 and then letting the model generate its own values for endogenous variables for subsequent years – the most interesting comparison is between the second and third columns of each section of Table 2.2. This is particularly so since this exercise concerns years within the period to which the model was initially fitted.

The results are largely self-explanatory. They show that the alternative policy would have caused a little more inflation early in the period (with, however, a steady decline subsequently), a steady build up of reserves and a gradual contraction of real income to its trend value. It is worth noting that the sharp downturn in real activity, shown by the counter-factual simulation to occur in 1969, results from the fiscal policies actually put in place at that time. Given that these

Table 2.2 Simulations, 1964–9

	1965	1966	1967	1968	1969
Rate of inflation					
Actual	4.61	3.81	2.62	4.59	5.24
Control simulation	3.22	3.59	3.79	2.82	5.28
Counter factual simulation	4.25	4.54	4.55	3.17	2.62
Level of reserves (£bn.)					
Actual	1.073	1.107	.992	.878	.922
Control simulation	1.216	1.179	1.108	1.022	1.264
Counter factual simulation	1.376	1.427	1.457	1.523	1.508
Rate of monetary expansion					
Actual	6.73	1.82	10.07	6.99	2.84
Control simulation	4.74	2.32	7.87	7.10	5.55
Counter factual simulation	6.88	4.47	3.83	3.87	4.59
Percentage deviation of real income from trend					
Actual	1.35	.60	.15	.02	−1.45
Counter simulation	1.14	.83	.70	−.12	−1.04
Counter factual simulation	1.30	1.02	.86	−.04	−1.74
Percentage unemployment					
Actual	1.21	1.32	2.04	2.13	2.13
Control simulation	1.33	1.38	2.70	2.85	3.02
Counter factual simulation	1.30	1.35	2.67	2.84	3.10

were in large measure a response to balance of payments problems which, according to Table 2.2, would not have arisen under the alternative policies, it would obviously have been possible to do better for that year. The only other point to note about Table 2.2 concerns the high levels of unemployment predicted by the mechanical extrapolation of the results for real income. These stem solely from the value of the post-1967 dummy variable. If the equation in question is fitted to data for 1954–70 instead of 1954–75, this variable takes the value .463, which would make these unemployment estimates more reasonable.

Episode 2: July 1970–July 1975

The Bretton Woods system was, of course, still in operation in 1970, though it was on its last legs. The stable and low world inflation rate no longer existed that in 1964 had made the maintenance of a fixed exchange rate a viable option for a country pursuing price stability as an important policy goal. Moreover, in 1967, sterling which had then probably been overvalued by about 5 per cent was devalued by 15 per cent. Over the period 1967–70 domestic prices had risen by only 2.5 percentage points more than had world prices. A further 7.5 percentage points thus had to be made good before long-run equilibrium was re-established at the new exchange rate, and that at a time when the world price level was itself rising at a rate in excess of 5 per cent. The maintenance of a fixed exchange rate in 1970 was thus a recipe for continuing and accelerating inflation. Hindsight provides ample justification for this judgement, because by mid-1972 an equilibrium price level had indeed been re-established given the exchange rate. (Once again the figures given here refer to the exchange rate against a weighted basket of currencies rather than to that on the US dollar.)

Of course, the situation in 1970 was characterised not just by high and rising inflation, but also by high and rising unemployment. Two factors had led to this state of affairs. First, a combination of demographic changes and a marked improvement in the relative economic status of the unemployed had shifted upwards the 'natural' unemployment rate. Second, and more important, monetary policy had been extremely tight from late 1968 onwards. On the assumption of a 3 per cent real growth rate, and a five-year period for the catch-up effects of the excessive devaluation of 1967 to work through, domestic credit should have expanded at a rate equal to about 8 per cent of the broad money stock to avoid putting downward pressure on domestic income and employment over the period 1967–70. Instead it had grown at close to 13 per cent over the first two years of the period, but then had actually fallen in 1969, and was expanding at only a 5 per cent rate in 1970. This tightness of policy from late 1969 onwards was bound to improve the balance of payments but also to depress domestic real income and employment.

By 1970 it was impossible to do more than mitigate the effects of previous policy on prices, income and employment. The most effective way in which this could have been accomplished would have involved an upward float, or straight revaluation of the currency to cut off what we might term the 'cost push' impulses that were arising both from the undervaluation of sterling and the high and rising world inflation rate. The abandonment of a fixed exchange rate of course would immediately have implied that the focus of monetary policy should have been shifted from regulating the DCE rate to the maintenance of balance of payments equilibrium to gearing the rate of monetary expansion to the achievement of a desired inflation rate. On assumptions already stated, a rate of increase of domestic credit of about 5.5 per cent per annum should have produced a long-run rate of inflation of about 2 per cent per annum. In point of fact, this is not far from the actual rate of credit expansion in 1970 and 1971, so that the domestic side of policy did begin the period on course. The initial appreciation of sterling would presumably have been about 7–8 per cent in 1970 and thereafter one might have expected further appreciation to take place at whatever rate necessary to reconcile a domestic inflation rate of about 2 per cent with that ruling in the world economy. Given what actually happened to the world inflation rate, the upward appreciation should have proceeded at a rate of 2 per cent per annum over the next two years, at about 5½ per cent in 1973, 8½ per cent in 1974 and 5½ per cent again in 1975.

It is hard to know how seriously simulations of our formal model for this period should be treated. They rest on the assumption that – with the exception of its long-run growth trend – the structure of the economy would have remained as it was during the 1950s and 1960s, had monetary and exchange rate policies other than those actually carried out been implemented. In fact it is clear that the economy's structure after 1970 is not properly represented by the parameter estimates given in Table 2.1. A dynamic simulation of the model beyond 1970, using actual values of the exogenous variables, produces results that are best described as nonsense. It is for this reason that Table 2.3, unlike Table 2.2 does not contain results for control simulations. For the counter-factual simulations in Table 2.3 to be treated as anything other than science fiction, a case must be made that the post-1970 changes to the economy's structure were the result of policies actually carried out.

Further, but as yet incomplete, work on the model over the post-1970 period suggests that some at least of the changes in question might plausibly be treated as responses to actual policy; but any interpretations of the post-1970 evidence whose characteristics are now sketched out must be extremely tentative. The Phillips curve equation changes radically after 1970. The parameter ϵ_1 goes to zero, while ϵ_2 becomes significantly larger. That agents should no longer believe that prices will converge on an equilibrium level, given the foreign price level and the exchange rate, is only to be expected when the authorities have announced that the exchange rate is in future to be allowed to become the 'slack variable' – that of course is what was done in 1972.

Moreover, the speeding up of the response of inflation expectations to experience, implicit in the growth of the parameter ϵ_2, might plausibly be put down to an increased consciousness of inflation generated by the high inflation rates of the 1970s. These changes, in short, might be thought to have been the result of policy, as might an apparent reversal of the importance of the parameters a_1 and a_2 in equation (1), not to mention inability to find a role for fiscal policy during this period. One would expect output to respond much less to the structure of relative prices between home and abroad if it is known that the exchange rate will be permitted to adjust to take care of any discrepancy between them, while a flexible exchange rate would tend to bottle up the effects of domestic monetary disequilibrium at home.

The difficulty with the above interpretation is, of course, that it was not just the United Kingdom economy that underwent violent fluctuations in the early 1970s. An equally plausible case can be made that the changes to the model's structure just noted were a response not only to domestic policy but also to happenings in the world economy, not least the breakdown of the Bretton Woods system. If that is the case, then it is inappropriate to use the parameter estimates listed in Table 2.1 for simulating the consequences of alternative policies after 1970, and particularly from 1972 onwards.

Two other problems ought to be mentioned. It is clear that simply to extrapolate the growth rate of real income of the 1950s and 1960s into the 1970s will not do, and yet the deviation of income from such a trend plays a vital role in the model. The 'solution' to this problem was to fit a separate trend to data for 1970–6, subject to the constraint that it began at the same value for 1970 as was generated by the original 1952–70 trend. The arbitrary hypothesis that the growth rate changed sharply and exogenously in 1970 is thus embedded in the results set out in Table 2.3, and is not an easy one to defend.

The second problem is just as serious. The structure of the model does not, when it is simulated even one year beyond its sample period – that is into 1971 – enable us to pick up the large balance of payments surplus, rapid monetary expansion and accelerating inflation of that year. Something – I would conjecture the influence of monetary disequilibrium abroad on the British balance of payments – is missing from the model that is all too present in the data for that period and its effects are in no way taken account of in the counter-factual simulations.

The results of these simulations, for what they are worth, are presented in Table 2.3. They were generated on the assumptions that, in the years 1970–4, fiscal policy was just as it in fact was, the rate of DCE was held at 5.5 per cent, the exchange rate appreciated by 8 per cent in 1970, 2 per cent in 1971, 2 per cent in 1972, 5½ per cent in 1973, 8½ per cent in 1974 and 5½ per cent in 1975 *and that exchange rate changes were fully foreseen.* Thus the rate of appreciation of the exchange rate for the following year was subtracted from the

Table 2.3 Simulations, 1971–5

	1971	1972	1973	1974	1975
Rate of inflation					
Actual	8.98	6.89	8.74	14.87	21.72
Counter factual simulation	.78	.16	−1.34	1.42	9.90
Level of reserves (£bn.)					
Actual	2.583	1.891	2.101	2.180	1.511
Counter factual simulation	.824	1.392	1.451	1.495	1.479
Rate of monetary expansion					
Actual	10.71	24.34	24.84	11.37	7.87
Counter factual simulation	3.60	3.79	3.79	3.33	3.31
Percentage deviation of output from trend					
Actual	−1.19	.55	3.49	−.10	−.27
Counter factual simulation	−3.29	−2.79	−.84	.76	1.45
Unemployment					
Actual	3.12	3.32	2.24	2.43	3.79
Counter factual simulation	3.43	3.34	2.98	2.69	2.57

world inflation rate in equation (5) in order to lower it to an expected rate of world inflation measured in domestic currency. The results are self-explanatory, showing virtual price stability until 1975, stability of reserves (after 1971) and a slightly deeper, and more prolonged, recession than actually occured in 1971–2. Clearly in the light of the high inflation rate that the model projects for 1975, a greater revaluation of sterling ought to have been prescribed for that year. In short, the results show that monetarist policies would have worked as expected *if* the structure of the British economy had remained as it was in the 1950s and 1960s into the 1970s.

Episode 3: Early 1977–December 1981

There would probably be a consensus that the policy problems of mid-1977 are more difficult than those of the other two episodes under consideration in this paper, and not only because we lack the extra information about them that can only come from hindsight. Once more, it will be helpful briefly to discuss the sequence of events that had led to the current state of affairs, which may be described as the trough (or the aftermath) of the most serious stop-go cycle of post-war years.

It has already been argued that it would have been better to permit the exchange rate to appreciate from 1970 onwards. Failure to do this ensured a continuing high inflation rate into 1971 and 1972, although the slack in the economy generated by the tight policy towards DCE in 1969–71 did begin to reduce inflation at the end of 1971. This error of policy was compounded by the budgets of 1972 and 1973, and the methods adopted to finance them. In 1972 DCE ran at about 29 per cent of the money supply, and at a slightly slower rate in 1973 – though in this case the annual figure is made up of an even higher rate early in the year and a sharp contraction later on. Because the exchange rate was finally floated in 1972 just at the time when an equilibrium exchange rate had been reached, this expansion nearly all materialised in an expansion of the money supply accompanied by an exchange rate depreciation. Thus the 1973 boom and the subsequent accelerating inflation of 1973–5 was set in motion. It has already been noted that monetary policy was reversed in late 1973. An extremely tight policy persisted throughout 1974, slackened somewhat in 1975, but then tightened up again in 1976, particularly in the second half of the year. However, it was only in 1976 that the public sector borrowing requirement began to come down. Before then, an acute imbalance between monetary and fiscal policy put particular pressure upon the private sector.

Finally, the reversal of monetary policy in late 1973 came at the very moment when the sudden increase in oil prices might have been thought to require an easing of monetary policy to offset any effects on real aggregate demand that it might have had. One should not exaggerate, however, the importance of this last factor as far as 1973–4 is concerned. The exploration and development of North Sea oil was well along in 1973 and the major effect of the oil price increase must have been to change the time profile of British income rather than to reduce its permanent level. The very fact that it proved possible to stabilise the exchange rate for eighteen months immediately afterwards, and to maintain national expenditure at a level substantially above national output in the interim by borrowing both on private and public sector account overseas must owe much to this often overlooked fact.

For Britain the importance of the 1973 oil price increase is that it complicates the policy problem of 1977 as a result of the balance of payments effects of North Sea production. It is worth digressing for a while to deal with this issue. Put briefly, oil revenues are contributing to a balance of payments surplus which is tending to push the exchange rate up and undermine the international competitiveness of the manufacturing sector, hence threatening to cause it to contract. The question then arises as to what state will the latter sector be in when the oil has run out. It is sometimes suggested that the exchange rate be held down to offset these effects. However, such a policy would be ineffective in achieving its goal, because monetary expansion would replace a rising exchange rate and the extra domestic inflation thereby generated would have an at least qualitatively similar effect on the international competitiveness of manufacturing. Even if the exchange rate were to be held down by a premature repayment of international debts, this could only delay matters. As Britain's international indebtedness fell, sterling would become a more attractive currency to hold, the balance of payments would begin to strengthen, and again either exchange appreciation or domestic monetary expansion would be the result. In short, one way or another, oil must compete with manufacturing for resources. There is nothing that *macro* policy can do to change that, but of course the way in which both the government and the private sector use their share of oil revenues will have a profound effect upon the future of the economy. The implication of the foregoing argument is, not that the problems raised by North Sea oil are insoluble, but the *micro* rather than macro policy tools should be deployed to deal with them.

Macro-policy instruments in 1977, as always, can influence output, unemployment and inflation. High unemployment is the inevitable consequence of extremely restrictive monetary policy, and my view remains as it was in 1974: that monetary policy has been, and is, too restrictive. Inflation, though high, has fallen markedly since 1975 albeit not continuously. It is usual to put this down to the operation of incomes policy. In the absence of any evidence that incomes policy did more than provide the institutional framework through which the downward pressure on inflation being exerted by excess capacity operated, I interpret this falling inflation rate as a manifestation of the Phillips curve mechanism (albeit an expectations augmented Phillips curve).

In short, and once more, the macro question resolves itself into one of choosing a time path for the money supply, DCE, and a related path for the exchange rate. It is compounded by the balance of payments effects of North Sea oil which make it far more difficult to come to any firm conclusion about the equilibrium value for the exchange rate than it was for other episodes. The case for a clean float of the exchange rate is thus far stronger in 1977 than it was in either 1964 or 1970. Hence the first aspect of my prescription for the present juncture is that the exchange rate be set free to find its own level. Given that the inflation rate has been running at 17 per cent, it is suggested that the rate of monetary expansion now (June 1977) be increased to 15 per cent for the next year, and thereafter be reduced at a rate of two percentage points per annum. This easing up on the monetary side does of course involve a slowing down of the rate at which inflation is brought under control, but it should help the level of real activity and hence make it possible to continue to bring fiscal policy, particularly as it influences the public sector borrowing requirement, back to a position that is compatible with the maintenance of a low rate of monetary expansion in the long run. At present the effects of excessively tight monetary policy on income and employment make it politically difficult, and, from the point of view of the unemployment problem, undesirable, to contract government expenditure by as much as one would otherwise like to see.

As the reader will already have inferred, it is not possible, given the current state of the development of the model upon which previous simulations have been based, to indulge in such exercises for this period. Whether the structure of the economy would have changed under alternative policies from 1970 onwards may be a moot question, but there is no doubt that in fact it did change, and in a way that has not yet proved completely amenable to formal modelling along the lines set out above. Certain relationships do, however, seem to have survived, which are key ones as far as the policy recommendations made in the previous section of this paper are concerned.

To begin with the demand for money function, even in the primitive form in which it appears in the model does not seem to have disappeared in the 1970s, at least according to preliminary work, nor does the relationship between excess demand and the rate of inflation. There are also signs that monetary disequilibrium has played some role in influencing domestic income and employment in these later years. What have not survived from the 1954–70 structure are the linkages between Britain and the rest of the world and, closely related, the mechanism whereby inflation expectations are formed, not to mention the firm links between fiscal policy variables and the level of activity. The extent to which the breakdown of the international monetary system, the oil price shock, not to mention the domestic political uncertainties of the period may have contributed to all this must be a matter for future investigation.

For the present discussion, forecasts would better be described as guesses. Since a clean float of the exchange rate is envisaged, the question of forecasting the behaviour of reserves does not arise. Moreover, the whole reason for recommending a clean float at present stems from uncertainty about what the equilibrium value of the exchange rate actually is. The estimates of the parameter 'a' are of no help here because they are based on data generated before the advent of the oil price shock and North Sea oil. And this is not to mention uncertainties concerning the policies that will be adopted by other countries. However, since a stable demand for money function still seems to exist, and an excess demand inflation relationship, it is possible to hazard a few guesses about the behaviour of inflation and unemployment. Given the rather slow monetary contraction that is envisaged – and that some expansion is actually recommended for the first year – it is hard to see that domestic inflation could fall any lower than 5 per cent by 1981, after remaining rather constant during 1978 as a result of the initial boost given to the economy. As to unemployment, one would hope that the same early bout of expansionary monetary policy might reduce it somewhat in the first year, but *if* the regression mentioned above does give a rough estimate of the natural unemployment rate, then it would be surprising if the rate had fallen to less than 3 per cent by 1981.

References

[1] Artis, M. J. and Lewis, M. K., 'The demand for money in the United Kingdom 1963–1973', *Manchester School* 44, June 1976, pp. 147–81.

[2] Ball, R. J. and Burns, T., 'The inflationary mechanism in the UK economy', *American Economic Review* 66, September 1976, pp. 467–84.

[3] Cross, R. J. and Laidler, D., 'Inflation, excess demand and expectations in fixed exchange rate open economies: some preliminary results', in Parkin, J. M. and Zis, G. (eds.), *Inflation in the World Economy*, Manchester University Press, 1976.

[4] Jonson, P. D., 'An investigation of the UK balance of payments with particular emphasis on the role of monetary factors and disequilibrium dynamics, 1880–1970', Ph.D. dissertation, University of London, 1975.

[5] Jonson, P. D., Moses, E. and Wymer, C. R., 'A minimal model of the Australian economy', Research Discussion Paper 7601, Reserve Bank of Australia, Sydney, 1976.
[6] Laidler, D., 'The finance of government expenditure and the control of the money supply', Evidence given to the House of Commons Expenditure Committee, London, HMSO, 1975.
[7] Laidler, D, *Essays on Money and Inflation*, Manchester University Press, 1975, chapter 9, 'Price and output fluctuations in an open economy'.
[8] Laidler, D., 'Inflation in Britain: a monetarist perspective', *American Economic Review* 66, September 1976, pp. 485–500.
[9] Mayer, T. (ed.), *The Structure of a Monetarism: A Symposium*, W. W. Norton, New York, 1977.

Sources of Appendix Data

Real income – Gross Domestic Product (*International Financial Statistics*, May 1977) line 99b deflated by consumer prices.

Consumer prices – *International Financial Statistics*, May 1977, line 64.

World prices – a GDP weighted average of the consumer prices of nineteen western industrial countries. The countries used were: Australia; Austria; Belgium; Canada; Denmark; Finland; France; Ireland; Israel; Italy; Japan; Netherlands; New Zealand; Norway; South Africa; Sweden; Switzerland; United States; West Germany. Data on GDP prices and exchange rates for these countries were obtained from *International Financial Statistics*, May 1977.

Exchange rate – a GDP weighted average of foreign currency values. *International Financial Statistics*, May 1977, lines rf and rh.

Money Supply – M3 end period.

* Official reserves – end period, Bank of England Statistical Abstract up to end 1966. Thereafter series generated by adding or subtracting Official Reserves, Drawing On ... etc. e.g., in Bank of England Statistical Abstract No. 2. Table 20.2.

* Loans – Official Reserves minus integral of total currency flow, as given in Statistical Abstract Table 20.2.

* Domestic credit – M3 – (R – L).

* Government expenditure – central and local government expenditure on current goods and services and capital formation. 1952–65. Based on data in Feinstein Tables 2 and 39. Thereafter various issues of the Blue Book.

* Taxes – tax receipts net of cash benefits and subsidies (excluding National Health Scheme transactions) 1952–65. Based on Feinstein Table 14. Thereafter various issues of the Blue Book.

* Data taken from Jonson [4].

Appendix: Data 1952–77

	Real income £bn.	Consumer price 1970 = 100	World prices 1970 = 100	Exchange rate £/F.C.U. 1970 = 100	Money supply £bn.	Official reserves £bn.	Loans £bn.	Domestic credit £bn.	Government spending £bn. at 1970 prices	Net taxes as % of GDP	Unemployment %
1952	27.77	56.4	64.5	88.0	8.65	.659	.237	8.2	7.18	.215	1.78
53	29.44	57.3	65.0	87.8	8.98	.899	.181	8.26	7.57	.219	1.44
54	30.53	58.3	65.5	87.9	9.35	.986	.142	8.51	7.56	.210	1.19
55	31.77	60.3	65.7	87.7	9.05	757	.142	8.44	7.46	.215	0.96
56	32.94	62.9	67.0	87.8	9.19	.799	.343	8.73	7.64	.208	1.10
57	33.72	65.0	68.7	87.8	9.52	.812	.343	9.05	7.78	.210	1.31
58	34.19	66.8	71.0	86.8	9.84	1.096	.337	9.08	7.72	.211	1.95
59	35.82	67.2	71.9	85.9	10.38	.977	.200	9.61	8.20	.205	1.94
60	37.60	67.9	73.2	85.7	10.57	1.154	.052	9.47	8.56	.195	1.46
61	39.07	69.8	74.2	85.9	10.78	1.185	.422	10.02	9.06	.200	1.39
62	39.41	72.5	76.0	85.8	11.09	1.002	.047	10.13	9.36	.209	1.74
63	41.12	73.9	77.9	85.8	11.79	.949	.052	10.89	9.76	.199	2.00
64	43.49	76.3	79.6	85.8	12.23	.827	.625	12.03	10.45	.199	1.39
65	44.57	79.9	81.8	85.8	13.08	1.073	1.224	13.23	10.91	.211	1.21
66	45.73	83.0	84.6	85.8	13.32	1.107	1.849	14.06	11.70	.221	1.32
67	47.08	85.2	87.0	86.8	14.73	.992	2.405	16.15	12.80	.229	2.04
68	48.61	89.2	90.4	99.9	15.80	.878	3.701	18.62	12.92	.236	2.13
69	49.38	94.0	94.7	99.8	16.26	.922	3.058	18.39	12.57	.254	2.13
70	51.02	100.0	100.0	100.0	17.78	1.047	1.763	18.49	13.21	.261	2.30
71	52.15	109.4	104.9	99.8	19.78	2.583	.028	17.73	13.50	.245	3.12
72	53.90	117.2	109.5	101.1	25.24	1.891	.477	23.82	14.01	.220	3.32
73	56.38	127.9	117.7	109.1	32.35	2.101	1.476	31.73	14.91	.212	2.24
74	55.24	148.4	132.5	113.0	36.25	2.180	3.227	37.30	16.06	.214	2.43
75	56.01	184.4	145.8	120.5	39.22	1.511	4.037	41.74	17.25	.218	3.79
76	56.24	215.0			44.54	.658	6.182	50.69	16.87		5.24

3 Stabilisation Policy in Britain 1964–81

by R. J. Ball and T. Burns*

Introduction

The object of this paper is to examine the history of stabilisation policy in the United Kingdom since 1964 and to project proposed policies to be followed to 1981 using the London Business School model of the economy. The exercise explicitly excludes consideration of problems of the underlying rate of growth of productive potential. It focusses on the question as to whether the pursuit of alternative macroeconomic policies could have resulted in more satisfactory paths of output, employment, inflation and the balance of payments over the historical periods 1964–9 and 1970–5, giving the prevailing underlying rate of growth of economic efficiency. A similar assumption underlies the projection to 1981. The exercise is therefore strictly limited and has little or nothing to say about important issues of industrial structure and performance which may be of far wider significance or about the effects of taxation on incentives or the detailed distribution of national resources.

Even within the terms of reference, there are difficulties in interpreting and analysing the results that have been well summarised by Blackaby [3]. Individual models of the behaviour of the economy will differ in structure and important differences in conclusions may be arrived at as a consequence of the structure rather than the manipulation of the models employed. This may lead to the view that conclusions drawn from a given model tell one more about the behaviour of the model rather than the behaviour of economic reality. Thus criticisms of policy do not necessarily take place within a common and agreed framework of how the economy functions, but may arise directly from a belief that policy making has been inadequate because

* The study reported in this paper has been supported by the Social Science Research Council, to whom we are extremely grateful. We are also very much indebted to Ann Aves, A. Gosling, Ruth Kosmin, Jan Laury, Ann Sheppard and Peter Warburton without whose constant help none of the results presented here would have been possible.

the wrong model of the economy has been employed. Nevertheless, comparative results are not without interest in that they may at least reveal the significance for policy of the alternative specifications pursued.

Simulation Analysis

The London Business School model of five years ago, described in Renton [7], was presented as a conventional Keynesian type, and contained a detailed specification of expenditure decisions relating to the components of GDP. It could also be described as Keynesian insofar as the main impact of monetary variables on expenditures came from the effect of interest rates, particularly on fixed residential and non-residential spending, rather than from changes in the monetary stock and explicit wealth variables. The first major addition to that model related to the endogenisation of the money supply and a full articulation of the flows of funds by sector, which followed the completion of work on the revenue generation of the public sector.

With some inevitable changes in equation detail, this version of the model, together with an important assumption about the behaviour of real wages, formed the basis for the simulation exercises with regard to the effects of a once-and-for-all shift of the exchange rate on the major economic variables in the economy and the balance of payments, that were reported in Ball, Burns and Laury [2]. The important assumption with regard to real wages was that eventually changes in prices would be offset by changes in pre-tax wages. As demonstrated in Ball, Burns and Laury [2], there exists a class of wage and price models which includes representations of behaviour as far apart as the long-run vanishing Phillips curve and the so-called Scandinavian model of price formation, which lead to the conclusion that, under a fixed exchange rate system, the domestic rate of inflation will ultimately be determined by the rate of change of import prices. For the purpose of simulation analysis, the rate of change of money wages was determined by the rate of change of prices, plus a long-term effect given by the rate of increase of average productivity. No allowance was made for any effect of unemployment or the pressure of demand on wage changes. The practical consequence of this specification was to leave the absolute price level indeterminate, the missing equation being provided by the import price level. This in turn depended on the world inflation rate that was assumed to be exogenous. Thus the domestic inflation rate under a fixed exchange rate was anchored by the world inflation rate.

Two important consequences stemmed from this specification of the model. The first was that, under a fixed exchange rate, the rate of inflation was ultimately determined by the world rate. This was consistent with that derived from conventional monetarism which approached the problem from a rather different route. It was shown that this conclusion could be derived from the assumption that, in the long run, the wage function was homogeneous in absolute wages and prices. It did not require either the acceptance of the 'natural rate' doctrine of unemployment and therefore a vanishing Phillips curve, or the criticised assumption of 'one price'. Secondly it was shown that the effect of an exchange rate change on the balance of payments depends on the fiscal policies pursued after the exchange rate change. While the lagged responses in the model were longer than those proposed by early versions of the New Cambridge economics, it was shown that, in the longer run, adjustment in the balance of payments required an offsetting adjustment in the public sector deficit. Under free collective bargaining and no fiscal or monetary measures other than the indexation of government grants and tax rates, the effects of an exchange rate change on the balance of payments were shown to be temporary. Any permanent effect could only be brought about by the deflationary effects of the exchange rate change which operated through the deflation of non-indexed government grants and through fiscal drag, which generated the required change in the public sector deficit. In either case, whether fiscal policy was such as to produce the required change in the public sector deficit or not, the effect of a given devaluation was to raise the domestic price level in the same proportion in the long run.

It follows that the specification of wage response is crucial to the way in which the model responds to policy changes as evidenced by the devaluation example. Moreover, as shown by Ball [1], the specification of the wage function is not only important for inflation theory but also for real multiplier analysis. The long-run properties of the model depend upon the extent to which there is a long-term trade-off between unemployment and real wages or, in the absence of an unemployment effect, the extent to which there is full passing through of price changes into wage changes. It should be noted that, for the purposes of the present exercise, the wage and price structure essentially reflects the Scandinavian model of wage-price behaviour. Export prices are determined in world markets. In turn they substantially influence domestic manufacturing prices, which enter into the determination of the own-product manufacturing real wage.

Failure to predict the sharp drop in consumers' expenditure in 1975 resulted in a reconsideration of the behaviour of consumers' expenditure and the impact of inflation on real spending. The failure to account for the substantial fall in consumers' spending in 1975 was judged to be a failure to model properly the response of consumers to the effects of inflation on personal balance sheets. Thus the rise in the savings ratio that occurred not only in the United Kingdom but also elsewhere was interpreted as an attempt by consumers to restore a normal ratio of wealth to income. In the model as it existed previously, inflation affected consumers' expenditure in a strictly traditional fashion, to the extent that inflation succeeded in reducing consumers' real incomes. No real balance or wealth effects entered as independent arguments into the consumer spending functions. We are now convinced by the data that these effects can be powerful if the inflation rate is fast enough and that previous empirical difficulties have arisen because, over much of the postwar period, inflation rates have not been high enough to reveal such behaviour. Hence simple flow analysis was sufficient to explain most of the historical variations in consumer spending.

The current model allows for such effects, which are potentially strong in two ways. Firstly, the behaviour of the savings ratio has been related to the rate of change of money rather than real incomes, which captures part of the impact of inflation on monetary assets. Secondly, the savings ratio has been explicitly related to the stock of liquid assets in the hands of the personal sector. The important consequence of this for the behaviour of the model is that effects of change in the inflation rate of the kind we have experienced in recent years can have quite powerful effects on real consumer spending that were not allowed for hitherto. If the hypothesis is correct, a sharp reduction in the rate of inflation could exercise a marked effect on the savings ratio and consequently on the rate of consumer spending.

In the model as it stands, balance sheet effects have no influence on real fixed capital expenditure by the company sector, which is still explained by a version of the neo-classical theory of capital accumulation. Effects of inflation on real capital spending largely operate through their effect on the real rate of return. However, stockbuilding has been related to the overall financial posture of the company sector as represented by the behaviour of the company sector financial deficit, and the behaviour of the deficit is significant in explaining some of the sharp movements in stockbuilding that have been seen in recent years. Interest rate effects on private housebuilding and the availability of funds in the mortgage market have, for several years, exerted a relatively strong effect in the model. Thus the overall effects of changes in wealth variables, interest rates and financial flows play a fundamentally more important part in explaining economic behaviour than in the versions of the model described previously.

The central problem, with which we have been confronted in the specification of the model for the purpose of the present exercises, concerns the behaviour of the model under floating rather than fixed exchange rates. The general thesis has been advanced elsewhere (for example, Budd & Burns [4]) with regard to the behaviour of the exchange rate and its relationship to monetary policy and has been designated by some as 'international monetarism'. We have been unable to model to our satisfaction the operation of a free floating exchange rate regime. The major problems lie with the satisfactory specification of the market clearing mechanisms for the foreign exchange market and the response of export prices to continuous depreciation.

The first problem lies in the failure to model the complete capital account. A necessary requirement of a floating exchange rate system is that the foreign exchange market should clear in response to a fiscal shock. Thus if we shock the system in such a way that a balance of payments deficit emerges then either private capital flows must emerge to finance the deficit or the exchange rate must behave in a manner to correct the current account. As we would not expect capital flows to indefinitely finance the current account, it is a requirement that the current account returns to balance. Three obvious channels are available to bring this about. If exchange rate depreciation generates a permanent increase in competitiveness there will be an improvement in net exports. Secondly, the higher inflation rate that follows the depreciation will depress private sector expenditure and hence imports. Thirdly, the problems of a rapidly depreciating currency may force the government to take measures to offset the initial shock.

The basic requirement is for a private sector capital flows equation that responds to exchange rate effects so that ultimately we can compute the exchange rate changes required to produce overall balance. In the absence of a fully specified capital account we have employed a reduced form exchange rate function to attempt to capture this effect. We have related the exchange rate to the relative money stock and a term to represent relative output movements. We have called the computed values from this relationship the 'normal' exchange rate. The gap between the actual exchange rate and this 'normal rate' is then related to its own lagged value, flows of sterling balances held by the OPEC countries and the cumulative current account level. This does not have the property of ultimately clearing the current account but it does enable us to see an outline of the adjustment mechanism.

The second issue is the response of export prices to continuous depreciation. In the current version of the model, export prices are related in the long run to the sterling value of world export prices with an adjustment mechanism to allow time for the exchange rate to have its full effect. The result of this formulation is that the level of competitiveness depends upon the change in the exchange rate and it is possible to obtain an improvement in exports by continuous depreciation. This appears to be consistent with the facts but we doubt its long run validity as we would expect exporters to adjust their expectations to offset this anticipated depreciation. The only lags then would represent orders made in sterling waiting to be delivered; but if the contract has been made, a subsequent depreciation would not affect export volumes. Thus in the long run we would expect competitiveness to adjust to continous depreciation unless it simply represented delivery lags and we would not expect these to increase export volumes.

The net effect of these developments of the model can be summarised in terms of the reaction to external shocks and changes in exogenous variables. Such shocks can be considered in the case of a fixed exchange rate or in the case of a changing exchange rate according to the function just described. Clearly for the reason given this function does not represent the consequences of fully floating the rate. For present purposes it is convenient to describe this case as one of *flexible* as compared to *fixed* exchange rates.

Under fixed exchange rates, the effect of a standard shock to the system of £100 million in real government current spending is not qualitatively different from the multiplier effects described in Renton [7], although in the case of a simple shock from public spending under a fixed rate the cycle is fairly weak. As in the case described in Renton, after allowing for the cycle the long-run multiplier looks to be something close to unity. In qualitative terms this is a fairly conventional result because of the strong leakages. Compared to historical Keynesian beliefs the computed multiplier is low but clearly not zero as in the case of conventional monetary models of the closed economy.

While for reasons already given the fully floating exchange rate case is deficient, some indication is given by looking at the effect of a change in government spending for a flexible exchange rate determined as above. The effects are markedly different from the fixed exchange rate case.

In broad terms the output response is less although behaviour is complicated by the fact that with a flexible exchange rate the five-year cycle that is present in the model is strongly activated. The rise in government spending causes the exchange rate to fall and subsequently interest rates rise more strongly than in the fixed exchange rate case. Both stockbuilding and fixed investment exhibit a stronger cyclical pattern. The fall in the exchange rate reduces the impact of the measures upon the balance of payments, primarily through its effect on inflation which crowds out consumers' expenditure. As opposed to the fixed exchange rate case, under flexible rates real consumers' expenditure falls sharply and the private sector surplus rises to offset the increase in the government borrowing requirement. The output effect is stronger than one would expect under a fully floating rate, which in part reflects the relatively slow elimination of the competitive advantage on the volume of exports, which at present is not consistent with our own *a priori* view of the likely pattern of adjustment. Part of the return to equilibrium in the balance of payments is achieved by the fall in the exchange rate but at the cost of a faster rate of inflation which in turn reduces real income and raises the savings ratio. Our view is that the model exaggerates in this form the permanent gain in output that would be obtained under a fully floating rate.

There are certain obvious similarities between the fixed and flexible rate cases for a tax cut, although the absolute effects on output are very much lower. The principal difference between raising government spending by £100 million and reducing real taxation by an equivalent amount lies in the import response. In the case of the tax cut obviously the major impact is on consumer spending with a pronounced effect on imports. For a real tax cut the long-run multiplier is as low as 0.5 in the fixed exchange rate case which reflects the large leakages in the system. Under a flexible rate the output response is even lower. Initially consumer spending rises strongly but faster inflation over twelve quarters reduces the increase.

Moreover, as in the case of an increase in public spending with a flexible rate interest rates rise more strongly and fixed investment is cut back. Thus both the flexible rate calculations for a rise in real public spending and a tax cut exemplify strong crowding out of private spending through the exchange rate/inflation mechanism, supported in addition by the rise in interest rates. These effects in the model are clearly quite strong although probably still an underestimate.

Money wage shocks and interest rate shocks in an upward direction both have negative effects on the behaviour of output in the longer run and such shocks are destabilising to the extent that they exaggerate the five-year cycle. At the trough of the cycle, a sustained increase in interest rates of 2 per cent above the control reduces the rate of fixed investment by as much as £400 million in the full year. In the case of a once-and-for-all change in the exchange rate, i.e. devaluation, the general effects are similar to those already described in Ball, Burns and Laury [2].

In the following sections we have only used the model in 'fixed exchange rate' form. Ideally we would have liked to have manipulated the model under conditions that reflected fully free floating but for reasons described this has proved difficult. Accordingly we have followed a less complete and less elegant two-step procedure which we believe should closely approximate the results of a more integrated exercise. The first step has been to stabilise the exchange rate, taking into account the relationship between the exchange rate, purchasing power parity and the position of the money supply relative to the world output at the beginning of each period. The second step has been to set fiscal and monetary policies that are consistent with this particular rate.

Policy Simulation of the Three Episodes

In principle the analysis of history and the derivation of policy recommendations might be carried out in the context of an optimal control application, but this has not been attempted here. We have begun each historical analysis with an attempt to use our model to categorise the monetary and fiscal stance represented by the economy at the outset. Both history and our subsequent recommendations bear comparison with what might be described as pursuing a neutral monetary and fiscal policy, but such a designation is not easy to uphold and conveys a degree of uniformity of understanding of such a term which might be misleading. In practice we have attempted to de-policise the historical periods in certain important respects, but what we have attempted to remove from history and what is left is obviously in part a matter of choice. We choose, therefore, to describe the course of events that is calculated according to the changes described below as representing the 'base case' for each episode.

At the outset, the actual course of history is adjusted to the model outturn by setting the residuals of individual equations at appropriate levels. To remove policies actually pursued and to build in the assumptions of the base case with regard to exogenous variables such as public expenditure is not as easy as it might appear at first sight. The general problem is that the model residuals reflect, in part, behaviour following policy changes such as incomes policies and the import surcharge. Hence the residual errors are correlated with the policy changes but the degree of correlation is not known. The case of incomes policy is a clear example. Although we include dummy variables to account for the impact of incomes policies, simply setting such dummy variables to zero does not adequately characterise the consequences of 'policy off' since there are other residuals in adjacent quarters which are affected by them. A similar and more complicated case is that of the operation of the temporary import surcharge that was in effect between 1964 and the end of 1966.

For the purpose of the historical exercises the base case policies were arrived at as follows:

(i) Government current and capital spending were set to grow at their trend rates of growth from the beginning of the period. The trend rates of growth were obtained by fitting trend lines to the series over the period from 1958–76. To avoid a sudden jump in spending at the beginning of the period these trend values were adjusted by a constant amount to make them consistent with recent experience.

(ii) Personal income tax rates and allowances and indirect taxes were indexed to the price level. In the case of income tax this was achieved by setting the ratio of tax to income levels to move with the growth rate of the economy. Local authority rates and the tax rates on beer, wines, spirits and tobacco, motor vehicles duties and hydro-carbon oils duties were adjusted to the price level.

(iii) The effective minimum deposit rate was set at 20 per cent throughout. This was taken as being close to the average value for the whole period.

(iv) Bank rate (subsequently MLR) followed the course of an estimated 'reaction function' where it was related to lagged values of the inflation rate, the change in the exchange rate, and the current account of the balance of payments. This was meant to capture average behaviour over the whole period and therefore the residuals were removed from the equation.

Table 3.1 Changes made to produce base runs

	1964–9	1970–5	1977–81
Tax rates/allowances:			
Standard rate of income tax		Kept at initial level[a]	
Betting and gaming duty		Kept at initial level[a]	
Purchase tax/VAT		Kept at initial level[a]	
Drink and tobacco		Indexed from initial level[a]	
Motor vehicle duties		Indexed from initial level[a]	
Hydro carbon oil duty		Indexed from initial level[a]	
Local authority rates		Indexed from initial level[a]	
Corporation tax	At 1966 rates	Kept at initial level[a]	
Allowances[b]		Kept at initial level[a]	
Other policy instruments:			
Public current expenditure	Fixed at trend level		White Paper[c]
Public non-housing investment	Fixed at trend level		White Paper[c]
Public housing investment	To grow at 0.75% p.q.		White Paper[c]
Minimum Deposit Rate	At average value		At initial value
Selective employment tax	Not introduced	At initial level	N/A
Personal income tax	Indexed[d]		
Value added tax	N/A	Not introduced	At initial value
Advanced corporation tax	N/A	Not introduced	At initial value
Stock relief	N/A	Not introduced	Maintained
Nationalised industry prices		Residual[e] set to zero	
Incomes policy	Effect[f] set to zero		Ended 1977.02
Dividend restraint	N/A	Not introduced	Maintained
Import surcharge	Effect removed	N/A	N/A
Import deposits	Effect removed		N/A
Exchange rate		EER fixed at initial value	
Competition & Credit Control	N/A	Not introduced	Maintained
Bank Rate/MLR	Residuals set to zero		Forecast residuals
Travel allowances	Removed	N/A	N/A
Other changes:			
1968 Budget[g]	Removed	N/A	N/A
Dock strike 1967.04	Removed	N/A	N/A
Three-day week	N/A	Removed	N/A
Prices policies	h	N/A	N/A

[a] *Of each period.*
[b] *For plant and machinery, vehicles and industrial building.*
[c] *Derived from White Paper.*
[d] *With elasticity greater than unity kept for real growth.*
[e] *On public sector trading surplus.*
[f] *On earnings and residuals.*
[g] *Anticipation effect.*
[h] *Residuals on wholesale prices removed.*

The dummy for the operation of Competition and Credit Control was removed.

(v) Incomes policies were removed by setting the dummy variables for incomes policy equal to zero. In addition the residuals on average earnings in manufacturing (and also on average weekly earnings and wholesale manufactured prices in 1968–9) were set to zero. This was felt to be necessary as the residuals reflected the actual behaviour of the incomes policy that was not covered by the dummy variables.

(vi) The exchange rate was held constant.

(vii) The import surcharge and import deposit scheme were both omitted.

(viii) The residuals on public sector trading profits were set to zero so that they grew in line with nominal output.

A detailed list of the replacement equations and variable changes are shown in Table 3.1 for all periods.

Episode 1: September 1964–September 1969

The calculations of the effect of the policies that were pursued between 1964 and 1969 are shown relative to the base case in Table 3.2. The magnitude of the policy changes can be best appreciated by an examination of the behaviour of the tax rate on final expenditure (the deflator for the factor cost adjustment), personal income tax receipts and the categories of public expenditure on current and capital account.

Government current expenditure was above trend from the second quarter of 1965 through until the beginning of 1969. The largest deviations were during 1967 and from then on spending was restrained until it falls below trend in the final periods. The pattern of public sector investment was similar. Non-dwelling investment was almost 3 per cent above trend in the second quarter of 1964. A further sharp rise in the third quarter took it to 7 per cent above trend. The peak deviation of 17 per cent is during 1967 and the first quarter of 1968 and by the final quarter non-dwelling investment is almost exactly back to the trend level. Government housing investment is above trend from the end of 1965 and remains at very high levels throughout the period. The net indirect tax deflator grew by 25 per cent more than the consumer price index over the period with the large measures coming in the second half of 1966, the second quarter of 1968 and the fourth quarter of 1968. Given a weight of over 20 per cent in the consumer price deflator this change can account for an addition of about 5 per cent to the price level by the end of the period for a given value of the GDP deflator.

Table 3.2 Comparison of base run with actual outturn, 1964–9

	1964[b]	1965	1966	1967	1968	1969[c]
Percentage change[a]						
GDP	−0.4	−0.4	1.0	0.6	1.4	5.3
Total final expenditure	0.2	0.3	2.4	1.5	3.4	8.7
Consumer's expenditure	−0.2	0.7	4.4	4.4	8.2	12.7
Public current expenditure	0.6	0.1	−0.8	−4.0	−2.1	1.2
Exports of goods and services	0	0	−0.1	−2.3	−1.6	−1.9
Imports of goods and services	0	2.9	7.0	2.7	7.6	15.8
Factor cost adjustment	−0.2	0.8	5.1	5.1	9.4	14.8
Stockbuilding[d]	0	−0.1	0.3	−0.1	0.1	0.8
Public non-dwelling investment	−6.9	−5.8	−8.0	−16.8	−12.4	−2.4
Public dwelling investment	4.7	0.5	−8.4	−18.1	−19.4	−15.7
Private non-dwelling investment	0.9	4.9	10.0	13.0	12.1	17.3
Private dwelling investment	0	−0.6	0.1	2.1	1.1	7.5
Private manufacturing investment P&M	0	5.7	10.3	15.9	11.4	16.6
Deflator for consumption (1970 = 1)	−0.7	−0.7	−1.9	−0.6	−5.0	−8.1
Deflator for GDP (1970 = 1)	−0.9	−0.4	0.2	2.6	−0.2	−0.3
Average earnings (1970 = 100)[e]	−0.6	0.2	1.0	2.1	−0.6	0.5
Stock of M3 (£m.)	−0.1	−0.7	−0.4	−0.8	0.2	7.0
Tax rate on final expenditure (1970 = 1)	0.7	−1.5	−8.8	−11.4	−17.2	−27.2
Personal income taxes (£m.)	−1.6	−6.6	−8.8	−12.7	−15.9	−15.8
Real disposable income	−0.1	1.6	4.1	4.7	7.4	10.3
Effective exchange rate (1970 = 100)	0.5	0.2	0.3	2.0	16.9	17.0
Absolute change[f]						
Net acquistion of financial assets:						
company sector	−11	−66	−23	−9	24	19
personal sector	7	50	−23	−27	−45	34
public sector	6	−33	−81	−15	−81	−365
overseas sector	−1	49	126	3	102	311
public sector as % of GDP	0	−0.4	−0.9	0	−0.8	−3.6
Public sector borrowing requirement	0	33	81	15	131	447
Wholly unemployed (000's)	−0.1	1.6	4.1	4.7	7.4	10.3

[a] *£m. 1970 prices unless otherwise indicated.*
[b] *Average of the last two quarters.*
[c] *Average of the first three quarters.*
[d] *Absolute change as a percentage of GDP.*
[e] *In manufacturing industry.*
[f] *Average quarterly values; £m. unless otherwise indicated.*

Although earnings are little changed between the base run and the actual case, for the latter the level of income tax receipts is 16 per cent higher. This amounts to a reduction in nominal disposable income of a little over 2 per cent for given levels of gross incomes. Once the impact of the devaluation and its multiplier effects are also taken into account the level of real disposable income is computed to have been lowered by 10 per cent as a result of the combined set of measures. The impact upon consumption is very similar. In the base case the level of private sector investment is also higher. In part this is the result of the accelerator nature of the investment function. In addition interest rates are lower in the second half of the period because although the balance of payments deteriorates the inflation rate is lower and there is no devaluation. The changes to the investment allowances and the impact of corporation tax changes raised the cost of capital, so the removal of these effects acts as a further stimulus. The combined impact of the policy changes, including the devaluation, is to reduce the level of output by 5 per cent by the end of the period and to raise the level of consumer prices by almost 8 per cent as compared with the base case. The level of earnings is little affected. The elimination of the incomes policy raises the earnings level in 1967 compared to actual, but the changes involved are very small. The impact of the higher exchange rate substitutes for the incomes policy in restraining the growth of nominal earnings.

The central feature of the comparison of the base case with the outturn is that for the period as a whole the base case is more expansionary. Output grows faster in the base case, inflation is lower due to the higher exchange rate but the balance of payments suffers inevitably. With the unemployment peaking at an annual average of around half a million and falling in the final quarters performance on the real side in the base case looks impressive. The problem is, of course, the balance of payments with a deficit throughout the period averaging 1¼ per cent and, towards the end, reaching 2 per cent of nominal GDP. This is reflected in the other sector balances by a private sector surplus averaging almost 2 per cent of income and the budget deficit of 3.5 per cent. We therefore conclude that the posture of fiscal policy in 1964 at 'normal' interest rates (as suggested by the reaction function) and at the existing exchange rate was inconsistent with a stable overseas account. The Labour government inherited an over-expanded economy which was not sustainable over the following years. The years of crisis and successive measures were the return for not recognising this sufficiently early, as gradually the government was driven by force of circumstances to introduce the measures. The end result was too much contraction and deflation as the price for having failed to adjust the situation at an early stage.

Episode 2: July 1970–July 1975

Our analysis of the period 1970–5 follows a similar pattern to that in the previous section. A comparison of the base run with the actual outturn is presented in Table 3.3. Current government spending follows a similar pattern, relative to trend, as in the earlier period. In the initial quarters spending is below trend but growth then picks up to above trend rates so that by 1973 it is 3 per cent above trend. There is a slight downward adjustment in the early part of 1974, but this is only temporary and spending rises rapidly during the last part of 1974 and 1975. Government non-dwelling investment is very erratic throughout the period on a quarter to quarter basis. In the early part of the period spending is above trend but subsequently falls back so that by 1975 the actual is almost 7 per cent below the base. Government dwelling investment falls during the early part of the period so that by 1972 it is 20 per cent below the base. There is then a rapid upturn from mid-1973 until early 1975 so that the shortfall below trend is only 2 per cent by the beginning of 1975. The second part of that year experienced a very sharp drop.

The major stimulus to spending came through a reduction of net indirect taxes (indirect taxes less subsidies). The deflator for net indirect taxes is 40 per cent lower than in the base case although consumer prices are almost 5 per cent higher and the GDP deflator over 12 per cent higher. This has the effect of reducing consumer prices by around 10 per cent for a given level of the GDP deflator and produces an equivalent increase in real disposable income. This effect manifested itself gradually over the period, initially through tax reductions and subsequently subsidy increases. Direct taxes were reduced relative to the base case until 1973 and as earnings were higher this represents an even greater 'real' reduction. However, by 1973 this only amounts to around 10 per cent, considerably less than the indirect tax give-away. After the oil crisis indirect taxes were increased and were a deflationary force in the final quarters.

Even with the effects of currency depreciation the combined effect of these measures was to raise real disposable income considerably compared to the base. The difference in 1972 is 6 per cent and it remains close to this figure for the remainder of the period. The impact

Table 3.3 Comparison of base run with actual outturn, 1970–5

	1970[b]	1971	1972	1973	1974	1975[c]
Percentage change[a]						
GDP	0.5	−0.5	−1.8	−0.9	0.4	−0.7
Total final expenditure						
Consumers' expenditure	1.3	−2.7	−5.1	−3.2	−3.4	−3.7
Public current expenditure	2.0	1.1	−1.0	−3.2	−3.3	−5.4
Exports of goods and services	−0.1	0	−0.1	−0.9	−0.9	−1.0
Imports of goods and services	1.5	−2.7	−5.6	−3.1	−3.9	−3.9
Factor cost adjustment	1.5	−3.1	−5.7	−3.5	−3.7	−4.1
Stockbuilding[d]	0.3	−0.6	−2.1	−0.5	−0.3	−1.7
Public non-dwelling investment	−6.3	−3.6	2.1	1.7	4.4	6.4
Public dwelling investment	1.6	11.3	20.3	24.3	10.8	9.1
Private non-dwelling investment	0.8	2.0	−1.4	3.5	11.0	14.1
Private dwelling investment	−0.1	1.0	−3.7	4.0	23.1	8.4
Private manufacturing investment P&M	0	4.4	0	10.7	15.6	24.3
Deflator for consumption (1970 = 1)	−0.2	3.2	3.1	−3.4	−3.2	−5.0
Deflator of GDP (1970 = 1)	−0.8	0.7	−1.7	−8.0	−10.7	−12.3
Average earnings (1970 = 100)[e]	−0.9	0.3	−2.4	−8.0	−10.1	−13.9
Stock of M3 (£m.)	−0.7	−4.7	−19.1	−26.7	−31.4	−37.2
Tax rate on final expenditure (1970 = 1)	1.9	11.5	22.2	20.3	39.4	39.4
Personal income taxes (£m.)	0.1	−1.3	5.6	1.3	−10.6	−22.1
Real disposable income	−0.8	−2.7	−6.2	−5.3	−5.8	−6.1
Effective exchange rate (1970 = 100)	0.6	0	3.5	14.5	18.0	25.7
Absolute change[f]						
Net acquisition of financial assets:						
company sector	21	−54	−145	−284	−72	−295
personal sector	−175	24	−53	−308	−509	−519
public sector	119	110	452	885	1015	981
overseas sector	35	−80	−233	−293	−434	−494
public sector as % of GDP	1.0	0.9	3.3	5.8	5.3	5.1
Public sector borrowing requirement	−215	−194	−452	−885	−1015	−1308
Wholly unemployed (000's)	−10	−16	123	161	11	14

Notes as for Table 3.2.

upon consumers' spending is substantial but less than in the case of real incomes. The higher inflation than in the base case produces a higher savings ratio and offsets some of the real income increase. Private sector investment falls short of the base case by large amounts in 1974 and 1975 although there is little difference in the earlier years. This change is brought about by higher interest rates than follow from the faster inflation and worse balance of payments situation.

The net effect of the measures upon GDP is expansionary except in 1974 (we have removed the 3-day week from the base run). Output in 1972 is 1.8 per cent higher, falling back to around 0.7 per cent in the final year. The balance of payments is much worse in the actual case than in the base, predominantly because of the rapid increase in imports resulting from the expansion in consumer spending. By 1972 the loss is £930 million rising to £1975 million in 1975. This deterioration in the external balance is less than half the increase in the fiscal deficit as the growth rate and faster inflation produce a much higher private sector surplus than in the base case. The money supply grows much faster than in the base case with a gap of over 30 per cent opening up by the end of the period. Much of this is due to the higher fiscal deficit, but higher stockbuilding figures and inflation rates also play a significant part.

We would conclude that the posture of fiscal policy in 1970 at 'normal' interest rates and the existing exchange rate was excessively contractionary when compared with the requirement for overseas balance. The position is hence almost the reverse of that in 1964. Within the framework of our discussion this would suggest either an expansion of the fiscal deficit as a proportion of national income and/or an appreciation of the exchange rate. There is possibly a case for exchange rate appreciation in 1970 in an attempt to offset some of the inflation that emerged in 1971 in the base case. The second occasion upon which it might have been sensible to allow the monetary pressures to bring about a revaluation was in 1973, to attempt to offset some of the world inflation that emerged later that year. Fiscal reflation at the beginning of the period could have been substantial. On the other hand, it would have had to be offset in 1973 with the arrival of the world boom to prevent a deficit emerging. Intervention was also necessary to precent monetary growth from being inadequate in 1971–2 and excessive in 1973.

Episode 3: Early 1977–December 1981

We have continued to apply the principles developed for the base runs in the historical period to compute a similar run for the next four years. The major exception is that we have taken the 'White Paper' figures for government spending to 1979. Otherwise the same principles apply; tax rates are indexed, hire purchase controls are constrained, the exchange rate is fixed, and incomes policy is dismantled. The major difference is that it has been necessary to forecast values for world output and prices. The cyclical nature of world output continues with the peak of the current cycle in the beginning of 1978 and the trough in end-1979. Residuals in the equations were based on the experience of the latest forecast at the time of writing (September 1977). In most cases these are constant and based upon recent experience although in some cases they have been gradually reduced to zero.

The values from the base run are shown in Table 3.4. Government spending (both fixed and current) is planned to fall in both 1977 and 1978. Above average increases are expected during 1979 to 1981 for fixed investment and in 1981 for current spending as spending levels return to levels expected prior to the IMF cuts. Export volumes follow the assumed world trade cycle with rapid growth in 1980–1 and slower growth in 1978–9. Real personal disposable income increases broadly in line with GDP in 1980–1, but grows faster in 1978 and 1979 as earnings catch up following the end of the pay policy and the terms of trade improvement expected with the increase in North Sea oil production. Consumer spending therefore increases rapidly as, in addition to this increase in real incomes, we project a fall in the savings ratio to 12 per cent in 1981 in line with the expected reduction in the inflation rate. This fall in the inflation rate emerges due to the stable exchange rate and the behaviour of foreign prices. The growth of world prices is expected to slow to around 5 per cent in the latter years of the period, giving inflation of 6 per cent per annum in 1980 and 1981.

The average growth rate in this base run is 2.3 per cent with the high growth rates coming in the final years of the period in line with the world trade cycle. Unemployment continues to increase until end 1978 but then falls slowly back in 1980 and 1981. The borrowing requirement as a share of nominal output declines sharply between 1976 and 1979 from almost 8 per cent to 4.5 per cent reflecting the fall in government spending; current expenditure is expected to fall as a proportion of nominal income throughout the period as first government current spending falls, and then subsequently the rate of increase in interest payments declines, whilst grants are only indexed to prices and do not rise with increases in real output. Taxes on the other hand keep pace with the increase in nominal GDP.

The balance of payments is in strong surplus in 1978 but this surplus declines afterwards and moves towards balance in 1980–1. This is due

Table 3.4 Base run 1977–81, computed outturn

	1977	1978	1979	1980	1981
Percentage change[a]					
GDP	1.0	2.0	2.3	3.7	2.7
Consumers' expenditure	−0.4	1.3	3.9	4.7	3.1
Public current expenditure	−0.3	−1.1	1.4	2.3	2.9
Exports of goods and services	6.9	4.9	3.1	5.5	5.8
Imports of goods and services	4.2	4.4	8.6	10.1	7.2
Factor cost adjustment	−2.1	1.1	4.2	5.1	3.4
Stockbuilding[b]	0.3	0.3	0.9	1.3	1.0
Public non-dwelling investment	−8.0	−1.4	8.1	12.0	7.7
Public dwelling investment	−25.7	−8.2	9.7	8.1	13.6
Private non-dwelling investment	0.4	11.7	2.8	6.8	2.4
Private dwelling investment	−17.2	19.9	7.5	2.7	7.0
Private manufacturing investment P&M	9.6	14.6	6.0	10.0	0.9
Deflator for consumption (1970 = 1)	13.6	13.7	12.1	6.2	6.8
Deflator for GDP (1970 = 1)	12.0	15.2	14.4	7.6	7.7
Average earnings (1970 = 100)[c]	10.7	15.1	15.2	9.3	9.2
Stock of M3 (£m.)	4.8	11.4	13.6	15.9	15.1
Real disposable income	−2.1	2.9	3.1	3.1	2.7
Personal disposable income (£m.)	11.2	16.9	15.5	9.5	9.6
Public current grants (£m.)	17.5	20.2	16.9	6.4	7.3
Absolute change[d]					
Net acquisition of financial assets:					
company sector	−47	−467	−383	−948	−891
personal sector	2116	2633	2896	2721	2829
public sector	−1878	−1421	−1902	−1584	−1842
overseas sector	−705	−705	−571	−150	−56
private sector as % of GDP	6.8	6.1	6.0	3.9	3.8
public sector as % of GDP	−6.2	−4.0	−4.6	−3.4	−3.6
Public sector borrowing requirement	2116	2095	2193	1804	2070
Balance of payments as % of GDP	0.6	2.0	1.4	0.3	0.1
Bank rate/MLR (%)	10.0	7.6	7.5	6.4	6.6
DCE as % of money stock	11.3	8.5	15.3	17.7	17.7
Effective exchange rate (1970 = 100)	62.1	62.1	62.1	62.1	62.1

[a] *£m. 1970 prices unless otherwise indicated.*
[b] *Absolute change as a percentage of GDP.*
[c] *In manufacturing industry.*
[d] *Average quarterly values; £m. unless otherwise indicated.*

to a very rapid growth in non-oil imports in line with the growth of consumer expenditure – the implied elasticity is two – and a large stockbuilding boom. This is sufficient to offset the gain from the North Sea; the major increments to the balance of payments from the North Sea are in 1977–9 and by 1980–1 the increments are slowing down.

The increases in money supply are in line with nominal income from 1979 onwards but the DCE figures as a percentage of the money supply are very high – 17.7 per cent. Thus the DCE figures, reflecting the strong growth of inventories, do suggest that the economy is unlikely to be able to maintain the high surpluses of 1978/9.

This is a similar situation to that observed in the first two episodes. Once the world output improvement emerges it brings with it a large inventory cycle that leads to rapid growth. The implications are similar to those in the previous episodes. There is room for expansion during the period of slow world output growth in 1977–8; indeed it is necessary if DCE figures are to be kept in line with nominal income. However, when we come to 1980–1 the problem is reversed. Not only do the original injections need to be removed but further deflation is required to prevent rapid monetary expansion at 'normal' interest rates.

Summarising the historical results of the last section, both episodes begin at (opposite) positions of severe disequilibrium; in 1964 the existing policy stance was excessively expansionary; in 1970 it was excessively deflationary. This shows up in relationship to the subsequent behaviour of money supply, the fiscal deficit/surplus and the balance of payments in the computed base runs. In the former case rapid monetary growth and the high fiscal deficit relative to the underlying growth of nominal income was accompanied by a balance of payments problem. The second episode is characterised at the outset by slow monetary growth, a budget surplus and a current account surplus. In both episodes the policy that was followed can be described as 'too much, too late'. Action was not taken at the outset to offset the problems outlined above. Eventually the deflation of 1968 and the reflation of 1972–3 were in excess of what was required.

Analysis of Recommended Policies

The subsequent analysis is based on certain observations and principles that stem from the earlier discussion. They are as follows:

(i) In the absence of exchange rate changes the United Kingdom inflation rate will tend to follow that in the rest of the world.

The mechanism for bringing about differences in relative inflation rates will be predominantly movements in the exchange rates themselves, resulting from imbalances in fiscal and monetary behaviour. If it is desired to have a lower inflation rate than average, this will involve tighter fiscal/monetary policy than elsewhere and an appreciating exchange rate and *vice-versa*.

(ii) The choice of target inflation rate should involve the consideration that a continuous unexpected change in the exchange rate will have an impact upon competitiveness. Continuous currency appreciation will tend to lead to a deterioration in competitiveness and depreciation to an improvement in competitiveness.

(iii) Given a target a inflation rate, fiscal policy should be directed towards the balance of payments. (The appropriate concept is the current account plus long-term capital movements.) Because of the behaviour of the savings ratio outlined above a higher target inflation rate will involve a higher fiscal deficit.

(iv) The economy is prone to cyclical disturbances. These derive from movements in world output and prices and the evolution of the inventory cycle. During periods of cyclical upturn the fiscal deficit consistent with external balance will be lower than normal. Fiscal changes may be necessary to offset large increases in output.

(v) The behaviour of the monetary aggregates is a useful measure of the combined impact of the fiscal deficit, the inventory cycle and the external position, and it is a better measure than any of these factors in isolation. For a given world inflation rate, a fiscal deficit that is inconsistent with external balance at the existing exchange rate will show up as a rate of DCE inconsistent with the rate of world monetary expansion.

Within the framework of these observations and assumptions it is important to highlight the fact that we consider only the impact of changes in fiscal and monetary policy on the possible outcome. That is to say, we have not attempted to introduce incomes policies or import controls. Our concern with import controls is that, apart from any views we may have concerning the general desirability of such controls, their imposition would have side effects that do not fall solely within the field of stabilisation policy. Our model is not in our view capable of reflecting the full consequences of import controls. Similar arguments could, of course, be brought forward concerning incomes policies, but this is not the reason for rejecting the use of incomes policies here.

The introduction of incomes policy involves making certain exogenous assumptions about the behaviour of wages, which we regard as a political rather than simply an economic act of faith; and the history of incomes policies since the war indicates a low probability of survival. We therefore state as a matter of prediction that combining incomes policies with floating exchange rates has little chance of success. This seems to us, if not to others, a more realistic assumption than a pious hope that powerful trade unions can be expected to adjust money wages in ways that are economically acceptable to the government. Accordingly, our search for alternative policies is confined to changes in fiscal and monetary policies as outlined below. Our analysis would therefore be regarded by some as an extreme case insofar as the balance of payments becomes the central constraint on policy for a given exchange rate, a constraint which incomes policy and import controls both try to break in somewhat different ways.

In the previous section we identified situations in both 1964 and 1970 where existing fiscal and monetary policy was inconsistent with the current exchange rate; in 1964 policy was over-expansionary and in 1970 the opposite was the case. Clearly, any inconsistency between fiscal/monetary policy and the exchange rate can be brought about by either changing the fiscal/monetary policy or changing the exchange rate. If we take the 1964 position then balance could have been restored by a reduction of the fiscal deficit as a proportion of national income. Alternatively, a faster rate of inflation and exchange rate depreciation would have reduced the real value of certain elements of government spending and possibly raised taxation, whilst at the same time raising the private sector savings ratio. The result would have been broadly the same for output, but in the second case the price level would have been higher.

Because of the results described earlier whereby exchange rate depreciation is offset by increases in prices, it is not possible within our system to both improve the balance of payments and increase the level of output by exchange rate management. This has been described at length elsewhere (Ball, Burns and Laury [2]). Once we exclude the possibility of direct action to assist the balance of payments, the degree of improvement that we can make to the aggregate level of output is limited, as the level of sustainable output is given by the relative position of the volume of exports and the marginal propensity to import as demonstrated in McKinnon [6]. Only if real wages fall can this ratio improve and lead to an increase in potential output.

We have attempted to assess any imbalance in the opening exchange rate in each period by reference to relative price movements and relative monetary growth. In looking at relative price movements there are two major difficulties. The first problem is to adjust for variations between countries in the extent to which overall price indices grow faster than manufactured prices. Any computation of purchasing power parity must be based upon traded goods prices, whereas it is well known that average prices tend to outpace traded goods prices as productivity growth is faster in the traded goods sector. The second problem is to determine where the 'correct' level of the exchange rate is, even if it is possible to gauge the correct movement through time.

In order to allow for the first problem we have examined the behaviour of the ratio of the aggregate price level to the price level of exports both in Britain and in our four major competitors. We find that in the British case the ratio grows at 1.2 per cent less per annum than for our competitors. This is to be expected from a country where manufacturing productivity is growing less than average. Using this difference we have computed purchasing power parity based upon a base of 1970 equal to 100. It is clear that the movement in this series is very similar to that of the actual exchange rate.

The second problem is to adjust this computed purchasing power parity to the 'correct' level. The ideas set out earlier suggest that the actual value of the exchange rate will be below the 'equilibrium' level when a currency is depreciating. When the depreciation comes to an end, relative prices will then adjust according to the long-run behaviour of real wages. Our judgement, based upon observation and upon attempts to estimate export price relationships, is that the effective exchange rate was 'correct' in 1971 and 1972 as by then the adjustment to the 1967 devaluation was complete. Our final purchasing power parity calculation is therefore based upon 1970 equal to a little over 105. These calculations are shown in Table 3.5.

A second method of judging the appropriate level of the exchange rate is to compare the outturn with the movement of the relative money stock per unit of output as shown in Burns and Warburton [5]. An equation relating the exchange rate to the money stock in the world relative to the United Kingdom is shown in Table 3.5 with the computed values from the equation. The coefficient on relative money has been constrained to unity, a time trend represents the differences in productivity between the United Kingdom and elsewhere and the

Table 3.5 Calculation of computed exchange rate (indices 1970 = 100)

T	Effective exchange rate EER	Competitors consumer prices[a] PW	UK consumer prices PC	Purchasing[b] power parity 1970 = 100 PPP1	Purchasing[c] power parity 1970 = 105.3 PPP2	Computed exchange rate CER
1959	117.5	69.7	67.5	118.2	124.4	
1960	117.5	71.3	68.1	118.4	124.6	
1961	117.5	73.1	70.1	116.5	122.6	
1962	117.5	75.4	72.7	114.4	120.4	
1963	117.5	78.1	73.8	115.3	121.4	117.9
1964	117.5	79.9	75.9	113.4	119.4	115.1
1965	116.9	82.6	79.6	110.3	116.1	113.5
1966	117.2	85.5	82.8	108.5	114.2	111.6
1967	115.1	87.6	85.2	106.7	112.3	110.7
1968	100.6	90.7	89.3	104.0	109.4	108.4
1969	100.8	94.8	93.9	102.2	107.6	108.2
1970	100	100	100	100	105.3	105.4
1971	99.9	105.2	109.5	94.9	99.9	103.9
1972	96.5	110.2	117.0	91.9	96.7	94.7
1973	87.3	118.7	126.7	90.3	95.1	83.6
1974	84.6	133.7	147.0	86.5	91.1	83.2
1975	78.1	145.7	183.0	74.8	78.7	73.4
1976	66.1	155.7	213.2	67.8	71.4	68.2

[a]*Competitive consumer prices are a weighted average of prices in US, Japan, Germany and France with the weights of .32, .20, .34 and .15.*

[b]*Relative prices adjusted by 1.2% per annum (see text) to allow for traded/non-traded differentials.*

$$PPP1 = \frac{PW}{PC} \cdot 100 \cdot (0.9878)^{(T-1970)}$$

[c]*Computed values from equation*

$$EER = \frac{KM3W}{KM3£} \cdot e^{(0.765 + 0.000154\,OIL - 0.0119T + Q_i)}$$

$\bar{R}^2 = 0.936$
DW = 0.32
SE = 3.89
6301–7604

where KM3£ and KM3W are the broadly defined money stocks of the UK and its competitors, and OIL is the flow of OPEC sterling balances.

flow of sterling balances held by the OPEC countries captures some of the effect of portfolio movements.

The relative movement of the exchange rate and the computed values based upon relative prices and monetary growth figures are as we would expect. The exchange rate in 1964 seems to be about 'correct'; between then and 1967 money supply increases faster than is justified by the exchange rate, despite the monetary outflow through the external account. Prices only partially adjust to this because of the dampening effect of the exchange rate (and possibly the incomes policies). After the devaluation, prices adjust downwards faster than the monetary figures suggest because of the influence of world prices. The analysis suggests that both in terms of monetary aggregates and relative prices the exchange rate was undervalued by around 5 per cent in 1970. From 1972 onwards the mechanism is mainly one of excess monetary growth forcing down the exchange rate with the relative price movements lagging behind. The OPEC inflow in 1974 gives some stability but the outflow in 1975–6 suggests that in mid-1977 the exchange rate was undervalued by some 10 per cent, whilst relative prices (having adjusted faster) suggest only 5 per cent.

Episode 1: September 1964–September 1969

Given the decision to maintain the exchange rate in 1964, our task is to design fiscal and monetary policy appropriate to it. The analysis in the previous section suggested that cuts in the fiscal deficit were necessary. The next stage is to assess the magnitude of the fiscal contraction that was required. The behaviour of the balance of payments deficit and DCE in the base case suggested a 12.5 per cent increase in tax rates (direct personal and indirect) at the beginning of the period. This would have implied an increase of around £900 million in tax revenues after indexing the tax system. A further small increase of 2.5 per cent was then necessary in the beginning of 1966 and a further 10 per cent at the beginning of 1968.

The results of this set of policies is compared in Table 3.6 with what actually happened. There is still a cycle in the economy which follows the pattern of world output and the final years of the period show strong growth. By 1969 GDP is 2 per cent higher than history and consumers' spending is up by 3.4 per cent. Government current spending and private fixed investment are also higher, whilst government non-dwelling investment and exports are slightly down with public-dwelling investment sharply down. Although output is higher in the final year, it is lower in the previous four years which is when the effective deflation occurs relative to what actually happened.

Despite the absence of incomes policies, prices are 5 per cent lower and earnings 2 per cent lower than actually happened, largely due to the absence of any exchange rate depreciation, but also because indirect taxes are lower at the end, despite the increases that are programmed as part of our policy. The balance of payments is very

Table 3.6 Comparison of final run with actual outturn, 1964–9

	1964[b]	1965	1966	1967	1968	1969[c]
Percentage change[a]						
GDP	−1.4	−1.8	−0.7	−1.1	−1.0	2.2
Total final expenditure	−1.9	−1.9	−0.2	−1.3	−0.7	3.0
Consumers' expenditure	−2.8	−2.7	−0.3	−0.7	0.6	3.4
Public current expenditure	0.6	−0.2	−0.8	−4.0	−2.3	1.2
Exports of goods and services	0	0.1	0	2.2	−1.5	−1.8
Imports of goods and services	−3.1	1.3	1.7	−2.6	−0.4	5.5
Factor cost adjustment	−3.2	−3.2	−0.4	−0.8	0.6	4.0
Stockbuilding[d]	−0.4	−0.5	0	−0.3	−0.3	0.8
Public non-dwelling investment	−6.9	−5.8	−8.1	−16.8	−12.6	−2.5
Public dwelling investment	4.7	0.3	−8.7	−18.1	−19.5	−15.8
Private non-dwelling investment	0.7	4.0	9.5	13.4	12.9	15.3
Private dwelling investment	0	−1.4	0	2.2	0.9	5.8
Private manufacturing investment P&M	0	16.4	9.8	15.9	13.0	14.7
Deflator for consumption (1970 = 1)	1.3	0.9	0	1.4	−1.7	−4.8
Deflator for GDP (1970 = 1)	−1.6	−1.3	−1.0	1.4	−1.7	−2.4
Average earnings (1970 = 100)[e]	−1.6	−0.9	−0.2	1.0	−2.3	−1.4
Stock of M3 (£m.)	−1.7	−5.2	−8.4	−11.1	−13.0	−10.9
Tax rate on final expenditure (1970 = 1)	13.2	10.1	4.5	2.3	2.4	−7.8
Personal income taxes (£m.)	7.9	1.8	1.0	−3.5	−2.1	−0.9
Real disposable income	−4.2	−2.7	−1.3	−1.0	−1.5	3.1
Effective exchange rate (1970 = 100)	0.5	0.2	0.3	2.0	16.9	17.0
Absolute change[f]						
Net acquisition of financial assets:						
company sector	−4.5	−92	−75	−45	−45	−46
personal sector	−65	3	−76	−19	−140	−70
public sector	161	120	125	172	252	36
overseas sector	−28	−26	25	−111	−67	80
public sector as % of GDP	2.2	1.5	1.5	2.0	2.5	0.4
Public sector borrowing requirement	−160	−120	−125	−175	−205	46
Wholly unemployed (000's)	15	123	147	73	152	−7

Notes as for Table 3.2.

close to balance and DCE as a proportion of the money stock rises on average by 6.2 per cent per annum. This is a very similar increase to that in nominal GDP although the growth of the money supply is a little less at 4.5 per cent per annum. The borrowing requirement at the end is slightly higher both absolutely and as a percentage of output. Thus the effect of the policies is broadly as we intended. The growth of the monetary aggregates is closely associated with the growth of nominal output, the external position is secure and interest rates are kept at normal levels.

In principle, it might be argued that an assessment of the suggested policy path against the actual can only be carried out after specifying an appropriate criterion function which would involve output, employment, the inflation rate and the balance of payments and also possibly some of the policy instruments. Obviously taking the period as a whole year by year, the suggested policy does not in all significant respects dominate the outturn, so that some question of choice and valuation arises. An obvious example relates to the path of output and employment above what actually happened for five of the six years. But it is evident that the high level of output was purchased at considerable expense, the consequences of which were not apparent until a later stage and which led the government of the day to over-adjust. The lower levels of output in the policy run reflect a slower and more continuous adjustment to an excessively loose fiscal and monetary policy, which is eventually achieved within the model without any reduction in the exchange rate, resulting ultimately in a distinctly lower inflation rate. Thus, by the end of the period, the policy produces higher output, lower inflation and a surplus in the balance of payments. But what is equally important is that the calculations are consistent with the view that, given the necessary action in time, these adjustments could have been made without the crises that did occur and which were manifestly debilitating to expectations and morale. Moreover, the reduction in the inflation rate is achieved without the politically-disturbing incomes policies which had such an effect on the Labour government's relations with the trade union movement in its later stages. Thus, while the improvement overall may not look particularly dramatic at one level, at the psychological level it could have been very profound indeed.

Episode 2: July 1970–July 1975

To correct for the imbalances outlined earlier we chose to revalue the currency by 5 per cent in 1970. Further revaluations were made in 1973 and 1974, taking the exchange rate back to 1967 levels to help offset some of the pressure of world price increases. Some fiscal reflation was still possible. Selective employment tax was halved in 1971 and abolished in 1972 – a year earlier in each case than actually happened. In addition, tax rates were reduced by 15 per cent at the outset. With the onset of the world boom in 1972–3 these tax reductions were rescinded and rates were increased by 5 per cent in mid 1972 and 10 per cent at the beginning of 1973. Once the world boom was over we were in a position to reinstate some of the reductions and rates were reduced by 10 per cent in the third quarter of 1974. The effect of Competition and Credit Control upon bank-lending was not introduced. The results of this set of policies is compared with what actually happened in Table 3.7. Overall, the actual exchange rate is 33 per cent lower than is used in this policy run. The major impact of this change is upon the inflation rate. By 1975 prices are 20 per cent below the actual outturn even though the indirect tax rate is little changed. Money supply is 33 per cent below the actual level, which is consistent with the exchange rate figures we chose at the outset. The lower money supply figures result from the lower borrowing requirement figures in 1973–5, higher interest rates in 1971 and 1972, the removal of the Competition and Credit control dummy and the impact of lower prices in generating a lower demand for bank lending to meet the higher value of stocks. The balance of payments is satisfactory; there is overall balance in 1972 and a £280 million deficit in 1973, whilst the deficits of 1974 and 1975 at £2.4 billion are very close to our share of the OPEC surplus. Domestic credit expansion averages 10 per cent through the period and is relatively stable; this is not inconsistent with an average inflation rate of 7½ per cent and growth rate of 2 per cent which has been achieved. Thus in terms of the behaviour of DCE, money supply and the balance of payments, it is clear that the combination of the exchange rate policy and fiscal/monetary policy is appropriate.

Real disposable income is lower than actual in 1973 and 1974, but in the remainder of the period is higher; in particular, in 1970 and 1971 the difference is almost 6 per cent. Consumer spending is higher throughout as the lower disposable income figures are offset by lower savings ratios. Import volumes are higher as a result of the higher consumption figures, and export volumes are down because of the loss of competitiveness which, by the end, is 7 per cent worse than the actual. The current account is better than the actual in 1973–5 because the terms of trade are better with the exchange rate path used here. Output is higher in this policy run throughout, with the improvement at its largest during the slump of 1970–1 and again in 1974–5, with only a modest increase in the upturn of 1972–3.

The major financial improvement was achieved by maintaining control of the price level and monetary aggregates. The key to this

Table 3.7 Comparison of final run with actual outturn, 1970–5

	1970[b]	1971	1972	1973	1974	1975[c]
Percentage change[a]						
GDP	2.0	2.3	1.0	0.2	1.8	2.1
Total final expenditure	3.6	3.4	1.7	0.6	2.2	2.9
Consumers' expenditure	6.6	4.9	3.0	1.6	3.5	4.2
Public current expenditure	1.1	0.5	−1.0	−2.6	−2.0	−3.6
Exports of goods and services	−0.4	−0.5	−0.6	−1.4	−1.9	−2.3
Imports of goods and services	7.3	6.4	3.0	1.3	2.5	5.0
Factor cost adjustment	7.6	5.6	3.4	1.8	3.8	4.7
Stockbuilding[d]	0.5	0.6	−0.1	−0.2	0	−0.1
Public non-dwelling investment	−6.3	−3.6	2.1	1.7	4.4	6.4
Public dwelling investment	1.6	11.3	20.3	24.3	10.8	9.1
Private non-dwelling investment	1.8	6.7	1.9	3.4	7.3	18.0
Private dwelling investment	−0.6	5.2	−1.5	1.9	24.5	16.5
Private manufacturing investment P&M	0	11.2	5.0	12.8	9.0	27.5
Deflator for consumption (1970 = 1)	−4.8	−3.4	−3.6	−8.7	−13.9	−18.5
Deflator for GDP (1970 = 1)	−1.1	−0.6	−2.7	−10.7	−16.9	−20.6
Average earnings (1970 = 100)[e]	−1.3	−0.7	−3.7	−11.5	−17.4	−22.7
Stock of M3 (£m.)	1.9	2.5	−9.4	−20.2	−27.1	−32.1
Tax rate on final expenditure (1970 = 1)	−14.5	−11.5	−4.8	5.0	11.8	4.3
Personal income taxes (£m.)	−12.6	−13.3	−4.1	−0.6	−17.4	−30.6
Real disposable income	5.8	5.7	1.9	−2.0	−0.9	0.8
Effective exchange rate (1970 = 100)	5.7	5.0	8.7	22.2	37.8	50.9
Absolute change[f]						
Net acquisition of financial assets:						
company sector	122	60	6	−264	117	−118
personal sector	−65	40	−56	−434	−768	−794
public sector	−215	−284	2	826	903	1025
overseas sector	158	184	48	−128	−251	−113
public sector as % of GDP	−1.9	−2.3	−0.1	5.1	4.5	2.5
Public sector borrowing requirement	119	200	−2	−826	−903	−1025
Wholly unemployed (000's)	−26	−189	−178	−58	−101	−178

Notes as for Table 3.2.

was the maintenance of an appropriate fiscal policy. Expansion at the outset not only raised personal incomes but also prevented interest rates falling to the extent they did. Combined with the removal of the effects of Competition and Credit Control, money supply in 1972 was then 10 per cent below outturn. This enabled us to hold the exchange rate and keep the current account roughly in balance. The cumulative spiral of exchange rate depreciation, inflation, a soaring budget deficit and monetary disorder was avoided. We were able to maintain lower interest rates, control the borrowing requirement and again avoid the problems associated with incomes policy, which produces a solid financial background with a reduced incidence of crisis and conflict. And our calculations suggest that this strategy would have been consistent with higher spending levels and lower unemployment. Within the framework, it has not been possible to avoid the recession of 1975. It is not possible to move significantly away from the behaviour of the rest of the world without significant effects on external stability and the financial framework, with the inevitable consequences for the exchange rate, for inflation and the resulting repetitive crises, when the world is subject to major synchronising shocks.

Episode 3: Early 1977–December 1981

The approach we have adopted entails decisions about the exchange rate at the outset, the extent of any initial stimulus to the economy that might be required and the deflation response as the world output cycle turns up again in 1980–1. In addition, it is necessary to review the public expenditure figures to see whether any changes need to be made as against plans that have already been announced.

The discussion in the early part of this Section indicated a higher exchange rate than that ruling today (62.5 on our index). It is not possible to fix this with any precision, but our judgement is that a free floating rate would be in the region of 65–70. For the purposes of these calculations we have chosen 67.5 as the appropriate rate from early 1978, following a gradual revaluation in the second half of 1977. For the remainder of the period, we have held this rate. The world inflation rate is expected to fall in 1979–80 and a stable exchange rate will be sufficient to bring inflation down sharply. The combination of the exchange rate function and world price assumption, allowing for 'catch-up' effects following the end of the pay policy, suggests an inflation rate of almost 10 per cent on average for the period 1977–81, with rates of around 6 per cent at the end of the period. The results of these policies are shown in Table 3.8

In the previous periods we have aimed to hold the current account roughly in balance. In this third episode there is a strong argument for maintaining some current account surplus initially to offset some

Table 3.8 Final run 1977–81, computed outturn

	1977	1978	1979	1980	1981
Percentage change[a]					
GDP	1.1	3.5	1.7	2.3	1.9
Consumers' expenditure	−0.1	3.1	3.2	2.9	1.8
Public current expenditure	−0.3	−1.1	1.4	2.3	2.9
Exports of goods and services	6.9	4.5	7.3	5.4	5.6
Imports of goods and services	4.4	7.6	7.0	6.9	5.5
Factor cost adjustment	−1.8	3.1	3.5	3.1	1.9
Stockbuilding[b]	0.3	0.8	0.8	0.8	0.5
Public non-dwelling investment	−8.0	7.2	1.8	5.2	7.2
Public dwelling investment	−25.7	12.6	2.6	0	2.6
Private non-dwelling investment	0.7	15.0	3.5	4.0	−2.1
Private dwelling investment	−17.2	23.8	9.3	−1.6	7.5
Private manufacturing investment P&M	9.7	18.6	7.5	7.7	−4.4
Deflator for consumption (1970 = 1)	13.1	9.1	10.8	6.1	6.4
Deflator for GDP (1970 = 1)	11.8	10.4	12.9	6.2	7.2
Average earnings (1970 = 100)[c]	10.4	10.9	13.2	7.7	8.3
Stock of M3 (£m.)	4.8	12.4	12.9	9.9	6.9
Real disposable income	−2.1	3.7	2.9	0.3	1.8
Personal disposable income (£m.)	10.8	13.2	14.0	6.7	8.3
Public current grants (£m.)	16.9	15.3	15.7	6.2	6.9
Absolute change[d]					
Net acquisition of financial assets:					
company sector	−26	−544	−468	−1061	−715
personal sector	2079	2237	2526	2097	2237
public sector	−1844	−1415	−1792	−807	−1139
overseas sector	−222	−238	−226	−189	−334
private sector as % of GDP	6.8	4.9	5.2	2.4	3.2
public sector as % of GDP	−6.1	−4.1	−4.5	−1.9	−2.4
Public sector borrowing requirement	1984	1786	2150	1166	1539
Balance of payments as % of GDP	0.7	0.7	0.6	0.4	0.7
Bank rate/MLR (%)	9.6	6.4	7.4	6.3	6.3
DCE as % of money stock	11.3	14.3	15.7	9.6	10.4
Effective exchange rate	63.9	67.5	67.5	67.5	67.5

Notes as for Table 3.4.

of the previous deficits. It is not easy to judge the extent to which this is necessary given the support of capital flows but we have refrained from reflating as much as we possibly could in the early part of the period.

There is a strong argument for using the small amount of flexibility in the early years to correct the projected movement of government spending. The effects of the cuts in 1977 and 1978 lead to a fall in spending in the period ahead, with a sharp increase in 1980–1 when the effects of the cuts come to an end. The problem with this projection is that it is highly correlated with our expected movement of output and is inversely related to the fiscal measures under consideration. Most of the cuts in 1977–9 are in government investment and there is a strong case for greater stability than is suggested here. Thus to the extent that there is room for reflation in 1977–8 it could usefully be achieved by smoothing the projected path for government expenditure.

Thus our chosen measures are based upon allowing the exchange rate to rise to 67.5 and remain there, and designing policy around this. We have then smoothed the path of government spending to avoid a further fall in 1978 and the sharp increase in 1980–1. Finally, we have increased taxes in 1980 by 5 per cent as world output accelerates.

The results of this set of policies are not dramatically different from the base run described in the previous Section. The growth rate for output over the period is 2.1 per cent per annum; disposable income is only projected to grow at 1.4 per cent, with consumers' expenditure growing at 2.2 per cent per annum due to a fall in the savings ratio from 14.3 per cent in 1976 to 11.6 per cent in 1981. The balance of payments is in surplus throughout the period. The inflation rate is reduced in 1978, reflecting the exchange rate appreciation despite the fact that the backlog of the incomes policy comes through. The decline is rapid towards the end of the period. The budget deficit falls as a per cent of nominal GDP from 6.2 per cent in 1977 to 2 per cent in the final two years, whilst DCE is on average 12 per cent of the money stock over the whole period. The average growth of money supply itself is 9.8 per cent per annum, although a sharp increase is predicted in 1978 following the squeeze of early 1977, before falling to around 10 per cent per annum at the end of the period.

The major restraint on growth is the rapid increase in import growth that accompanies the recovery of consumer spending. The result is that North Sea oil is not capable of generating an above-average growth rate for long and still keeping the balance of payments in surplus. Nevertheless, if care is taken to maintain the financial improvement that is now under way, there is every possibility of reducing the inflation rate to more satisfactory levels. This could provide the base for a period of low interest rates and higher rates of capital investment.

Conclusion

This paper has been directed at the problem of economic stabilisation, using the familiar tools of fiscal and monetary policy. Our examination of the three episodes concerned was initially directed at an appraisal of the stance of policy at the beginning of the period. The three episodes are very different in this respect. In 1964, existing policy was excessively expansionary when measured as the likely progress with fixed real tax rates, trend government spending and the existing exchange rate. The position in 1970 was exactly the reverse, with the budget in surplus and the likelihood of continuous external surplus on the basis of the exchange rate and the stance of fiscal policy. The situation in 1977 appears to be nearer to equilibrium, given the likely behaviour of exports and imports. Surpluses on the current account and a strong exchange rate are in prospect over the next two years on the basis of current policy, although this surplus is reduced in the final years as consumer spending expands.

Given this starting position, we have attempted in the third part of the paper to prescribe policies that would remove the obvious positions of disequilibrium. The starting point of this exercise has been the intention to stabilise the exchange rate once the appropriate starting position has been established, with the exception of 1973–4 when appreciation could have successfully offset some of the world inflation. Technically, the exercise has been characterised by first setting the exchange rate and then designing appropriate policy. This is not to suggest that we support the operation of a fixed exchange rate throughout the period. Only in a technical sense is the exchange rate fixed. In reality, we are advocating the adoption of a target exchange rate that is stable, and then designing policy that is appropriate. We do not advocate hanging on to an exchange rate that is inconsistent with the financial policies that are being pursued. The sense in which this is an equilibrium exchange rate is very different from that which is normally interpreted in the context of demand management. There is no guarantee that our exchange rate will achieve the combination of full employment and external balance. It has the more limited aim of clearing the foreign exchange market at whatever level of unemployment is involved. Any excess of unemployment over desired levels is then a combination of inadequate world output or inappropriate real wages. The first is beyond our control, whilst the second will be settled by the behaviour of productivity, not by exchange rate management.

Once the exchange rate was decided upon, the next step was the design of appropriate fiscal and monetary policy. We have taken a passive approach to monetary policy by setting interest rates according to an estimated reaction function. The monetary aggregates that follow depend upon the design of fiscal policy and the conjunctural behaviour of private sector demand. The aim was to achieve a rough balance on the external account. We were not able to achieve this by the establishment of a fiscal rule at the beginning of the period. The base runs that we computed with 'neutral' fiscal policy showed very sharp fluctuations which coincided with the movement of world output. During these periods output and stockbuilding grew rapidly and the balance of payments deteriorated. Some discretionary fiscal intervention was necessary to offset these movements generated from outside and the unwinding of the inventory cycle. In general this meant designing fiscal policy to move inversely with world output and, by implication, export growth.

Our approach suggests that to achieve relative monetary stability it is necessary to use discretionary fiscal policy. If interest rates simply followed inflation and any external crisis, then periods of rapid world output growth and inventory accumulation generated rapid monetary expansion which showed up in particular in the figure for DCE. The DCE figures provided an important indicator within our system as they are the most comprehensible guide to the requirement for fiscal intervention. In general it was the case that the measures that we took operated in the direction of stabilising the value of DCE as a percentage of money supply. We therefore have an important paradox that in an economy where interest rates are kept at some 'normal' level, monetary stability requires discretionary fiscal policy. Furthermore, the resulting discretionary policy tends to stabilise output growth and maintain external balance. The average values for some of the indicators under our chosen policies are shown in Table 3.9.

Thus the policies that broadly achieved current account balance had the characteristic of producing DCE as a percentage of the money supply broadly equal to the growth of nominal output. The money supply itself tended to grow slightly less rapidly but there was not a great deal of difference. The fiscal deficit as a proportion of nominal output tends to be around 20–30 per cent of growth of nominal income and the rate of DCE expressed as a percentage of the money supply. The earliest period was at the lower limit and the final period towards the upper limit.

In terms of the debate on fine tuning, our calculations give support to the broad methodology employed by the IMF in its dealings with

Table 3.9 Indicators of chosen policies (average annual percentage change)

	1964–9	1970–5	1977–81
GDP	3.6	1.9	2.1
World industrial production	6.7	1.9	4.6
Inflation (consumer prices)	3.3	7.3	9.1
World inflation (manufactures)	1.6	9.2	6.6
DCE as % of money supply	5.9	10.0	12.3
Fiscal deficit as % of GDP	1.2	2.25	3.8
Money supply	4.4	9.6	9.8
Exchange rate	0	4.0	0

the British authorities. Given a target exchange rate, together with assumptions about world inflation and the growth of the world economy, it is possible to compute the rate of DCE that is consistent with external balance. This will normally be the same rate as the target growth of nominal GDP. Fiscal policy should then be designed to produce this target rate of DCE at 'normal' interest rates. We have also suggested that this will on average imply a fiscal deficit as a proportion of nominal output of around 25 per cent of the target growth of nominal income, but that discretionary changes could profitably be made in line with the movement of world output. During periods of world expansion, the fiscal deficit needs to be reduced if the DCE target is to be maintained and *vice-versa* in periods of world recession.

The extent to which we were able to improve on the performance for output was limited. We were aware of this at the outset, as we chose to eschew the magic of incomes policies and import controls and did not exogenise wages, imports or competitiveness on the grounds that this had not been successfully achieved in the past – and we did not wish to bias the results by the appearance of some *deus ex machina*. We were able to improve performance without the aid of incomes policies and at little cost in terms of output.

Our major conclusions are that it could have been possible to operate fiscal and monetary policy with the aim of creating a stable currency, overall external balance, tolerable interest rates and an absence of permanent crises. Viewed in this way, stabilisation policy has only a limited role in long-term full employment policy. Employment is a problem associated with the long-run development of productive potential, real wages and competitiveness which belong in the world of micro rather than macroeconomics. Stabilisation policy can create the appropriate stable financial framework, but an exaggerated belief in our capacity to create full employment through fiscal and monetary means is only likely to destroy financial stability, in much the same way as we have experienced in the last ten years.

References

[1] Ball, R. J., 'The theory of employment revisited', in *Quantitative Wirtschaftsforschung – Festschrift für Wilhelm Krelle*, December 1976, J. C. B. Mohr, Tubingen.

[2] Ball, R. J., Burns, T. and Laury, J. S. E., 'The pole of exchange rate changes in balance of payments adjustment – the United Kingdom case', *Economic Journal*, March 1977.

[3] Blackaby, F., 'British economic policy, 1960–74: a general appraisal', *National Institute Economic Review*, National Institute of Economic and Social Research, May 1977.

[4] Budd, A. P. and Burns, T., *Economic Outlook*, London Business School, April 1977.

[5] Burns, T. and Warburton, P. J., 'International aspects of UK inflation – some preliminary empirical results', *Econometric Forecasting Unit Discussion Paper*, London Business School, September 1976.

[6] McKinnon, R. I., 'Portfolio balance and international payments adjustment', in Mundell, R. A. and Swoboda, A. V., *Monetary Problems of the International Economy*, University of Chicago Press, 1969.

[7] Renton, G. A., *Modelling the Economy*, Heinemann Educational Books, London, 1975.

4 Demand Management in Britain 1964–81

by M. J. C. Surrey and P. A. Ormerod

Introduction

In our analysis of the three periods 1964–9, 1970–5 and 1977–81 which follows, we have employed our current forecasting model of the British economy to try to explore the extent to which 'conventional' demand management techniques, together with the appropriate use of exchange rate and incomes policies could have led to a more satisfactory evolution of the economy than in fact happened (or, in the last case, than seems probable).

We stress the conventional nature of our interpretation of demand management: our approach was, essentially, to take each episode year by year and to design a series of policy adjustments aimed at producing steady progress towards a favourable conjunction of (again conventional) economic targets: high employment, low price inflation, an acceptable balance of payments, and so on. We deliberately eschewed possible alternative approaches to the management of aggregate demand – for example, setting public expenditure growth paths, or tax rates, at some level thought to be appropriate in the medium term, and avoiding short-term adjustments. We also decided not to consider the use of 'unconventional' policies – for instance quantitative import controls – on the grounds that these were not in fact employed between 1964 and 1977 and, quite apart from any implications that this has for their feasibility as policy instruments during that period, it follows that our forecasting model based on past behaviour of the economy would necessarily provide little reliable evidence on their effects. We therefore restrict ourselves to the major macroeconomic instruments – fiscal and monetary, incomes and exchange rate policies – which have in fact been employed over the last fifteen years.

Although we present quite detailed figures in the tables, we stress that these figures are not intended to be more precise than the general statements in the text.

The National Institute Model

The National Institute model belongs to the mainstream tradition of income–expenditure macroeconomic models and is built round the expenditure GDP account: consumers' expenditure, stockbuilding, private fixed investment, exports, imports and the adjustment to factor cost are determined in the main endogenously, while government expenditure is treated broadly as exogenously given.

Consumers' expenditure is a lagged function of real personal disposable income and an exogenous debt term intended to allow for the effects of changes in hire purchase terms and changes in bank advances.

Fixed investment is disaggregated by sector: private dwellings, manufacturing and other private investment are treated as endogenous; public dwellings, shipping, mining and quarrying and mainly-public industries and services as exogenous. Private dwellings investment depends on a variety of factors, including the availability of mortgage finance, the real cost of mortgages, real disposable income, the rate of increase of house prices and local authority rents. This sector represents one of the strongest links between monetary and real variables in the model. The equations for investment in manufacturing and in other private industry are flexible accelerator functions in which lagged changes in manufacturing output and consumers' expenditure respectively are the principal determinants of the rate of investment. In the manufacturing equation there is in addition a capacity utilisation term. Investment in stocks is similarly determined by a flexible accelerator.

Exports of goods are disaggregated into manufactures, food and basic materials and a small exogenous residual category; there is also an equation for exports of services. The determinants of exports are world trade and relative prices, and the relationship is dependent on the level of domestic capacity utilisation. *Ceteris paribus*, export volumes are higher at high than at low levels of utilisation, presumably reflecting the influence of lower unit costs, although the relationship is non-linear.

Imports are disaggregated only into goods and services: in both cases the independent variables are total domestic expenditure, relative prices and, in the case of goods, capacity utilisation.

Output, capacity utilisation and employment are disaggregated into five sectors, of which three (mainly public industries and services, public administration and defence and imputed services of dwellings) are treated as exogenous. The behaviour of the other two sectors (manufacturing and other private industry) is modelled in terms of CES production functions. Actual output is a function of weighted disaggregated expenditure and the production functions are used to obtain both potential output (and thus capacity utilisation) and, on inversion, actual employment. Unemployment is obtained by relating it to aggregate employment with an exogenous allowance for changes in the labour force.

Wage rates are determined by an augmented Phillips curve in which the rate of change of money wages is a distributed lag function of the unemployment rate and the past change in consumer prices. When an incomes policy is in operation that equation is overriden, and the rate of increase of wages taken as exogenous. Together with employment and average hours worked, the rate of change of wages leads to the rate of increase of the wage and salary bill. Income from self-employment is related to the level of current-price GDP and a time-trend. Net personal sector property income is related to the personal sector's net financial assets and to a weighted average of various interest rates, again with various lags. The other components of personal income – current grants, forces' pay and rent – are treated as exogenous. Personal tax payments are related to total personal income with an imposed (and variable) elasticity significantly greater than one, reflecting fiscal drag. Net contributions depend on exogenous contribution rates.

The rate of change of consumer prices depends, again with lags, on the rates of change of wage costs, import prices, productivity, manufacturing output, interest rates and indirect taxes.

The exchange rate equation, essentially a reduced-form specification, relates the rate to purchasing power parity (relative export prices), modified by terms reflecting changes in the covered United Kingdom/United States short-term interest rate differential (reflecting the effect of imbalances on the short-term capital account) and the visible balance in real terms (proxying overall disequilibrium in the external sector).

The banking sector is modelled around the identity between changes in bank lending to the personal and public sectors on the one hand, and in net deposits, net lending overseas and net other liabilities on the other. The demand for real balances (M3 deflated by the GDP deflator) is a function of real GDP, the Consol and Certificate of Deposit rates and the rate of inflation. A similar equation is used to explain the demand for currency; the difference between this and M3 then gives the change in net deposits. Bank lending to the private sector depends on net deposits, on expenditure on stockbuilding and consumer durables, and on the differential between the average overdraft rate and the cost of alternative finance (represented by the local authority rate). Net lending overseas and net other liabilities are taken as exogenous and, given the identity mentioned earlier, bank lending to the public sector is obtained as a residual. The model contains the government budget constraint, in which the net acquisition of public sector debt by the overseas sector is treated as exogenous and the net acquisition of public sector debt by the non-bank private sector is determined as the residual. The overall net acquisitions of financial assets by sectors are derived from the income and expenditure decisions briefly outlined above.

The main linkages in the model can be seen by considering the effects of a rise in public expenditure. This rise increases real GDP and thus employment and incomes, with consequential standard multiplier repercussions. There is, however, a variety of other reactions. The rise in output increases imports, worsens the visible balance and lowers the exchange rate. This raises domestic prices, and wages will rise in response to this as well as to the reduction in unemployment. The rise in GDP, with a fixed nominal money supply, increases the demand for real balances, as does the increase in the rate of inflation. If control of the money supply is to be maintained, interest rates will have to rise. This tends partially to offset both the initial stimulus to demand (by depressing, for example, housing investment) and the initial fall in the exchange rate (by improving the interest rate differential).

Like all models, that of the National Institute is in a constant state of change. A much fuller account of the model as it stood in mid-1977 is to be found in [4], [5] and [6].

Episode 1: September 1964–September 1969

The crucial strategic decision to take in reforming economic policy for the period 1964–9 is when the pound should have been devalued. That it had become overvalued by 1964 is not in doubt, and that the devaluation of 18 November 1967 was forced rather than rationally chosen is similarly not at issue. Many commentators have suggested that devaluation would have been politically impractical when the Labour government came into office in October 1964 (that is, for practical purposes, at the outset of our period) and have therefore plumped for mid-1966, when Labour had been returned with a comfortable majority rather than the knife-edge margin of 1964. Thus

Graham and Beckerman [1] state baldly: 'Those who assert that the pound sterling should have been devalued in 1964 know their economics but not their politics'. This is an appealing and pithy judgement, but is it correct?

There are three main factors to bear in mind. First, there was the emerging balance of payments deficit for 1964, estimated by the National Institute Economic Review in November as 'perhaps £700 million' on current and long-term capital account, though now put somewhat lower (a precise comparison is difficult because the distinction between 'long-term' and other capital transactions is no longer drawn). Secondly, there was the dangerously low level of the reserves – a little over £800 million at the end of 1964 of which nearly £600 million represented official borrowing. And thirdly, the Labour majority of only 5 overall meant that there was a compelling need to frame economic policy in a way which would preserve Party unity, in particular by attempting to maintain full employment.

In the short run, the deficit could be financed by further official borrowing, but in the longer run it had to be corrected and the corrective measures had better be taken sooner than later. There were three choices – deflation, devaluation or some new 'unorthodox' measures. In the event, the last course was chosen: the temporary import surcharge and export rebates with, in the longer run, an incomes policy to restrain the rise in wage costs and a National Plan to improve productivity. The measures proved inadequate to correct the underlying deficit particularly because of the limited extent to which the import surcharge could be applied, and need not detain us. The government should, therefore, have chosen deflation or devaluation. Both of these – indeed any measures to correct a balance of payments deficit starting from full employment – involve a relative fall in living standards via a fall in real wages or a rise in unemployment or both. The choice between them, given that a choice *had* to be made, is thus not affected by the political situation in the House of Commons. In fact, of the two, devaluation was preferable in that, unlike deflation, it offered the possibility of a return to an equilibrium with external balance and full employment.

We thus begin with the assumption that the pound was devalued by 15 per cent at the outset. To conform with the rules of the game, we assume that the devaluation took place in January 1965, the implicit assumption being that the deficit was financed by official borrowing between October 1964 and then. It follows that we have also assumed that the temporary import surcharge and export rebates were never introduced, and this is incorporated in our estimates. In order to release resources for the ensuing switch into the balance of payments, we assume that in the following April budget, cuts of £400 million a year, at 1970 prices, in public authorities current expenditure and £200 million a year in public investment were implemented, together with increases in personal income tax amounting to £500 million, again at 1970 prices, in a full year; a smaller increase, of some £200 million, in indirect taxes; and a slight tightening of hire purchase controls. The latter in fact took place in July 1965.

On these assumptions, and with no further significant fiscal action during the year, we estimate that the current balance would have been about £150 million in deficit compared with the actual deficit of £26 million, unemployment virtually unchanged at 300,000 and consumer price inflation approaching 7 per cent per annum rather than the actual 5 per cent (see Tables 4.1–4.6). The deterioration in the balance of payments reflects, of course, the net effect of the devaluation-induced deterioration in the terms of trade and the

Table 4.1 Policy simulations 1964–9: gross domestic product at factor cost

	1964	1965	1966	1967	1968	1969
£m. 1970 prices						
Gross domestic product	37890	38917	39376	40888	42237	43350
Index 1964 = 100	100	102.7	103.9	107.9	111.5	114.4
Consumers' expenditure	28330	28292	28424	29245	30097	30742
Public current	8138	8057	8195	8675	8888	9000
Gross fixed investment	7541	7903	8022	8819	9282	9318
Stockbuilding	1148	674	340	275	649	817
Exports[a]	7991	8631	9304	9840	10724	11237
Total final expenditure	53148	53557	54279	56854	59635	61107
Imports[a]	8487	8144	8343	9146	10180	10487
Factor cost adjustment	6771	6497	6560	6821	7218	7270
Percentage changes						
Gross domestic product		2.7	1.2	3.8	3.3	2.6
Consumers' expenditure		−0.1	0.5	2.9	2.9	2.1
Public current		−1.0	1.7	5.9	2.4	1.3
Gross fixed investment		4.8	1.5	9.9	5.2	0.4
Exports[a]		8.0	7.8	5.8	9.0	4.8
Total final expenditure		0.8	1.3	4.7	4.9	2.5
Imports[a]		−4.0	2.9	9.6	11.3	3.0
Factor cost adjustment		−4.0	1.0	4.0	5.8	0.7

[a]*of goods and services.*

improvement in trade volumes. Exports of goods and services would have been 8 per cent higher than in 1964 while the volume of imports, assisted by a sharp fall in the rate of stockbuilding, would have fallen by 4 per cent. This marked stimulus to demand would have been offset by small falls in both public and private consumption, leaving GDP growing at or a little below the rate of growth of productive potential. Given the extent of the limits of credit which were in fact negotiated in 1964–5, we assume that sterling could have been adequately protected during the initial deterioration in the balance of payments.

Table 4.2 Policy simulations 1964–9: gross fixed investment

	1964	1965	1966	1967	1968	1969
£m. 1970 prices						
Total	7541	7903	8022	8819	9282	9318
Public sector	3667	3852	4129	4740	4761	4616
Private sector	3874	4051	3893	4079	4521	4702
Manufacturing	1561	1765	1860	1824	1837	1979
Percentage change						
Total		4.8	1.5	9.9	5.2	0.4
Public sector		5.0	7.2	14.8	0.4	−3.1
Private sector		4.6	−3.9	4.8	10.8	4.0
Manufacturing		13.1	5.4	−1.9	0.7	7.8

By the beginning of 1966, with the balance of payments moving steadily into surplus and unemployment remaining low, attention would inevitably have turned to the problem of inflation. With consumer prices having risen by nearly 7 per cent in 1965, and with real personal disposable income having actually fallen a little, considerable upward pressure on wages could be expected – we estimate that average earnings would have been rising at an annual rate of nearly 8 per cent by the beginning of 1966. We therefore assume that from April 1966 an incomes policy was introduced which restrained the rise in average earnings to 5 per cent per annum. At the same time, partly to offset the temporary deflationary impact of the introduction of the incomes policy at a level lower than the contemporary rate of price inflation but, more importantly, to help its acceptance, we assume that the regulator power to reduce indirect tax rates by 10 per cent was employed (about £300 million), and that income tax concessions amounting to £200 million at 1970 prices were announced. We see no reason to disapprove of the introduction of either corporation tax or the selective employment tax in 1966; apart from these, we assume no other changes in fiscal policy.

Table 4.3 Policy simulations 1964–9: the balance of payments (£m. current prices)

	1964	1965	1966	1967	1968	1969
Imports of goods	5021	5660	5834	6401	7131	7243
Imports of services	1691	2019	2147	2348	2367	2470
Exports of goods	4583	5395	6232	6592	7236	7355
Exports of services	1753	1889	2084	2372	2628	2760
Trade balance	−375	−395	335	215	366	403
Current balance	−355	−144	521	514	805	894
Exchange rate (IMF)	108.5	93.5	94.8	96.4	98.0	101.6

On this basis, steady progress towards the achievement of the major objectives of demand management could have been expected in 1966: an external surplus required to repay the debts incurred up to 1965, high employment, a sustainable rate of economic growth and a tolerable rate of price inflation. The current balance would have been over £500 million in surplus. Unemployment, though rising from about 300,000 at the end of 1965 to about 400,000 at the end of 1966, remained low. Helped by stable import prices and by the regulator cut, the effect of the 5 per cent incomes policy would have brought the rate of consumer price inflation down to about 4 per cent by the end of the year. There would, it is true, have been some anxieties: the growth in output was slower than that of capacity, the 1965 boom in manufacturing investment (in turn largely reflecting the rapid expansion of demand in 1964) was ending, and unemployment was,

Table 4.4 Policy simulations 1964–9: net acquisition of financial assets (£m. current prices)

	1964	1965	1966	1967	1968	1969
Personal sector	592	625	888	717	765	866
Company sector	−49	−416	33	713	826	182
Public sector	−1004	−351	−540	−1277	−1011	−45
Overseas sector	355	144	−520	−510	−806	−895
Residual error	−386	−1	117	357	227	−107

if low, nevertheless rising. But reflation, the only fiscal option open, would have to some extent jeopardised the balance of payments surplus. More important, it would clearly have had to be reversed in 1967 when much more rapid expansion was in view as a result of the rapid expansion of public expenditure, particularly on capital account, and the fall in the rate of accumulation of stocks coming to an end.

In 1967, then, there would have been no need to make any discretionary fiscal changes, though we in fact assume a further minor cut of £200 million in direct taxation to assist the continuing acceptance of the incomes policy. The rapid expansion of public spending, however, with a consequential increase in the public sector borrowing requirement on the supply side, together with the rapid expansion of nominal income on the demand side, would at the prevailing low level of interest rates probably have led to a rapid rise in the money supply. We therefore suppose that interest rates were gradually raised during the year.

Table 4.5 Policy simulations 1964–9: other indicators

	1964	1965	1966	1967	1968	1969
Unemployment (000's)	360	297	324	443	428	420
Average earnings	100	107.9	115.8	121.7	127.8	134.1
Consumer price index	75.8	80.9	85.9	88.5	89.7	91.2
PSBR £m.	1098	712	497	1545	1143	−94
% of GDP	3.7	2.3	1.4	4.2	3.0	−0.3
M3 £m.	12398	11398	13456	14512	16170	17039
Consol rate	6.0	6.4	6.9	7.5	8.5	8.5
Percentage change						
Average earnings		7.9	7.2	5.1	5.0	5.0
Consumer price index		6.7	6.2	3.1	1.4	1.7
M3		5.1	8.5	7.8	11.4	5.4

The outcome for 1967 thus sees the balance of payments continuing in substantial surplus, GDP growing by 4 per cent, unemployment reversing its rise to end the year as it began, at about 400,000, and inflation continuing to fall, so that by the end of the year it is down to about 2 per cent.

By early 1968, with world trade beginning to expand very rapidly, the balance of payments remains in comfortable surplus despite the rapid growth of domestic demand. With unemployment falling steadily, some degree of deflation would have been required. We assume that the April budget aimed to reduce public authorities' current expenditure by some £400 million (at 1970 prices) in a full year and increased personal taxation by £150 million. A further rise in interest rates is also assumed. While these measures would have stabilised the unemployment rate, they would not have prevented the balance of payments surplus from increasing still further – to the perhaps embarrassingly high level of some £700–£800 million.

At this point, the options for the management of the economy would have become almost completely open. There would no doubt have been pressure to revalue the pound, and our simulation incorporates a modest 5 per cent revaluation in late 1968 which, of course, actually improves the balance in 1968 and 1969. There are no signs of overheating: unemployment remains at about 400,000, or about 1.9 per cent. Manufacturing investment, after stagnating in 1967 and 1968, recovers strongly but steadily in 1969. Price inflation levels out in 1969 at 1–1½ per cent per annum. While we have assumed that average earnings continue to rise at the 5 per cent rate set by the incomes policy, it seems highly probable that at this level of price inflation such a rate of increase could be sustained without the necessity of such a policy.

Table 4.6 Summary of fiscal policy changes 1965–9 (financial years, £m. annual rates)

	1965–6	1966–7	1967–8	1968–9	1969–70
Public current expenditure	−300	—	—	−450	—
Public fixed investment	−150	—	—	—	—
Direct taxes	+720	−200	−200	+150	—
Indirect taxes	+200	−300	—	—	—

This analysis suggests that, in the period 1964–9, a prompt devaluation with the induced switch of resources from consumption into net exports safeguarded by a subsequent and effectively maintained incomes policy, coupled with judicious fine-tuning of domestic demand, would have produced within three to four years remarkable economic success. It is worth stressing, though, that this conclusion depends critically on the assumed success of the incomes policy in restraining price inflation – an assumption which is also critical in later episodes.

Episode 2: July 1970–July 1975

If the reassessment of the conduct of demand management during the period 1965–9 is dominated by the question of whether sterling should have been devalued earlier, the 1970–5 period is by no means so simple. To anticipate, the following analysis rests on three broad judgements. First, the reflation in the earlier part of the period should have begun earlier and proceeded in a more stepwise fashion. Secondly, given the political climate, an incomes policy could not have been introduced earlier than late 1972 but, in retrospect, should not have included either the Phase I freeze or the effective indexation of wages implied by the threshold agreements of Phase III. Thirdly, the commodity price rises of 1973, and in particular the oil price rise of late 1973, need not have been allowed to be so contractionary on demand nor so inflationary on prices.

When the Conservative government came to power in 1970, the outlook was for economic growth rather below the growth of productive potential, at about 2–2½ per cent per annum, with unemployment drifting upwards from its then current level of some 550,000. The balance of payments on current account was expected to be in comfortable surplus in both 1970 and 1971, in the range £500–750 million. The rate of consumer price inflation was expected to remain steady at about 5 per cent a year [2].

On conventional demand management criteria, that is ignoring the apparent intention of the Government at the time simply to reduce the scale of intervention in the working of the economy, there would thus have been a strong case for some significant reflation. We judge that an autumn 1970 budget could appropriately have reduced direct taxation by some £800 million per annum, and indirect taxes by £500 million at current prices, with a further reduction of about £700 million in personal taxes in the spring 1971 budget. At the same time, we assume that, given the political climate, public expenditure on both current and capital accounts could not have grown faster than it in fact did. We also incorporate the £250 million reduction in SET and the £400 million reduction in indirect taxes in 1971.

The net effect would have been to raise the growth of GDP in 1971 to about 3¼ per cent, halting the rise in unemployment. With exports rising as a result of a continued fairly rapid growth of world trade, with stocks falling in the face of the rapid expansion of demand, and with the terms of trade improving a little, the current account in 1971 should have remained in substantial surplus. The rate of growth of average earnings, however, could have been expected to remain at about 10 per cent per annum, with the rate of consumer price inflation edging up to about 5½ per cent a year (see Tables 4.7–4.12). The public sector borrowing requirement would have become substantial in 1971, at about £2.7 billion or 5.6 per cent of GDP. There must be some doubt about whether a deficit of this size and, to look ahead, the even larger deficits of 1973–5 could have been financed without

Table 4.7 Policy simulations 1970–5: gross domestic product at factor cost

	1970	1971	1972	1973	1974	1975
£m. 1970 prices						
Gross domestic product	43546	44934	45909	47512	48130	48224
Index 1970 = 100	100	103.2	105.4	109.1	110.5	110.7
Consumers' expenditure	31645	33363	34883	35120	35766	34950
Public current	9095	9344	9725	10123	10328	10797
Gross fixed investment	9449	9798	10085	10169	9912	10118
Stockbuilding	474	−187	280	1125	259	11
Exports[a]	11501	12395	12655	14121	15401	14943
Total final expenditure	62165	64714	67628	70657	71666	70819
Imports[a]	11092	11818	13189	14386	14724	13958
Factor cost adjustment	7527	7962	8530	8758	8812	8637
Percentage changes						
Gross domestic product		3.2	2.2	3.5	1.3	0.2
Consumers' expenditure		5.4	4.6	0.7	1.8	−2.3
Public current		2.7	4.1	4.1	2.0	4.5
Gross fixed investment		3.7	2.9	0.8	−2.5	2.1
Exports[a]		7.8	2.1	11.6	9.1	−3.0
Total final expenditure		4.1	4.5	4.5	1.4	−1.2
Imports[a]		6.5	11.6	9.1	2.3	−5.2
Factor cost adjustment		5.8	7.1	2.7	0.6	−2.0

[a] *of goods and services.*

very substantial increases in the money supply. In our view it was a mistake in 1971 for the Bank of England to introduce the greater flexibility of control of the banking system, which had been foreshadowed in the Bank's consultative document *Competition and Credit Control* of May 1971. If the Bank had retained its former powers – notably those in connection with the tighter control of reserve asset ratios, the imposition of ceilings on various categories of bank lending, and the power directly to control Bank, or Minimum Lending, Rate – the control of the money supply need have caused no serious

Table 4.8 Policy simulations 1970–5: gross fixed investment

	1970	1971	1972	1973	1974	1975
£m. 1970 prices						
Total	9449	9798	10085	10169	9912	10118
Public sector	4517	4584	4537	4566	4611	5127
Private sector	4932	5214	5548	5603	5301	4991
Manufacturing	2129	2034	1835	1904	2038	1917
Percentage change						
Total		3.7	2.9	0.8	−2.5	2.1
Public sector		1.5	−1.0	0.6	1.0	11.2
Private sector		5.7	6.4	1.0	−5.4	−5.9
Manufacturing		−4.5	−9.8	3.7	7.1	−5.9

difficulties in 1971 or in later years. It would be extremely difficult to quantify how much difference this would have made: the figures for the changes in M3 and for the levels of interest rates shown in Table 4.11 are intended to suggest only broad patterns of likely developments given the size of the public sector's financing needs.

By the first half of 1972, two problems would have been emerging: a rate of price inflation edging inexorably upwards, and a deterioration in the current account which was sliding steadily from surplus towards bare balance and into deficit. On the other hand, with world trade in manufactures expected to increase by 13–14 per cent in real terms in 1973, the balance of payments situation would not have been particularly worrying and, although a case could perhaps be made for some minor deflationary action in the spring of 1972, there was no need to reverse the substantial reflation of 1970–1. We assume that

Table 4.9 Policy simulations 1970–5: the balance of payments (£m. current prices)

	1970	1971	1972	1973	1974	1975
Imports of goods	8128	8762	10217	13885	19766	19109
Imports of services	2949	3291	3529	4307	5128	5248
Exports of goods	8125	9014	9365	12012	15838	17653
Exports of services	3363	3764	4012	5019	6007	6185
Trade balance	412	724	−369	−1162	−3049	−519
Current balance	757	956	−149	−309	−2321	−482
Exchange rate (IMF)	100.1	102.1	98.1	89.0	91.9	93.0

the change to a system of floating rates in June 1972 in fact occurred. This too, given the impossibility of foreseeing the scale of the commodity price rises of 1973, would have reassured economic managers that the medium-term balance of payments posed no serious problems.

In total, our reflationary stimulus amounts to nearly £2.7 billion by 1972–3, which is of the same order of magnitude as the reflation which actually took place, though smoothed forward quite significantly. In consequence, our level of GDP in 1973 is close to the recorded level though the growth path from 1970 is much smoother.

Table 4.10 Policy simulations 1970–5: net acquisition of financial assets (£m. current prices)

	1970	1971	1972	1973	1974	1975
Personal sector	1330	1233	952	1565	3339	3532
Company sector	−896	970	956	648	1083	4486
Public sector	414	−1672	−1776	−2577	−6993	−8706
Overseas sector	−757	−956	149	309	2321	482
Residual error	−91	425	−281	55	250	206

Our earnings equation suggests, however, that by the end of 1972 average earnings would have been increasing at 11–12 per cent per annum, and showing no signs of deceleration. An incomes freeze, of the kind that was in fact introduced for 90 days in November 1972, we think to be mistaken. By removing all negotiating flexibility such a freeze almost certainly creates more problems for ensuing stages than are warranted by the brief hiatus it provides. We therefore assume the introduction of a more flexible policy at the end of 1972 designed to contain the rise in average earnings to 6 per cent over the following year, against a rise in consumer prices in the previous twelve months of some 7–8 per cent.

Fuelled largely by a substantial increase of 9½ per cent in the volume of exports of goods and services, GDP would have grown by about 3½ per cent in 1973, with unemployment falling steadily to a little under 550,000 by the end of the year. The commodity price boom of 1973 would nevertheless have taken the current account into deficit. Between the third quarters of 1972 and 1973, that is before the major oil price rise of December 1973, the prices of imports of fuels and basic materials rose by 56 per cent. For the year as a whole, the overall terms of trade would have worsened by some 8 per cent, giving a small current account deficit of some £300 million.

Table 4.11 Policy simulations 1970–5: other indicators

	1970	1971	1972	1973	1974	1975
Unemployment (000's)	570	675	658	546	547	645
Average earnings	100	109.9	121.3	130.1	141.2	157.1
Consumer price index	99.6	105.0	111.3	119.9	129.9	144.6
PSBR £m.	272	2725	2090	3972	7795	9738
% of GDP	0.5	5.6	3.9	6.6	11.4	12.7
M3 £m.	17329	18786	19967	21964	24965	26483
Consol rate	9.2	10.0	10.8	11.7	15.0	14.7
Percentage change						
Average earnings		9.9	10.3	7.3	8.5	11.2
Consumer price index		5.5	6.0	7.7	8.4	11.3
M3		8.4	6.3	10.0	13.7	8.1

Up to late 1973, then, the problems of the period had been essentially the familiar ones of demand management, exacerbated only by the refusal of wage inflation to respond to limited reductions in the pressure of demand. The commodity price boom, and particularly the quantum jump in the price of oil, posed problems which had not arisen since the Korean War, and then only in an attenuated form. The effect was akin to a sharp increase in the level of indirect taxation. Matters were made worse for most industrial countries by the very low price elasticities of the commodities affected, so that the deflationary impact could not be avoided by the substitution of domestic products. They were made acutely worse in the case of Britain by the virtual indexation of wages through the threshold agreements of Phase III of the incomes

Table 4.12 Summary of fiscal policy changes 1970–5 (financial years, £m. annual rates)

	1971/2	1972/3	1973/4	1974/5	1975/6
Public current expenditure[a]	—	—	—	—	—
Public fixed investment[a]	—	—	—	—	—
Direct taxes	– 1500[b]	—	+ 100	– 500	+ 200
Indirect taxes	– 1150[bc]	—	– 600[d]	– 1950	—

[a] *Actual path of public expenditure assumed.*
[b] *Part in autumn 1970.*
[c] *Includes reduction in SET.*
[d] *Includes changes in 1974, first quarter.*

policy which operated from November 1973 until its suspension in November 1974. This latter factor intensified the wage-price spiral which was not brought under control until the next round of incomes policies began in July 1975. In addition, there was the massive deterioration in the current balance of payments.

Taking the balance of payments problem first, there were four possibilities. First, assuming industrial capacity was adequate, the deficit could have been self-correcting if the commodity producers could have increased their imports *pari passu* with the rise in their export earnings. This was rightly recognised to be implausible, given the low propensity to import of most commodity producers and in particular many of the OPEC countries. Secondly, each country could have attempted to compensate for the commodity deficit by balance of payments corrective measures – devaluation or protection. But both these would have affected predominantly trade in manufactures, and thus merely have represented an attempt to shift the total deficit around among the industrial countries. Thirdly, massive deflation could have been used to reduce imports, but this would have concealed rather than solved the problem, and again would have been essentially a beggar-my-neighbour solution. Finally, the current account deficit could have been financed by capital account borrowing, notably through the recycling of oil surpluses. This would have avoided the need for any corrective action involving the domestic economy; it is what to a considerable degree happened, and we believe, with hindsight, that the balance of payments 'problem' need not have led to such deflation as in fact happened.

Turning to the domestic economy, the question is whether the commodity price boom, and specifically the oil price rise, could have been neutralised by fiscal and monetary policy. Our view is that it could and should have been neutralised, at least in great part, by means of substantial reductions in rates of indirect taxation. In the limiting case, these reductions could have been on such a scale as to leave the aggregate price level where it otherwise would have been. This would of course have immediately removed the deflationary impact of the oil price rise itself on domestic real incomes. Perhaps more important, it would have cancelled the sharp rise in domestic prices which, whether through formal indexation or more loosely through the response of money wages to price rises, would inevitably give a sharp twist to the wage-price spiral.

The problems with such a strategy would of course have been financial. A sharp increase in the public sector borrowing requirement would have been entailed, with the risk of very rapid increases in the money supply. The risks should not, however, be overstated. The direct impact of the oil price rise was estimated at 2–2½ per cent on consumer prices (see [3], especially pp. 33–4). Making some allowance for other commodity price rises, though not for completely neutralising the impact of imported inflation, it might have been appropriate to reduce indirect taxes by an amount equivalent to about 3½ per cent of consumers' expenditure, or some £1¾ billion: this is the figure we assume. This is not an enormous increase in the public sector borrowing requirement and it would have been offset to some degree by the higher direct tax revenue resulting from a more buoyant economy than there would otherwise have been. Our simulation suggests a public sector borrowing requirement in 1974 of about £8 billion which, as later experience suggests, is by no means impossible to finance without excessive monetary expansion.

We also assume that there was no index linking of wages to the cost of living but that the 6 per cent limit of the 1973 incomes policy was relaxed to 10 per cent for 1974.

Despite the neutralisation of the oil price rise, there would nevertheless have been considerable deflationary pressure in the economy in 1974. The fall in investment and the sharp decline in stockbuilding would have held GDP growth to only about 1¼ per cent in 1974, with unemployment hovering at about 550,000. The rate of inflation of consumer prices would have been about 8½ per cent compared with the actual rate of over 16 per cent and, despite the substantial deterioration in the current balance attributable to the commodity price rise, the markedly lower rate of domestic price inflation would have produced a deficit of some £2.3 billion, actually smaller than the recorded deficit of about £3.3 billion.

Given the scale of the public sector's financing needs in 1974 and again in 1975, we see no way in which Britain could have been further insulated from the world recession by means of demand management. The volume of world trade in manufactures fell by nearly 5 per cent in 1975; United Kingdom exports of goods and services by 3 per cent. Assuming the incomes policy to have been further relaxed to 12 per cent for 1975, but with the world recession holding down foreign prices severely, the terms of trade would have improved sharply, cutting back the current account deficit to about £500 million. Despite the fact that we eliminate the tax increases of the 1975 Budget, GDP growth is reduced to less than ½ per cent in 1975 and unemployment would probably have risen to about 750,000 by the end of the year. But with the scope for demand management techniques now exhausted, there was probably little more which could have been done. Even so, the economy would have been in a much better condition in 1975 on our policy assumptions than it in fact was with inflation at over 20 per cent a year, unemployment reaching over a million by the end of the year, and a current account deficit of over £1½ billion.

Episode 3: Early 1977–December 1981

The analysis of demand management policies over the next five years is dominated by three interconnected policy choices: first, how should the North Sea oil revenues be used? Secondly, what should anti-inflation policy be? And thirdly, how should the exchange rate be managed? We explored a number of permutations of different choices in each of these areas, and summary descriptions are given below for a few key cases. In addition, we present detailed figures for our own 'best buy'.

As a base, we explored the implications of simply continuing with 'present policies', that is, our interpretation of policy as it stood in early 1977. This we took to mean the following. First, some form of incomes policy prevented any catching up of the real income losses of Stages I and II, but no more than this. Technically, we employed our average earnings equation with zero residuals from mid-1977, thus implying that the incomes-policy-induced negative residuals are never reversed but that average earnings changes from then on are in line with those which would have occurred in the absence of an incomes policy. Secondly, the exchange rate was maintained at about its 1977 first half level until the end of the year, allowed to float freely in 1978, with the upward movement partially restrained thereafter. Thirdly, existing public expenditure plans were continued and no discretionary fiscal action was taken other than indexing personal tax allowances from 1979 onwards so as to make personal tax payments rise in line with personal income.

The combination of a fairly loose incomes policy and the upward drift of the exchange rate gradually brings down the rate of consumer price inflation to about 3 per cent by 1981. The absence of any reflationary action, however, restricts the rate of growth of GDP to an average of 1.6 per cent per annum over the period and, given the expected increase in the labour supply of 150–200,000 a year, unemployment rises to 2.2 million by 1981. Export competitiveness worsens until mid-1978, but thereafter improves gradually and the balance of payments on current account is in substantial surplus throughout. The accumulated surplus amounts to some $22 billion by 1981, almost exactly matching the total of scheduled debt repayments between 1977 and 1985.

This scenario, then, reflects the likely outcome if the benefit to the balance of payments from North Sea oil is used very largely to repay debt and only to a limited extent to allow an upward movement in the exchange rate. A similar picture would emerge if the current account surpluses were used to a greater or lesser extent to finance overseas investment, another possibility which has been suggested. In either case, there is little or no benefit to employment, and it is worth noting that by the end of the period investment in manufacturing would be only about 5 per cent higher than in 1976.

We next explored the implications of pursuing the same policies, but with a significant degree of fiscal reflation in addition to the indexing of personal tax payments. Specifically, we assumed cuts of some £2.4 billion in personal taxation at current prices from the end of 1977, together with increases of £900 million in public authorities' current expenditure and £600 million in public investment in the spring of 1978 and a further £600 million increase (at 1978 prices) in public investment in the spring of 1979. The consequential expansion would reduce the upward pressure on the exchange rate and, correspondingly, we assume a slightly lower rate by 1981 (an effective rate of about 73 rather than 78).

The effect of this reflation is to raise the average rate of growth of GDP over the period to about 2.6 per cent per annum, and to stem the rise in unemployment which is, in 1981, some 1.5 million. Private investment is significantly stimulated: manufacturing investment in 1981 is some 20 per cent higher in real terms than in 1976, for instance. Consumer price inflation is worse, though only fractionally: the rate of increase is 5 per cent in 1981 compared with 3 per cent in the base case, reflecting the effect on average earnings of the more rapid expansion and of the slightly lower exchange rate. The current account is, of course, considerably worsened: the cumulated surplus to 1981 is some $10 billion, implying a need (if the capital account is ignored) for at least some recycling of debt. For a surplus country, however, this should prove both easy and relatively cheap.

A combination of reflation with relatively loose control of both average earnings and the exchange rate thus leads to a potential conflict between the achievement of a reasonable employment objective and a sufficient balance of payments surplus. In order to explore the extent to which it is incomes policy rather than exchange rate policy to which this conflict is sensitive, we next investigated the consequences of abandoning any attempt to control average earnings while simultaneously fixing the exchange rate rather than letting it float up. At the same time, in addition to indexation, we assumed reflation of £1 billion at current prices in the second quarter of 1978 and a further £2 billion in the second quarters of each of 1979, 1980 and 1981.

The immediate effect of this conjunction of policies is, of course, to produce very rapid rates of inflation of both average earnings and consumer prices in the early years of the period. The rate of increase of earnings peaks at about 22 per cent a year in 1978, and consumer prices rise at about 15 per cent per annum until 1980. The progressive improvement in the terms of trade is more than sufficient to compensate for the relatively poor trade performance in volume terms, and the current balance improves to nearly £5 billion in 1980 and over £6 billion in 1981. However, the almost static level in real terms of net exports and the very slow growth of private investment virtually offset the reflationary fiscal stimulus. GDP rises by only 1.9 per cent

Table 4.13 Policy simulations 1976–81: gross domestic product at factor cost

	1976	1977	1978	1979	1980	1981
£m. 1970 prices						
Gross domestic product	47394	48195	49294	50632	53002	54980
Index 1976 = 100	100	101.7	104.0	106.8	111.8	116.0
Consumers' expenditure	35290	35305	35565	36557	38050	39343
Public current	11101	11220	11220	11332	11580	11950
Gross fixed investment	9562	9279	9810	10094	10658	11109
Stockbuilding	−464	96	193	348	618	854
Exports[a]	15551	16484	17053	17664	18488	19359
Total final expenditure	71040	72385	73840	75994	79393	82615
Imports[a]	14589	15094	15419	16011	16700	17655
Factor cost adjustment	9057	9096	9127	9350	9691	9981
Percentage change						
Gross domestic product		1.7	2.3	2.7	4.7	3.7
Consumers' expenditure		0.0	0.7	2.8	4.1	3.4
Public current		1.1	0.0	1.0	2.2	3.2
Gross fixed investment		−3.0	5.7	2.9	5.6	4.2
Exports[a]		6.0	3.4	3.6	4.7	4.7
Total final expenditure		1.9	2.0	2.9	4.5	4.1
Imports[a]		3.9	2.2	3.8	4.3	5.7
Factor cost adjustment		0.4	0.3	2.4	3.6	3.0

[a] *of goods and services.*

Table 4.14 Policy simulations 1976–81: gross fixed investment

	1976	1977	1978	1979	1980	1981
£m. 1970 prices						
Total	9562	9279	9810	10094	10658	11109
Public sector	5071	4494	4510	4667	4876	5025
Private sector	4491	4785	5300	5427	5782	6084
Manufacturing	1650	1827	2127	2143	2110	2206
Percentage change						
Total		−3.0	5.7	2.9	5.6	4.2
Public sector		−11.4	0.4	3.5	4.5	3.1
Private sector		6.6	10.8	2.4	6.5	5.2
Manufacturing		10.7	16.5	0.7	−1.5	4.5

per annum on average. Unemployment rises steadily, reaching 2 million by 1981 and despite the gradual deceleration in the growth of average earnings which this causes, the rate of consumer price inflation is still at 8 per cent a year at the end of the period.

For our final scenario, therefore, we combined reflation with a managed exchange rate and a continuous incomes policy (see Tables 4.13–4.18). The incomes policy is such as to prevent any 'catching up' of real wages after the end of Stage II in mid-1977, together with policies designed to keep the rise in average earnings to 10 per cent in 1979, 8 per cent in 1980 and 6 per cent in 1981. In addition to the increases required for indexation, incorporated in all previous cases, reflation comprises:

(i) reductions in personal income tax of £2 billion in 1978 II (at 1978 prices, £1 billion in 1979 II, and £1½ billion in 1980 II and 1981 II, the higher figures for the last two years to offset the squeeze on real disposable incomes which would otherwise be entailed by the relatively tight incomes policy;
(ii) increases in public investment of £600 million (at current prices) in the financial year 1978/9, £600 million more in 1979/80 and a further £300 million in 1980/1;
(iii) cumulative increases in public authorities' current expenditure of £400 million (at current prices) in 1978/9, £250 million in 1979/80 and £250 million in 1980/1;
(iv) increases of £600 million (at current prices) in current grants in each of 1979, 1980 and 1981.

Table 4.15 Policy simulations 1976–81: the balance of payments (£m. current prices)

	1976	1977	1978	1979	1980	1981
Imports of goods	28886	34118	36315	38830	42810	47312
Imports of services	7418	8295	9035	9722	10524	11513
Exports of goods	25294	31222	34688	37831	42068	46960
Exports of services	9358	11456	13074	14310	15328	16616
Trade balance	– 1652	266	2412	3589	4062	4750
Current balance	– 1433	131	1335	2121	2246	2714
Exchange rate (IMF)	66.2	61.9	62.2	62.5	62.4	62.4

The exchange rate is maintained throughout at around 62–62.5 (IMF weighted index, December 1971 = 100).

The net effect of these policies is to produce average annual growth in GDP of 3.3 per cent. Unemployment, after rising a little up to 1979, falls to about 1 million by the end of the period. The rate of inflation is down to 5 per cent by 1981, and the ratio of United Kingdom manufactured export prices to world manufactured export prices is, in 1981, at almost precisely its 1977 level. The current balance is in comfortable and growing surplus throughout: the cumulative surplus from 1977 to 1981 is about $18 billion, implying no difficulty in both repaying foreign debt on schedule while at the same time accumulating adequate foreign currency reserves (for example, maintaining their mid-1977 level in real terms). Indeed, given the ease and economy, already noted, with which foreign debt could in these circumstances be refinanced, a case could be made for yet further reflation later in the period. Our assumption of a roughly constant personal savings ratio entails a substantial rise in the personal sector's net acquisition of financial assets in nominal terms (Table 4.14), but in real terms, the average growth

Table 4.16 Policy simulations 1976–81: net acquisition of financial assets (£m. current prices)

	1976	1977	1978	1979	1980	1981
Personal sector	7617	7379	9546	11803	12850	14661
Company sector	– 1670	– 2467	– 1364	– 1633	– 772	45
Public sector	– 8569	– 5877	– 6847	– 8104	– 9832	– 11991
Overseas sector	1423	– 133	– 1335	– 2121	– 2246	– 2714
Residual error	1199	1097	—	—	—	—

rate is little higher than that of GDP. A smaller rate of acquisition (lower savings ratio) would, other things being equal, reduce the need for discretionary fiscal stimulus. It is important to note that, in the present scenario, manufacturing investment is 30 per cent higher in real terms in 1981 than it was in 1976. Nevertheless, the bulk of this recovery takes place in 1977 and 1978; if North Sea oil is to be used at least in part to ensure that industry emerges from the oil era with a substantially modernised capital stock, a sustained expansion of demand is required in order to generate and maintain a sufficiently high level of investment.

Table 4.17 Policy simulations 1976–81: other indicators

	1976	1977	1978	1979	1980	1981
Unemployment (000's)	1223	1280	1382	1458	1295	1010
Average earnings	100	112.1	127.0	141.9	154.3	164.6
Consumer price index	100	114.6	128.0	139.7	149.0	156.8
PSBR £m.	9489	6779	8000	9416	11232	13391
% of GDP	8.9	5.5	5.7	6.0	6.4	7.0
M3 £m.	43065	45417	50777	57086	64611	73583
Consol rate	14.3	12.7	14.0	13.2	10.8	8.1
Percentage change						
Average earnings		12.1	13.3	11.7	8.7	6.7
Consumer price index		14.7	11.7	9.2	6.7	5.2
M3		5.5	11.8	12.4	13.2	13.9

Our analysis suggests, then, that the three major objectives of demand management – higher growth of output and lower unemployment, an adequate balance of payments surplus, and a tolerable rate of inflation – can be met over the next five years if and only if an

Table 4.18 Summary of fiscal policy changes 1977–81 (financial years, £m. annual rates)

	1978/9	1979/80	1980/1	1981/2
Public current expenditure[a]	+400	+250	+250	—
Public fixed investment[a]	+600	+600	+300	—
Direct taxes[b]	−2000	−1000	−1500	−1500
Indirect taxes[b]	—	—	—	—
Current grants[b]	—	+600	+600	+600

[a] *Changes to announced plans as at mid-1977.*
[b] *These changes are in addition to indexation.*

appropriate combination of planned reflationary fiscal policy, preservation of trade competitiveness via the management of the exchange rate, and control of cost inflation through an incomes policy, is chosen. In this episode, the incomes policy, as measured by comparison with the behaviour of earnings in a non-incomes policy run, is not in fact particularly restrictive; it serves more as an insurance policy to prevent any unexpected upward pressures on earnings which might emerge.

Conclusions

Throughout the period, we have assumed that the pursuit of the three major aims of macroeconomic policy – internal and external balance and the control of inflation – required the use of three policy instruments – in our case, the management of aggregate demand through fiscal and monetary policy, exchange rate policy and incomes policy. The results of our analysis suggest that in each episode, a good deal of progress could have been made towards a satisfactory conjunction of the objectives. By 1969, our recommendations for the first episode would have resulted in unemployment of about 1.8 per cent (compared with an actual figure of 2.3 per cent), a current account surplus approaching £1000 million compared with £400 million and consumer price inflation below 2 per cent per annum instead of the actual 5½ per cent. Starting again from the actual position in 1970, by 1975 our policies produce unemployment of 2.8 per cent instead of 3.9 per cent, a current account deficit of less than £500 million compared with the actual £1700 million and consumer price inflation of about 11 per cent per annum instead of 24 per cent. Again beginning with the actual situation in 1977, our projections give unemployment of just over 4 per cent, a current account surplus of over £2500 million and consumer price inflation of about 5 per cent per annum.

These represent significant achievements for conventional demand management policy. Given our self-imposed restriction to the kinds of macroeconomic policies which have in practice been used over the last two decades, they do not, of course, necessarily reflect what could have been (or could be) achieved with a wider range of policy instruments. But they do suggest that 'fine tuning' could on the whole achieve a good deal more than its critics, on the basis of past experience, often suggest.

There is one important aspect of our analysis to which attention should be drawn. At a number of points, our results depend critically on the assumption of a successful incomes policy. Indeed, for substantial parts of each period (1966–9, 1973–5 and the whole of the third episode) an incomes policy is assumed to operate. This near continuous 'policy-on' assumption is, however, in some respects deceptive. In each case, the function of the policy is to provide a once-for-all safeguarding of a pause in the growth of net earnings such as is required by a successful devaluation: given this once-for-all effect and the associated reduction in inflationary expectation, succeeding stages of incomes policy hold the increases in money earnings close to the levels which we estimate would have taken place in the absence of a policy. Thus the second and subsequent years of control of incomes represent an insurance policy rather than a crucial component of our analysis.

We conclude, therefore, that while demand management is not by itself enough to provide the basis for the macroeconomic control of the economy, it should in conjunction with exchange rate and incomes policies continue to play the central role.

References

[1] Beckerman, W. (ed.), *The Labour Government's Economic Record*, Duckworth, London, 1972, p. 38.
[2] *National Institute Economic Review*, May and August 1970.
[3] *National Institute Economic Review*, February 1974.
[4] *A Listing of National Institute Model 3*, National Institute of Economic and Social Research, Discussion Paper No. 7, 1977.
[5] Ormerod, P. A., *The Structure and Properties of the National Institute Model*, National Institute of Economic and Social Research, Discussion Paper No. 4, 1977.
[6] Laury, J. S. E., Lewis, G. R. and Ormerod, P. A., 'Properties of macroeconomic models of the UK economy – a comparative study', *National Institute Economic Review*, National Institute of Economic and Social Research, February 1978.

PART II

Assessment of the Model Builders

5 The Main Issues

by M. V. Posner

This paper attempts to summarise the main issues of the three historical episodes before the conference. It is intended to assist the discussion and to help readers to approach the record of the discussion in Part III with a notion of the state of play as it seemed to one representative participant before the argument started.

Episode 1

The stereotype point of view with which I think most of us begin consideration of the period from 1964 onwards and which was implanted in my mind most by Wilfred Beckerman's account [1] runs as follows. The Labour government came to precarious power in 1964 with the objective of achieving a steady increase in output of around 4 per cent a year or more, together with an incomes policy to control inflation and a healthy balance of payments. This programme could conceivably have been achieved if the exchange rate had been lowered early enough and sharply enough to ensure that the increment of demand came largely from net exports. In those circumstances too the ill-fated National Plan, itself built on the assumption of an increased export success, might even have had a chance to achieve its implied objective of increasing the warranted rate of growth through its influence on business expectation [2].

Well before reading the papers for this conference I would have been inclined to modify this stereotype for three reasons. First, the international trade *demand* elasticities, both for exports and for imports, are probably a bit lower than most of us believed five or six years ago. Secondly, the lags in the response of *supply* are rather long, longer than even seemed likely when the Beckerman volume was being composed. Thirdly, the ability of the British economy to squeeze net exports out of the industrial sector in times of high employment and a high degree of capacity working, now seems highly questionable. Some observers might be inclined to add a fourth cause for caution about the benign effect of exchange rate changes, namely the importance of non-price factors in international trade [3]. I myself have always supported the view that non-price factors are important [4]. But the fact remains that, even taking account of the long time-lags over which exchange rate variations may have to work, changes in non-price competitiveness are extremely hard for governments to achieve. They take far longer to come into effect than do the results of fiscal or monetary policy or of the exchange rate itself. So it seems to me that those of us who argue now, and even those of us who argued in 1964, that non-price factors were important, still have to acknowledge the strength of the stereotype case.

How do the papers in Part I fit in with the stereotype? The National Institute and the Cambridge Group essentially agree, at least as far as the exchange rate strategy is concerned. Laidler is not far out. The London Business School looks backwards bravely, imposing their present outlook on the relationship between fiscal and monetary policy on to the experience of 1964. Many of us with long memories will discern an ironic resonance between that view and central bank gossip of the early 1960s. Exchange rate devaluation was much feared by those of a conservative frame of mind, on the grounds that it would encourage a slipshod and casual approach to the problem of containing inflation at home. Once the authorities came to believe that a too rapid rate of increase of prices and wages at home could be accommodated by allowing exchange rate depreciation, so their view (embodied no doubt in fiscal and monetary policies appropriate to their frame of mind) would be signalled to price setters and wage bargainers, with a consequent effect on price and wage levels. The money illusion necessary to prevent a continuing acceleration of inflation might survive one move in the exchange rate, but would not survive two or three, and *a fortiori* would not survive a downward float. It was I think this notion of the fragility of the structure of counter-inflationary policy, perhaps not as well articulated at the time as this summary in modern language would suggest, that lay behind official resistance to exchange rate changes in the early 1960s. And this sentiment was reinforced by some doubt as to how strong or weak our underlying position was on the balance of payments (see page 227) and a belief in non-price factors, all combining to produce a potent brew. The London Business School would insist of course that, once the authorities had chosen not to move the exchange rate, certain strict fiscal and monetary consequences should have followed, which the authorities were reluctant to adopt.

Indeed the main focus of the discussion of this period would seem to me to centre on fiscal and incomes policies. The actual record of the period seems with hindsight to have been too active and too mutable by almost any standard. But here is a period in which very little in the way of external perturbation was offered to the system, and in which therefore those economists with a penchant for steady medium-term settings of their policy instruments may ring up some success, at least on simulation paper, for their points of view.

Stability aside, the question of the pressure of demand, of the terms of trade, the path of real wages and the path of money wages, these are the interrelationships which should most be illuminated by a study of this first historical episode. The Cambridge Group, which always stresses particularly the concept of real wage resistance, will doubtless wish to explain how it comes about that their simulated devaluation of 1964 is accommodated with very little more eventual price inflation by the end of episode 1 than took place in reality, and indeed with less 'stored up' inflation for the future. (The key here, I suspect, is the greater increase in real output that the Cambridge Group simulations suggest for 1964–70). The National Institute will wish to defend their choice of a pressure of demand at which to run the economy, and to face the question of whether the increased strain on the real wage imposed by the exchange rate depreciation would not have made incomes policy even harder to pursue during the period 1964–8.

The most paradoxical result, to those brought up to accept the stereotype criticism of the 1964–70 episode which I outlined above, comes from the London Business School; their results are certainly not miraculous, but they are, as they point out, better from almost any point of view than the path actually followed by history, whatever the specified objective function.

One important property of the policies actually followed by the authorities in episode 1 is the disequilibrium stance in which they left the economy in 1970. The several first-round authors take differing lines, as we see in the next episode, as to how this disequilibrium should have been resolved, but it certainly did not correspond to the stated aim of the authorities, nor to the general establishment interpretation of events in 1969–70. The National Institute was forecasting at that time the need for some fiscal relaxation, but Mr Jenkins' last budget was clearly based on the premise that the economy would continue to expand satisfactorily without any fiscal or monetary manipulation. It seems to me important to ask how it was that the authorities were wrong at that stage and what mode of analysis might be available to prevent such errors in the future.

Episode 2

Three factors characterised the economic experience of Mr Heath's government. The fixing of a parity for sterling at the Smithsonian Conference which to many observers seemed too high, was followed by the decision to float in 1972 and the deliberate doctrine that the exchange rate would become what Laidler calls the 'loose variable' in the system of prices. Secondly the persistence for nearly two years with the rather severe budgetary stance inherited from Mr Jenkins gave way in the spring of 1972 to fiscal concessions, soon to be accompanied by a city boom which by any standards was excessive. And thirdly, the about-turn on incomes policy, starting from an almost 'hands off' posture, through the vicissitudes of the n−1 doctrine to the fully fledged legal elaboration of the Pay Board, the Price Commission, and the threshold agreements. The timing of the various changes of policy and their combination would have been remarkable enough, even if there were no substantial external events to shock the system. But in fact, all these internal events were dwarfed by the simultaneous boom of the OECD countries, the sharp rise in world raw material prices, and the eventual OPEC crisis of the autumn of 1973.

The choice of a policy *ex post* to steer through this extraordinary combination of self-inflicted errors and externally imposed misfortunes is itself an extremely complex task, as the first-round papers demonstrate. To have chosen a set of policies in 1970 that would have been robust, not only to our changing discernment of the nature of the problems facing us, but also to the accumulation of shocks from abroad would have been virtually impossible. The warning I therefore gave in the introduction about the impropriety of confusing hindsight with foresight applies above all to this episode. With the exception of the mistaken parity for sterling agreed at the Smithsonian Conference (and this itself was more *force majeure* than an error of British official thinking), I supported, largely from the side lines, most of the major policy measures of this period. Even in the summer of 1973 I argued that whilst it was undoubtedly correct to desire the pace of economic expansion to slow down markedly, it was still moot whether this would come about by itself, or would need deliberate government action to bring it about. (I offer this autobiographical comment partly as a warning against hubris by my colleagues, partly because I believe that some of the criticism of the Heath regime has been excessive.)

I shall start with a question about fiscal policy, which is partly answered in Artis' paper. In a system where fiscal drag is substantial, and at the beginning of history the fiscal stance is appropriate, assume an economy in which the Cambridge Group regularities do *not* hold within a three year period, and consider in this closed economy the optimal structure of fiscal policy. One attractive device is to allow the authorities freedom in the timing of their tax indexation measures, so that they can either delay or accelerate the offsetting of fiscal drag by a year or two. Successful countercyclical operations, and apparently large concessions or budget deficits can be safely allowed because they will by their nature be reversible. On this argument, the 1972 budget contained measures which combined in one year the indexation corrections appropriate to 1971, 1972 and 1973. If the Chancellor had then announced 'no budget' in 1973, and events had allowed themselves to work out, the fiscal stance would have come more nearly right in 1974: it was just a matter of waiting for things to work out.

Now I acknowledge that this model is deficient for many reasons, not least because it underestimates the runaway of public expenditure in the period 1973–4. As I understand it, however, these public expenditure excesses were more a sign of a lapse in control than the result of consciously taken aggregate decisions by the chief Economic Ministers (the loss of control was in my judgement at least as much a matter of ministerial failure as of bureaucratic failure, but that is largely beside the present point).

To go to the other extreme of policy, as I understand it all observers would now agree that, as it turned out, the timing of the switch in methods of monetary control (the introduction of Competition and Credit Control) and the actual numbers chosen for the various ratios and rules, were most unfortunate. The monetary strains of the large fiscal deficits might have been harmless on their own; and the monetary consequences of an effective relaxation in the ability of banks to create M3 might have been absorbed without difficulty. The combination of the two events was too much for the economy to endure, however, and there was some overspill, through some mechanism, from excess money balances to excess demand for physical assets.

Between these two extremes of substantial agreement (on the monetary policy mechanism) and in my view substantial disagreement (on fiscal policy tactics) lie the cases of exchange rate policy and incomes policy. On incomes policy, I think there is little doubt in anyone's mind that it would have been better to abort the threshold agreements at almost any cost. In the autumn of 1973 they were seen to lead unavoidably to the escalator effect, forcing up wage levels and prices by at least 10 per cent. Of course, it could still be argued that it was better to have the formal escalator rather than a series of increasingly contentious wage negotiations at three or four monthly intervals: and I admit that at the time some of us did console ourselves with this justification for the threshold. I suggest that this fear was exaggerated, however, given the experience of other countries and of the degree of realism shown by trade union leaders in the last two or three years. Even with hindsight it is not clear that we can make such adverse judgements about the rest of Mr Heath's incomes policy arrangements. They seem in retrospect imaginative, institutionally sensible, designed to incorporate flexibility in the face of both market pressures and social attitudes – just the sort of combination of measures which appear implicit in the notion of the social contract launched under the successor Labour government in the summer of 1975. (I certainly cannot bring myself to condemn the Heath incomes policy, lock, stock and barrel, although of course we all know it did not work too well!)

Even more puzzling is the attitude now to be adopted on exchange rate policy. The stereotype which characterises a lot of vulgar economics thinking in the mid-1970s (I admit I believed in this stereotype myself) would describe the exchange rate episode since 1970 in the following way. In 1970 the full employment balance of payments was still substantially in deficit, although low levels of activity and growth disguised this fact except to the most percipient. The world was doing quite nicely at this time, so that it would have been consistent with international good neighbourliness as well as our internal needs had the British authorities forced sterling down in the summer of 1970, probably through a managed float accompanied by a judicious appearance of fiscal laxity so as to scare away the bulls of sterling. If this had been done, the incipient export demand would have discouraged the excessive fiscal expansion of 1972, and would have provided that sort of incentive to industrial investment which Mr Heath was striving to seek through other means. The nominal effective exchange rate reached along this route may not have been very much lower by mid-1973 than the historical level, but it would have been reduced earlier and export demand would have replaced demand generated by fiscal action. We would then have approached the inflationary recession to 1973–4 with greater strength, and conceivably have ridden out the shocks since then more robustly.

I think the National Institute paper would give some support to this hypothesis, and the Cambridge Group are not unsympathetic but believe that the elasticities and the trends of Britain's world performance were too unfavourable to make this counter-factual story at all plausible. This of course drives me to ask what is there about the world which in the view of the Cambridge Group makes the exchange rate an appropriate weapon for episode 1 but inappropriate for episode 2.

Laidler and the London Business School take a clearly different view. Laidler actually argues, as I understand him, that we could have damped out the internal inflationary effect of the rise in world prices by allowing the exchange rate to appreciate, which I think implies that money wages per man week in home currency would have risen by less than half the OECD average. I know that the National Institute team and I are open to severe criticism for the excessive belief that we express in the possibility of an incomes policy, but the mind boggles at the labour market mechanism which would have brought about this sort of result in Laidler's world.

There is just one other strand in the complex and exciting history of this period to which I would draw attention. How would the British economy have fared if the world commodity boom had been only, say, half as marked, and if the oil price rise of autumn of 1973 had taken the price of oil to no higher than the $6 per barrel that some of us were forecasting in 1972–3? Could we have ridden out this very modest international storm, and would our internal policies have been sufficiently coherent? I believe the papers in Part I enable answers to be given on this point, although I doubt whether they can be unanimous.

Episode 3

Suppose that the flow from the North Sea (both hydrocarbons and money) were to start in 1978 and remain steady thereafter until the end of time. Then the target balance of payments rationally sought would not be different from that which we were contemplating before North Sea oil was dreamt of – save for the fact that we would therefore be a little richer than we had expected, and therefore would wish to rearrange somewhat our portfolio of assets. The question of whether it is better for Britain to continue to borrow from overseas rather to lend is conventionally answered by a comparison of rates of return at the margin at home and overseas. But for practical purposes I think one could take it that some repayment of the foreign currency denominated debt of the public sector would be desirable, and most analysts would also agree that some rebuilding of our free reserves would be sensible: and I have elsewhere estimated that a current account surplus of £2 billion a year for the next decade would meet both these needs.

The fact that the North Sea will begin to tail off probably rather rapidly suggests to some of us at least that a more cautious attitude should be adopted when the North Sea benefit is added to the balance of payments. As a rule of thumb I suggest that this might mean running a surplus of nearer £3 billion in the earlier 1980s, although it could be argued that a slightly more generous approach could be allowed in the next year or two.

Against this sort of background it is hard to see what freedom of manoeuvre on conventional demand management is now open to the authorities. The balance of payments surplus forecast on current policies is no larger than the minimum figures that I have floated above, and the degree of slack in the economy cannot therefore be taken up unless world trade expands faster than forecast, or the real exchange rate sags further than forecast, or British productivity rises very much more sharply than in the past (in which case our competitiveness increases at a constant real wage) or very much slower than in the past (in which case unemployment could fall even though output was growing at no more than two or three per cent per year).

On inflation, there seems every prospect of the rate of price increase dipping well below 10 per cent in the first six months of 1978, but then beginning to accelerate again despite the monetary guidelines, however strictly observed. This of course implies, from a monetarist stand point, that unemployment will increase, but how long it will take to persuade wage bargainers of this proposition is unknown, and sensible trade unionists may well expect that at some future date a once-for-all monetary readjustment will allow the established price level to be accommodated at a higher level of employment.

This conventional stereotype of our present difficulties has to be read in the same way as the counterpart stereotypes that I offered for the first two historical episodes. It leads to the conclusion that the old fashioned short cuts to prosperity are no longer available. We cannot use money illusion to reduce the real wage through exchange rate devaluation, because the wage earners will tumble to the trick, and wages and home costs generally will be pushed sharply upwards. We cannot use a slow growth in the money supply to adjust our rate of inflation, because the rate of increase of money wages is obstinately hooked on high numbers because of anomaly corrections, wage-leapfrogging and comparability wage fixing [4]. The *deus ex machina* of incomes policy on which the National Institute team and I would wish to rely is to say the least as hard to create as it has been over the last twenty years.

In face of this gloomy scenario the authors in Part I are mildly optimistic, although none of them produce really joyful projections of the future. The mild optimism is partly due, in the case of the Cambridge Group, to the extension into the future of their new policy instrument of import controls – another way of avoiding the nastier aspects of the stereotype I sketched above. However it is illuminating to examine the options that are available while continuing to accept the spirit of the conventional approach.

The first set of questions refers to the taking up of slack under present circumstances. How much slack is there? Would an increased public sector borrowing requirement really crowd out private sector spending? Is there a substantial mis-match between available resources and potential demand? And would the Phillips curve start to operate at levels of unemployment, as conventionally measured, above the one million mark?

These issues, it seems to me, are susceptible of analysis using the analytical details and the empirical information available to all the authors without regard to the school or model which they adhere to. It really should be possible for economists to provide the bones of a collective answer to this type of question without prevarication.

A second set of questions arises from the treatment of monetary policy. It should be possible to avoid the sort of trap presented by the following typical dialogue: 'If you believe in monetary targets it is impossible to allow expansionary fiscal policy today.' 'But to take that point of view is to suggest that the total of effective demand must be constrained, and more demand from the government requires that there be less from the private sector.' The issue here concerns the degree of rigidity with which we have to adhere to one particular set of monetary guidelines – those that happen to have been chosen in April 1977. As I understand recent utterances from the London Business School and from David Laidler, wise monetarists are more sensible than that, and there is no reason why monetary guidelines should not be revised upwards if the other elements in the policy simulation are satisfactory: an increase in the rate of growth of money supply need not imply an acceleration in inflation if there are reasons to suppose that the real output of the economy may itself be increasing.

But it is the third set of questions, about the exchange rate and the balance of payments, that once again are the most intractable. The notion that there is no way for Ruritania to increase employment by increasing net exports is surely quite unacceptable. Those who most strongly take the view that a depreciation in the real exchange rate will not help us, would say of Ruritania that her share of world trade could increase only if the skill and diligence of the Ruritanian workforce were to increase. But it is a strange doctrine to suggest that full employment can be achieved if we work harder for a given basket of goods, but cannot be achieved if we merely undertake to accept a smaller basket of goods for a given expenditure of effort.

References

[1] Beckerman, W. (ed.), *The Labour Government's Economic Record 1964–1970*, Duckworth, London, 1972.
[2] Posner, M. V., 'Industrial policies', in Cairncross, Sir Alec (ed.), *Britain's Economic Prospects Reconsidered*, Allen & Unwin, London, 1970.
[3] Stout, D., *International Price Competitiveness. Non-Price Factors and Export Performance*, National Economic Development Office, London, 1977.
[4] Posner, M. V., 'Wages, prices and the exchange rate', in Artis, M. J. (ed.), *Proceedings of the 1977 AUTE Conference*, forthcoming.

6 A Statistician's View

by A. J. Boreham

Introduction

Part of my role is to comment on the difference between the policy problem as it seems to those operating within the machine at the time, and as it seems now, with the benefit of hindsight. Being a statistician I am a little obsessed with the need to distinguish between the past and present (sometimes embodied in facts) and the future (sometimes embodied in forecasts). Of course in practice past, present and future get muddled up, but if the conceptual difference gets lost some people, especially economists, start to confuse what ought to be (the forecasts) with what is (the facts) and then we are in trouble.

Before I received the first-round contributions, I wrote a number of assessments of the 'current' economic situations on the lines of those prepared regularly in the Central Statistical Office. During the last five years the emphasis in those current assessments has shifted from a report on the quality of the statistics towards an assessment of the latest situation. In fact, however, it is often difficult to know whether a point being made in the report is a quality point or an assessment point.

From the beginning the current assessment has striven to be exactly that – *current*. We have tried to estimate 'now', what it will turn out that the trend 'now' was, when we have, not only the figures for 'now' but also for the following twelve months or so. It is obvious that current assessment, so defined, includes an element of forecasting. It is, after all, not possible to estimate what the trend 'now' will turn out to be without having at least an implicit view of what the next few actual figures will be. I have always insisted that the view should remain implicit.

It was not possible for me truly to do that exercise in respect of two of the three episodes that we are dealing with at this conference because I know too much. However, I did my best to set aside everything I have learnt since October 1964 and since October 1970 and to write economic assessments as if they were being done at the time. Another imperfection is that I was obliged to do the work without the aid of a computer, so that my assessments of the trends at the various 'nows' have been even more subjective than what we do for the Central Statistical Office reports.

I then did the exercises again but making use of the information available to the four first-round authors. I chose October, which is in accord with the spirit, if not the letter, of the rules of the game so as to have the benefit of the full run of quarterly national accounts data consistent with the *Blue Book*.

Finally I looked up the answers, to see how the trends at the two Octobers look now with the aid of the figures for succeeding months and years. That makes four economic assessments. The points which I think are valuable for this conference all emerge from comparing the 'at the time' assessment with the assessment made from hindsight.

There was a problem of method – and even of morals – over the 'with hindsight' assessment. It is possible to take two degrees of hindsight. The first is merely to know what the finally revised figures up to August of the year in question are now, but not to know how September onwards turned out. The second, and much more beneficial, is to know what the underlying trend at October turned out to be (that would call for the finally revised figures for all the months up to about the October twelve months later). I carried out the 'with hindsight' exercises in two stages, using the figures for the months up to September, and using the figures for all the months that are available now.

Episode 1: 1964

Reconstruction of lost times is what we have to do. On 26 October 1964 the new government published a White Paper on the Economic Situation which forecast a balance of payments deficit of £700 million at least for 1964 and said that there was no undue pressure on resources calling for action. In October there was no quarterly index of GDP (Output). There was no seasonally adjusted monthly index of average earnings. Seasonally adjusted unemployment was not officially published as such, although normal seasonal changes were. The argument was that people who were only skilled enough to read figures from tables could not be trusted to make sensible use of seasonally adjusted figures whereas people who were skilled enough to add together figures taken from different tables could. The same was true for vacancies. Monthly figures of imports, f.o.b. and on a balance of payments basis, were not available. No figures of money supply were published. Nor, needless to say, was the exchange rate.

October 1964 Economic Assessment at the Time

Activity and Unemployment

The pace of economic expansion appears to have been slow since the beginning of 1964, in contrast with the rapid expansion in 1963; indeed *industrial production* has been flat all this year. The underlying trend of the *volume of exports* is now flat after the rapid rise in 1963 but the *volume of imports* is still rising, though less rapidly than at the turn of the year. It is this deterioration in net exports, with the end of increase in *consumers' expenditure*, which has slowed, or even stopped, the growth of output. Only *fixed investment* is still increasing.

Some of the rise in *unemployment* in July and August may have owed something to the influx of school-leavers and the renewed fall in September tends to confirm that judgement. Nevertheless it is now likely that most of the sharp drop in unemployment since early 1963 is over and that the underlying trend is at best flat and may be rising a very little.

October 1964 Economic Assessment with Hindsight

Activity and Unemployment

GDP, which grew by over 5 per cent during 1963, has progressively slowed down this year and, if as we believe, stockbuilding has passed its peak, it is now increasing at an annual rate of no more than 2 per cent.

Domestic consumption, private and public, as well as *fixed investment* are rising moderately.

The *volume of exports* is not changing but the *volume of imports* is still growing moderately.

It is now likely that most of the sharp drop in *unemployment* since early 1963 is now over and that the underlying trend is a very slow fall or even flat.

Inflation and Costs

Wages seem to be rising at about ½ per cent a month. Although seasonal food prices are now moving favourably and the sharp rise in the index of *retail prices* that took place in the Spring (½ per cent a month, on average, between January–February and June–July) is unlikely to reappear, increases of 0.2 or 0.3 per cent a month are still possible.

Balance of Payments

The trends in export and import volumes have produced a sharp deterioration in the *current balance*.

Inflation and Costs

Average earnings are rising at a little over 1 per cent a quarter which is not out of line with the settlements at something under 5 per cent which are taking place. *Wholesale prices of materials and fuel* bought by manufacturing industry, after the rather sharp rise at the end of 1963, seem to have stabilised for the time being. Although seasonal food prices are now moving favourably and the sharp rise in the index of *retail prices* that took place in the Spring (½ per cent a month, on average, between January–September and June–July) is unlikely to reappear, increases of 0.2 or 0.3 per cent a month are still possible.

Balance of Payments

The trends in export and import volumes have produced a sharp deterioration in the *current balance* from a small surplus at the end of 1963 to a deficit now of about £40 million a month.

Differences between 1964 at the Time and with Hindsight

One difference between 'at the time' and 'with hindsight' on the monthly indicators is that with hindsight it is possible to say something about earnings. Since it is as usual consistent with what one would (and did) say about wages and settlements no change is made to the assessment. The assessment of unemployment changed because with hindsight the seasonal adjustment has smoothed out the fluctuation caused by school-leavers. The problem is still with us in 1977 however.

Chart 6.1 1964 At the time and with hindsight[a]

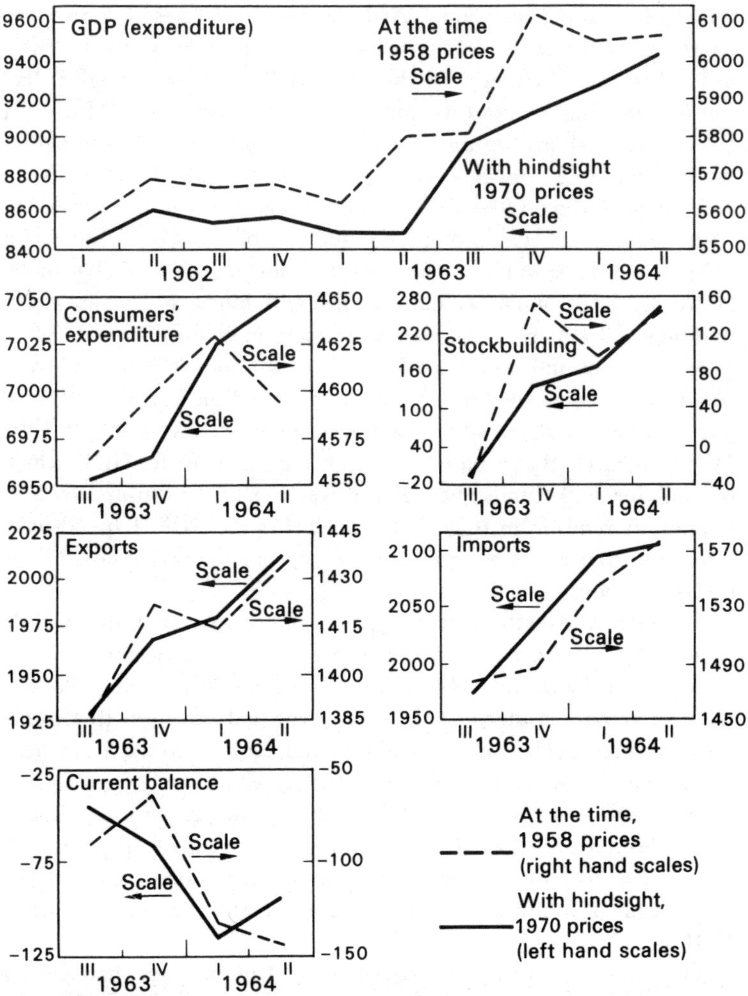

Source: Central Statistical Office, *Economic Trends* (various issues).

[a]£ million, seasonally adjusted.

Things are a bit different on the quarterly national accounts. A quick look at Chart 6.1 will help, but as the scales have *not* been carefully picked to produce equal gradients for equal rates of change the charts can only be used to spot differences in kinks, not differences in level or rate of change. At the time GDP looked as though it had stopped growing at about the turn of the year. From 1963 III to 1964 I there was a sharp 'up and down' owing a great deal to the figures for stockbuilding and exports of goods and services. Even if the up and down is discounted because of the perennial timing problems with figures of stockbuilding, the flatness of the GDP figures for 1964 I and II seemed at the time to confirm the end of growth. However, the up and down has vanished with hindsight because stockbuilding and exports of goods and services have been smoothed out to some extent and a small, offsetting, 'down and up' (in relation to trend) has been inserted into consumers' expenditure. As a result there seems to be a fairly steady growth of some 9 per cent between 1962 IV and 1964 II (that is based on the average estimate for GDP, which is available with hindsight). There was a kink (down-up-down in relation to trend) from 1962 IV to 1963 III in the GDP (Expenditure) series, but that is not of significance except for the way it could have misled in 1963.

The rate of growth of about 1¼ per cent a quarter from 1962 IV to 1964 IV, together with a much less marked deterioration in real resources for the balance of payments, bring about the changed assessment of activity. Indeed, if the assessment had not been that stockbuilding had reached its peak about mid-1964, it would have been reasonable to assess that GDP was still growing briskly in 1964 III. In the event, as we all know, GDP went on growing into 1965, though not so fast as in 1963. (The fourth quarter to fourth quarter rates were 6 per cent from 1962 to 1963, 4 per cent from 1963 to 1964, 2½ per cent from 1964 to 1965, all based on the average estimate of GDP.)

The National Institute's forecast in its August *Review* had been a growth of 3.7 per cent in GDP between the second halves of 1964 and 1965. The outturn based on the average estimate of GDP given in the *Annual Supplement to Economic Trends* in 1976, was a rise of 2.6 per cent. The Institute's forecast of the current balance of payments was that the deficit would be about £50 million a quarter in 1965. The outturn was a deficit of £26 million for the year as a whole.

Episode 2: 1970

In 1970, there was no seasonally adjusted figure of M3. Otherwise, apart from the exchange rate, which still did not arise, the full set of indicators now used in the Central Statistical Office's monthly economic report was published.

October 1970 Economic Assessment at the Time

Activity and Unemployment

The very moderate growth in *GDP* during 1969 has petered out. The main source of that growth had been a rise of 10 to 15 per cent in the *volume of exports* during 1969. This year the trend has been obscured, first by anticipation of, then by the fact and now by the after-effects of the dock strike. As far as can be seen at present, however, there has been no increase in the underlying trend since about the end of 1969. Not only the dock strike but also the arrival of the Jumbo jets had obscured the trend of the *volume of imports* and our judgement that the underlying trend is about flat or perhaps rising very slowly must be very tentative. If these judgements are right, the change in the volume of resources going to the balance of payments, which had added nearly 2 per cent to GDP during 1969, has by now taken 1 per cent off it.

Consumers' expenditure, which contributed a little to the slow growth in 1969, is still growing slowly, perhaps at a rate of ½ per cent a quarter. The other components of domestic demand are flat.

October 1970 Economic Assessment with Hindsight

Activity and Unemployment

The very moderate growth in *GDP* during 1969 has petered out. The main source of that growth had been a rise of just over 10 per cent in the *volume of exports*. This year the trend has been obscured, first by anticipation of, then by the fact of and now by the after-effects of the dock strike. As far as can be seen at present, however, there has been no increase in the underlying trend since about the end of 1969. Not only the dock strike but also the arrival of the Jumbo jets have obscured the trend of the *volume of imports* and our judgement that the underlying trend is still about flat or perhaps rising very slowly must be very tentative. If these judgements are right, the change in the volume of resources going to the balance of payments, which had added nearly 2 per cent to GDP during 1969, has by now taken 1½ per cent off it.

Consumers' expenditure, which contributed a little to the slow growth in 1969, is still growing slowly, perhaps at a rate of ½ to 1 per cent a quarter. The other components of domestic demand are flat.

The underlying trend of *unemployment* has been overlaid by large movements in the numbers of school-leavers but our view is that the trend is still upwards. That is based on the unemployment figures themselves; it is also consistent with our view of the petering out of the trend of output.

The underlying trend of *unemployment* is still upwards. That is based on the unemployment figures themselves; it is also consistent with our view of the petering out of the trend of output.

Inflation and Costs

Wages accelerated earlier this year – the new Forces' pay arrangements were a large factor. The index of *average earnings* rose by over 6 per cent between December 1969 and June this year and the rise continues at about 1 per cent a month.

On the other hand *import prices* are rising much more slowly than last year and may have stopped increasing, for the time being at least.

Wholesale prices of *materials and fuel* purchased by manufacturing industry have been falling since March. In August – the latest month for which an actual index is available – *retail prices* were nearly 7 per cent higher than a year earlier. However most of that rise had occurred by April; since then, and particularly now that seasonal food prices are moving favourably, the rate of increase is much smaller.

Inflation and Costs

Wages accelerated earlier this year – the new Forces' pay arrangements were a large factor. The index of *average earnings* rose by over 6 per cent between December 1969 and June this year and the rise continues at about 1 per cent a month.

On the other hand *import prices* are rising much more slowly than last year and may have stopped increasing, for the time being at least.

In August – the latest month for which an actual index is available – *retail prices* were nearly 7 per cent higher than a year earlier. However most of that rise had occurred by April; since then, and particularly now that seasonal food prices are moving favourably the rate of increase is much smaller.

Balance of Payments

The flat trends in the volume of imports and exports during 1970 have not been modified by any marked change in the terms of trade and the *current balance*, which was a surplus of around £60 million a month at the turn of the year, is about the same now – that is to say in October, when we assume that the effects of the dock strike have largely worked through.

Balance of Payments

The flat trends in the volume of imports and exports during 1970 have not been modified by any marked change in the terms of trade and the *current balance*, which was a surplus of around £70 million a month at the turn of the year, is about the same now – that is to say by October, when we assume that the effects of the dock strike have largely worked through.

Differences between 1970 at the Time and with Hindsight

There are few problems. Once again the effect of school-leavers on the unemployment series was smoothed out by the later seasonal adjustments. Even the quarterly national accounts show a remarkably similar picture. The one big difference concerns the four quarters from 1968 III to 1969 IV. At the time there was a marked up-and-down in GDP during that period. The wobble appeared in GDP (Output) as well as in GDP (Expenditure).

But that has all been revised out of existence by the time we have the 1976 *Annual Supplement to Economic Trends*. It hardly affects the assessment of the situation at October 1970 except that it is a little easier to see what happened in 1969 and 1970 starting from a fairly smooth 1968–9 instead of from a fluctuating period. The real difficulty with October 1970 was to know what the trends of exports and imports were. Both at the time and with hindsight (but not knowing any figures after September) I assessed that the volume of exports had stopped growing while imports might still be growing but only very slowly. Even with the aid of all the figures after 1970 II it is not too easy to detect a trend and to pinpoint turning points but a chart of the quarterly figures does suggest that, ex-dock strike, the volume of exports was not changing from late 1969 to early 1971. Similarly with the volume of imports, looking at Chart 6.2 right through to 1971 suggests that the trend, ex-dock strike, did turn upwards around the turn of 1969–70 and carried on up until about mid-1971. These results confirm the judgements I made 'at the time' and 'with hindsight'.

Chart 6.2 1970 at the time and with hindsight[a]

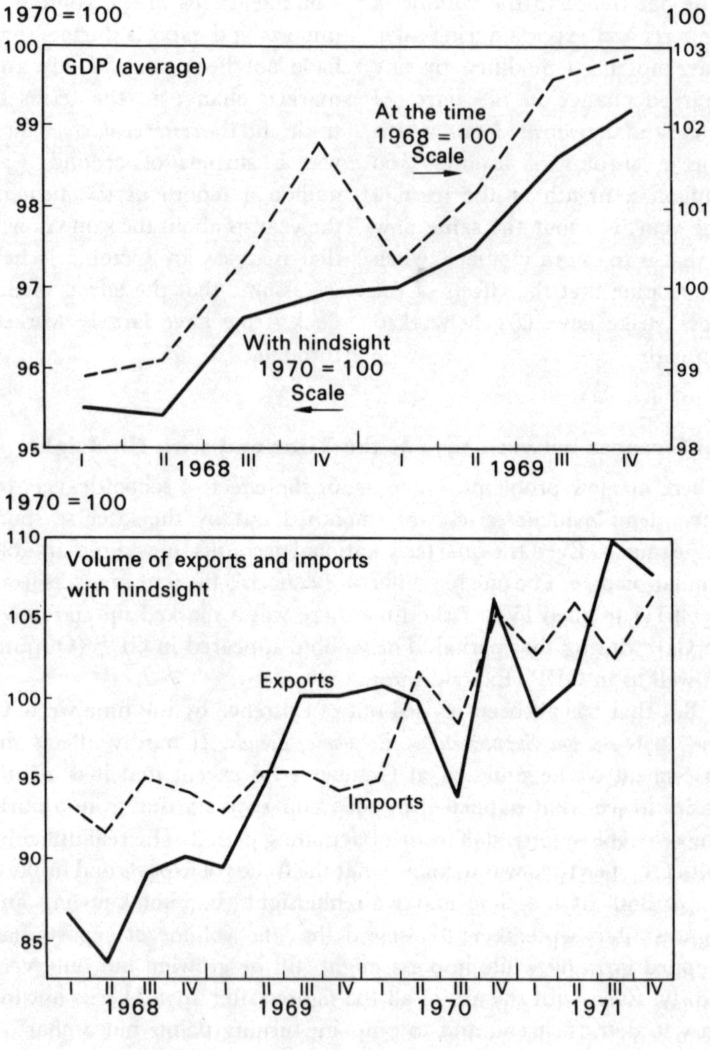

Source: Central Statistical Office, *Economic Trends* (various issues).

[a] seasonally adjusted.

Clearly all these assessments of the current economic situations are subjective and, if someone else did the work, a different picture might emerge. My experience over the past five years, however, has been that the differences are usually quite slight. That does not mean that they are not passionately argued and that the problems with seasonally adjusting unemployment in the school-leaving months are not real, persistent and painful. Nevertheless it seems to me fairly well established that, with occasional exceptions, the picture of the current economic situation which was painted with the aid of the figures available at the time is not changed at all seriously under the influence first of revisions and second of figures for subsequent periods.

There are however differences between the analyses and recommendations of the authors in Part I, and they require explanation. I do not think it is at all difficult to explain them without blaming the statisticians. In the first place the analysis and recommendations lie, latent but inexorable, in the structure of each model. Secondly it is almost impossible to deal adequately with the problem of practical possibilities. At one extreme it is possible to argue that anything not done was politically impossible. The argument does not depend on assuming that governments are perfect but merely on assuming that the governed are irresistible. At the other extreme it is possible to argue that everything is politically possible, given the will. The National Institute's assumption of a successful incomes policy comes near that.

It is not only figures that have changed; standards have done so too. Three examples of these are as follows. The National Institute clearly implies that 400,000 unemployed at the end of 1966 would have been considered low (page 108); whereas at that time it was considered very high. Later on (page 112) it is implied, but not all that clearly, that a rate of increase of prices of 5 per cent a year was quite acceptable in 1970; but at that time it was regarded as unacceptably high and had only been exceeded during exceptional periods such as the Korean War. Again the Institute state that £1¾ billion is not an enormous increase in the public sector borrowing requirement; it does not look like it now but I think it would have done in 1974. These examples of how standards of acceptability have changed illustrate how political compulsions and possibilities also change.

Three rather more detailed points are as follows. Firstly, I think carrying out the London Business School recommendations would depend on knowing, at the time, the rates of increase of world output and world prices. In the fact the information on those trends is 3–6 months behind what we have in Britain. Policies based on that knowledge would run the risk of being seriously out of phase.

Secondly, David Laidler's comment that the current state of affairs may be described as the trough, is really unacceptable. The Central Statistical Office's cyclical indicators all show quite clearly that the most recent trough was reached late in 1975. The recovery has been slow and hesitant and it is not yet at all clear either when the peak will be reached or how high it will be but that does not affect the assessment that it is now two years since the trough.

Last of all the London Business School complain about the seasonal adjustment of government non-dwelling investment: 'Each year the level of spending falls between the first and second quarters of the year, suggesting something wrong with the seasonal corrections'. The trouble is that there has been a change in the quarterly pattern of the local authority component of government fixed investment expenditure, especially since local authority reorganisation in April 1974, which is not yet fully explicable. The first quarters of 1971, 1972 and 1973 were quite high after seasonal adjustment but the first quarter of 1974, the final quarter under the old system of local government, was very high indeed. The 1974 phenomenon was taken to be due to the hastening of some expenditure in order to clear the accounts of the old authorities and so it would not have been appropriate to adjust it for seasonality. However, when the same thing happened in 1975 local authorities were asked for an explanation. Nothing specific emerged. The situation was further confused by changes of responsibility from local authorities to other sectors. The problem is now being looked at more thoroughly with the benefit of several years data showing an apparently new seasonal path. It is likely, whatever the outcome of the present investigation, that we shall soon be applying new seasonal factors to recent years' capital expenditure by local authorities, on the assumption that there has been a substantial break in the series.

7 Comparisons of the Four Econometric Models

by M. H. Peston

Introduction

The purpose of this paper is to interpret the four models in broad terms pointing out their key similarities and dissimilarities. This task, while fascinating, has been immensely difficult. The reasons are first the size and complexity of at least three of the models and second, and probably more important, the difficulty of interpreting the models from the outside, without experience of manipulating them and possibly without even the experience of estimating them. It is virtually impossible to maintain four different theoretical commitments in one's mind in order simultaneously to assess each individual model and to compare it with the others.

There is a sense in which the only useful critics of any econometric model are the creators of it themselves. I see my role, therefore, as chiefly that of asking questions in the hope of persuading the individual authors to take us further along the way with them and perhaps to reveal their own doubts and weaknesses. I hope this approach will also be helpful to the readers of the Conference report.

Size of the Models

The most obvious difference between the models is size. The Laidler model runs to only six or seven equations, the Cambridge one to more than 120, the National Institute to about 170, and the London Business School to more than 270 equations and endogenous variables. In part, therefore, in judging the models one may get into a subject of some methodological importance but which may be irrelevant to the direct policy problems that concern us, namely the importance of the difference in size. Does it remotely make sense to compare the Laidler model at one extreme with the London Business School at the other?

My own view is that one must exercise great care in order not to be unjust to either of the extremes. It is very easy to attack Laidler and monetarists in general by saying that they make life so much easier for themselves by avoiding the difficulties of estimating a large model. In many ways I would adopt this position. Nonetheless, it would be wrong to exaggerate the benefits of the size of any of the other three models especially that of the London Business School. For many purposes their extra equations are irrelevant and one should not be impressed simply by the thickness of the handbook. Paradoxically, there are a considerable number of questions which even the largest of these models are unable to answer; therefore, none of them can be regarded remotely as complete.

Let me now return to the Laidler model simply to utter a word of warning. He himself makes very explicit his commitment to a particular research strategy which he regards as most significantly different from that adopted by the other authors. He adds 'monetarists are much less ambitious in the degree of detail into which they go when explaining and forecasting macroeconomic phenomena'. We would all no doubt agree that the model one builds and estimates depends very much on the purpose in hand. No economists would expect to find a simple correlation between size and beauty. There is, however, a specific danger with a small model which must not be ignored – that so much is taken for granted. There is no harm in this if it is made explicit, but there is the pitfall of assuming that all things that are taken for granted are themselves well established and correspond to well defined and well estimated econometric relationships. In a sense a small model is embedded in a potentially large one. Certainly Laidler's is, and it is one in which a great many of the relationships which he assumes to exist have not yet been demonstrated empirically. What are the consequences of differences in the size of models? The answer lies partly in the degree of aggregation of the models and partly in the range of phenomena which they comprehend. I cite four examples.

Consumption

The London Business School distinguishes consumption of non-durable goods, drink and tobacco, oil, and durable goods. Moreover (a subject to which I will return) because these equations are in money terms, there are also relevant equations to be taken into account which enable the model to convert from expenditure in current prices to expenditure in constant prices. The Cambridge model's consumption function is much more highly aggregated essentially dealing only with consumer expenditure. It then has two conversion formulae from consumer expenditure at market prices into consumer expenditure at full cost and then into consumer expenditure at constant prices at full cost. The National Institute model is simpler still being a straightforward equation determining real consumer expenditure which, once a consumer price index has been determined, can convert into consumer expenditure at current prices. The Laidler model offers us even less. There is no explicit propensity to consume estimated, but built into his equation (1) must be some implied behavioural relationship relating consumption to his various other input variables.

Prices

The London Business School model has over thirty price equations. Many of these have to do with the disaggregation of the foreign trade sector of the model, but others do correspond to the disaggregation of consumption and to other expenditure functions. Here too equations which are estimated, and give all sorts of additional statistical material, are side by side with those which are not. The National Institute prices section is also large involving some seventeen relationships of which twelve are estimated. There are some half a dozen price equations in the Cambridge model and two in the Laidler model. However Laidler's equation (5) is to do with the expected inflation rate which itself is not directly observable. One must be very careful therefore in comparing his equations with those in the other models.

Exports

The London Business School model has eight equations, about twice as many as the Cambridge and National Institute models. The Laidler model has no explicit treatment of exports, but again it must be assumed that exports, and imports for that matter, are built in implicitly into his equations (1) and (3). In connection with exports it is also important to note that the Cambridge model has a separate and special treatment of the North Sea, whereas Laidler hardly mentions the oil problem at all until his fiscal policy section.

Employment

For once the London Business School does not present us with the most elaborate view. They have only one equation whereas Cambridge and the National Institute have three. The puzzling contribution is that of Laidler. He throws in, not an employment equation, but an unemployment equation as a sort of makeweight. He states that the equation was generated mechanically and the reason for doing it at all was simply to offer some estimates of the likely path of unemployment in the simulation exercises. What puzzles me is how a monetarist model which takes extremely strong views of the way the economy is likely to move towards the position of full employment is happy to do this without the very careful investigation of the available empirical material and an attempt to produce a sophisticated employment equation. I might also add that insofar as any of these models are intended to be used for policy purposes, and Ministers want forecasts of employment or unemployment, that in itself should be sufficient reason for including such equations.

I have referred to differences in the degree of aggregation. What this does is to restrict the range of phenomena to which the models can be applied. Obviously, if a model does not distinguish durable consumer goods from non-durables, it is unable to say much about the importance of the distinction between the two or to predict the two separately. Nonetheless in terms of fundamental theory and fundamental policy making the difference may not be important. Thus, I have not been able to see how the greater size of the London Business School model enables it to throw greater light on the general workings of the economy than the Cambridge and National Institute models. I hasten to add that I am not asserting that the London Business School model throws less light than these other two do, or that the extra detail is not worth knowing for its own sake.

Limitations of the Models

Although the models were set up with a particular class of question in mind, it is as well to remember that, once they are set up, they limit the kind of questions which they can be used to answer. This is obvious when one examines the difference in the degree of temporal aggregation of the models. The London Business School and National Institute models are quarterly whereas the Laidler and Cambridge models are annual. Obviously, he two latter are limited in the kind of dynamics they can take into account. It would be surprising, therefore, if an annual model did produce results which were all that helpful to policies of a fine tuning nature. Equally it might be expected that such models would themselves emphasise medium-term forecasts and long-run relationships.

As another example of the limitations that the models themselves impose let us look again at the employment equation. The dependent variables in the Cambridge model are total employment, public service employment, and employment in the business sector. No distinction is made between male and female employment, between employment of young people and older people, between employment in the export sector and in the rest of the economy, and between employment in the various regions. Thus, within this model we are unable to test any of the propositions that have been put forward in the last two or three years that the growth of unemployment in the economy has had special structural characteristics. This also means that we are unable to take direct account of policy measures intended to deal with those structural characteristics. In the case of the London Business School the position is even more limited. They have an equation for the change in the number of employees in employment which is related to the change in the number of wholly unemployed excluding school leavers. They also have an equation relating the rate of unemployment to what I take to be essentially a measure of the degree of utilisation. I have already remarked on the limitation of the Cambridge approach in this connection. But it is interesting that even a model as large as the National Institute's is only able to subdivide employment into public administration and defence, manufacturing, mainly public, and other private. Moreover, the unemployment equation (which is not an estimated one) simply relates the change in unemployment in aggregate to the lagged changes in employment in the aggregate.

There is yet one other sense in which the model limits the questions that one can ask or the policies that one can consider. This concerns not so much the numbers of the equations and their degree of fineness of detail, but the dependent variables which are to be found within them. Here too it is convenient at this stage to look at the employment equations.

In the National Institute model one of the independent variables is the ratio of the price of output of manufacturing to essentially an index of the cost of hiring labour. In other words, in broad terms the real cost of employing someone in manufacturing is taken into account. There are, therefore, built into the model classical elements of the sort that too high a rise in the real wage will lower employment and raise unemployment.

Theory behind the Models

The Cambridge model describes itself as Keynesian. It comprises the usual income expenditure set of inter-relationships with leakages into savings, taxes and imports. Both the consumption and the investment function are formulated in current prices rather than in constant prices or wage units and, I suppose, one could then argue whether that is truly Keynesian or not. Prices (a subject to which I shall return) seem to be largely cost determined. The wage equation seems to be built around something called 'the real value of the wage bargain' and involves some notion of the relationship between the desired real wage and the actual real wage. Here again I must point out that I cannot see anything specifically Keynesian about that. The treatment of the money supply takes explicit account of the government budget restraint, and of the overall accounting definitions pertaining to the whole economy. Thus, there is a linkage between the difference between public expenditure and taxation, the public sector borrowing requirement, DCE, the behaviour of the balance of payments on current account and the change in M3. A rate of interest variable and a measure of the degree of credit restriction appear in both the consumption and investment functions. I have considerable difficulty discerning where the latter variable comes from at all. As for the rate of interest the connection seems to be from world interest rates and the British inflation rate to the minimum lending rate which in turn determines, together with incomes and the sale of public sector debt, the yield on war loans. This is the input into the spending equation.

The National Institute model also retains the income expenditure framework. It seems to me to be much more Keynesian in that the income expenditure part is set in constant prices. The only monetary variable in the consumption function is what is called debt, that is hire purchase and personal bank advances. There are no monetary variables in the investment equations. Again, the model has within it the government budget restraint and the usual accounting identities, but it is very difficult to discern how the monetary side relates to the real side. The claim is made that 'the real and monetary sectors are linked through interest rates'. This actually appears to happen via the foreign trade sector and the price level. But I find the model and this explanation very confusing on this issue.

On wages, the National Institute's model postulates a Phillips curve with the percentage change in a wage rate the dependent variable and the unemployment rate and the percentage change in the consumer price index as independent variables. I am not clear that this is an estimated equation. It is noteworthy that within the equation the full effects of price changes are not passed on in higher wage rates, given the degree of unemployment.

The London Business School model has evolved from what they call a conventional Keynesian type to what is now sometimes referred to as international monetarist. Clearly, given its great proliferation of expenditure functions it still retains a very considerable Keynesian flavour. It has, however, developed in certain new ways, some of which it shares with the other models under consideration. It has a government budget restraint and all the usual connections between one sector's accounts and the others. In this sense the money supply has become endogenous. But where it differs most significantly from the other two large models is in its treatment of real wages. Essentially this seems to be made up in two parts – 'the important assumption with regard to real wages that eventually changes would be offset by changes in pre-tax wages', and 'the conclusion that, under a fixed exchange rate system the domestic rate of inflation will ultimately be determined by the rate of change in import prices'. This leads them to examine exchange rate changes in terms of the ability to achieve a permanent reduction in real incomes. However, I am not entirely happy with their account of this or the way in which it appears in the model. It is important to distinguish the real wage net of tax and all payments by employees from the real wage gross of tax and all payments by employers in analysing how this kind of theory works. This relates to a class of problems which I have difficulty in following within any of the models under consideration.

When exchange rates vary, both importers and exporters have pricing decisions to take. They may allow competitiveness to vary fully by the change in the exchange rate or they may modify it, which in turn may have an effect on profit margins. In practice, a rise in the sterling price of foreign currency may cause importers partly to quote lower delivery prices abroad and partly to trade up somewhat. I have a feeling that this distinction cannot be made within the London Business School model although it might be extremely important in the short to medium run. The model itself is also non-Keynesian, although as is now well known not against the spirit of Keynes, in the attention it places on real balance effects, cash balance effects and wealth effects.

This enables me to raise for the first time the whole question of re-estimating models. The London Business School authors are extremely honest in pointing out the difference between their earlier work and their presentation for this conference. Real balance effects and wealth effects used not to appear as inputs in their spending functions, but they do now. The reason given is that their significance depends critically on the rate of inflation itself. The question one asks, therefore, is whether their appearance is purely transitory, and if we do in due course return to low single digit inflation figures, we shall be able to ignore these effects from then on. The London Business School authors argue that there are good theoretical grounds for postulating these effects but in what sense are they to be regarded as important if they cannot be extracted from the data? I do not wish to go into the question of behaviour being determined by theories of behaviour, but I do think that one ought to be extremely wary of explanations that are too closely geared to one particular and rather short period of historical experience.

Finally, I turn to the monetarist model. While I have not been totally convinced of the purity of what the Keynesians mean by Keynesianism, Professor Laidler has made it abundantly clear what the monetarist position is. He places great emphasis on the existence of the aggregate demand for money function, the adjustment mechanism of the money market, and on the significance of certain exogenous real variables. On the last he maintains the hypothesis of the convergence to full employment and of the given real rate of interest. There is, so to speak, a convergence to full employment itself and also a convergence to the full employment level and rate of change in real wages. If the rate of exchange is fixed, the world price level will determine the domestic price level and therefore the domestic money wage.

There is one other way in which the Laidler model is notably monetarist, although I have never been able to understand why this particular aspect of economics is regarded as monetarist – his treatment of expectations. He is not the only contributor who mentions expectations. The National Institute refers to the expectations augmented Phillips curve. Ball and Burns refer to an 'unanticipated rise in the rate of inflation' and even postulate something called the 'expected' exchange rate. But it is Professor Laidler who has an actual equation for inflationary expectations.

Professor Laidler, like other monetarists, places great emphasis on the long run, both in terms of where we ought to focus our attention and in terms of where the economy is approaching. But he does not limit himself to commenting on the long run and does not deny that variation in particular exogenous variables will have quite different influences in the short run. He says 'I would not deny for an instant that changes in government expenditure on goods and services or in taxes, have a direct effect on the level of income and employment.'

I would not be in the least surprised not only that he did not deny this, but, if asked to give an account of what happened, it might well turn out to be Keynesian. It could well be that if this highly aggregative model were fully spelled out and attempts were made to estimate the short term adjustment mechanisms of the economy, a great deal of Keynesianism would emerge.

My last comment on types of theory relates to the multipliers. Within the National Institute model they are extremely low. On this, I must say that I am unconvinced, and uneasy about how they were achieved. The multipliers in the London Business School model are larger but still nowhere near as large as the old-fashioned Keynesians might have anticipated. I cannot say what the multipliers in the Cambridge model are because I have some difficulty in interpreting them and, of course, there are no multipliers within the Laidler model. Insofar as Keynesianism meant a significantly large multiplier, none of the models are all that Keynesian. Indeed, I am inclined to believe that they are all partially Keynesian, but that they all contain some monetarist elements, with the National Institute being least monetarist. They differ from their counterparts of some years ago in their explicit recognition of the complexities of the foreign trade sector, the balance of payments on both current and capital accounts, and the importance of the sectoral accounts in the sectoral budget relationships, but notably the public sector relationships.

Prices, Wages and Money

Prices

The Cambridge model concentrates on 'the price of business sector domestic sales at full cost'. The London Business School price equations include an estimated deflator for consumer durables, a calculated deflator for non-durable consumption, which then enables them to work out a deflator for all consumer expenditure. None of these correspond precisely to the price index in the Cambridge model, but the London Business School also has an estimated price equation which is for the wholesale price index of manufacturing output. The independent variables in this are the price index of world exports of manufactures, and unit labour costs in manufacturing industry, which is in turn determined by average earnings relative to producitivity. The key variable in the Cambridge equation is what they call current full cost per unit sales. This is a weighted average of domestic cost per unit of output and input cost per unit of output. Domestic costs per unit of output themselves are largely a function of average earnings relative to labour productivity.

Comparing the wholesale price index in the London Business School model with the price index used in the Cambridge model there are two noteworthy differences. Firstly, the London Business School model lets an index of export prices have an effect, but not an index of import prices. In addition, the same model allows for the effect of excess demand both as it works through earnings and as it works through productivity. The Cambridge model includes import costs as an independent variable determining prices, but it does not look as if excess demand influences prices either directly or indirectly via wages. The only possibility I can see is that standard weekly money earnings per male full time employee in the business sector, since this is partly affected by the level of money earnings at settlement, might on that account be influenced by demand and in turn transmit that demand effect to the price equation. The other way in which excess demand is important is, presumably, that it leads to a worsening in the balance of payments and an increase in the price of foreign exchange. This will then work itself through via import prices.

Going back to the London Business School model, the paper sees the world inflation rate as determining the domestic inflation rate under a fixed exchange rate. This is said to depend on the way in which money wages are dependent on real wages, with the export price index being the dominant influence on domestic manufacturing prices. While I understand the theory, I find it impossible to trace this through the model. Essentially the implicit deflator for consumers' expenditure depends on the implicit domestic value added deflator for private expenditure, and in the excess of that over the import prices index. The domestic value added deflator itself is obtained by dividing private expenditure at constant prices into private expenditure in current prices. It is at this point, namely where the export price index feeds into domestic private expenditure, that I fail to see the causation working through the model. If I now try to bring the National Institute price equation into the picture, once again concentrating on manufacturing industry, this too is a chiefly cost determined function of average earnings and the cost of capital, but a demand element can enter in both via an influence on average earnings and insofar as it pushes actual output above trend. What is noteworthy in the National Institute equation is that in determining the price index of manufacturing output, import prices do not appear and nor do export prices. The relevant linkage is between the 'price of output, manufacturing' which is an independent variable in the equation determining the 'wholesale price manufacturing'; the 'foreign price deflator, imports total' being another independent variable. The wholesale price of manufacturing is then an independent variable in the export price equation determining the 'deflator, exports manufacturing'. Thus demand effects occur because the degree of capacity utilisation is found in the wholesale price of manufactures equation and in the export price equation, and because import and export prices depend on the rate of exchange which in turn may be influenced by excess demand as it works through the balance of payments.

The Laidler price equation depends essentially on the growth of demand and on the expected rate of inflation. Both of these independent variables are themselves influenced by the behaviour of foreign prices, and the price of foreign currency relative to the domestic price level. Essentially the link is then made by the balance of payments equation enabling a surplus or deficit to feed through via the money supply and effective demand. For the Laidler model it is certainly the case that demand pressures work through into prices via an increase in the price of foreign currency, this happening both directly and via expectations. As I read the model, however, there is also a direct effect through excess demand itself.

Wages

I have emphasised already that it is difficult to say much about wage determination in the Laidler model. He says that it is typical of post-Keynesian macroeconomics that the money wage rate is determined exogenously. Nonetheless he clearly thinks that real wages are important, and indeed if the labour market is not based in at least full equilibrium on the demand for and supply of labour as functions of the real wage, the whole edifice of full employment, natural unemployment rate, and that kind of thing collapses. It is not necessary to stress the point that even if this real model holds in the long term, it does not have to hold in the short term; therefore, it may not be much help in assessing the behaviour of the economy over some relevant time interval.

The Cambridge equation for wages depends on current and lagged values of settlements, changes in normal weekly hours, and some cost of living adjustment. Settlements themselves were determined by something called the real value of the wage bargain weighted by the consumer price variable adjusted for direct tax rates. It is not clear where the real value of the wage bargain emerges from. It is also not clear in this kind of model how the desired real wage reacts to the actual real wage. The issue is complicated by the assumption made about public sector wages. It is asserted that these are projected on the basis of an assumed relativity with standard average money earnings in the business sector. The assumed relativity is set exogenously. This surely leaves the question of wage determination, in circumstances such as those occurring in the country in the present wage round, as hanging almost totally in mid air.

The London Business School wage equation works in a multi-stage way. Wages and salaries per employee are determined by average weekly earnings in manufacturing which are in turn determined relative to the wholesale price of manufacturing by disposable income relative to GDP, productivity in manufacturing, and an allowance for incomes policy. (Including real national disposable income relative to GDP means that the terms of trade effect is taken into account.) It is also stated that for 'the purpose of simulation analysis the rate of change of money wages was determined by the rate of change of prices plus a long term effect given by the rate of increase of average productivity'.

The National Institute's wage rate equation is essentially a price expectations augmented Phillips curve. The National Institute go on to explain average earnings in terms of average earnings in manufacturing which is itself determined by output in manufacturing relative to expected output and the degree of capacity utilisation.

Starting from the wage and price equations, one ought to be able via employment and hours, to work through to income from employment, disposable income and real disposable income, and thence to consumption. These linkages can certainly be seen with the utmost clarity in the National Institute model. In the London Business School model too it is possible to trace the connection. The Cambridge model also meets this test but in terms of its own specific definitions of the variables.

Money

All four models take some account of the demand for and the supply of money. The demand for money equation is critical in the Laidler analysis. He puts the matter very clearly in saying that the demand for real balances is a function of permanent income. The omission of the interest rate variable from the equation is justified on the grounds of simplicity, which suggests that Laidler would regard it as important to include it in any extension of his model. In the model as formulated, theoretically the excess supply of money can influence the level of real income. In the model as estimated, the relevant coefficient takes a zero value which means this direct money supply effect disappears. There is no effect on the interest rate because that is missing. The outcome is that monetary policy has its chief effect on the balance of payments. The difficulty with that, once the interest rate is missing, is to limit the analysis of the capital account especially in the short term. It is possible for the supply of money to differ from the demand. In other words the money market does not equilibrate instantaneously. But the only data we have on money is the money supply.

The London Business School model has an equation for the change in money supply as a function of DCE and the balance of payments surplus on current account. This is related to a rather complicated equation for DCE itself. If I understand the model correctly, there is no equation for the demand for money. Instead we are concerned with such phenomena as the net flow of bank lending to the personal sector and to the corporate sector. As far as the propensity to consume by the personal sector is concerned, what is relevant is the stock of liquid assets and there is an equation for that. I have had considerable difficulty in marrying up all these. But starting (say) from the public sector borrowing requirement, I am unable to trace the financing of this through in such a way as to see at the end how the liquid assets effect on consumption and expenditure is arrived at. *A fortiori* I find it hard to see what role the money supply itself plays in the expenditure side of the model. In particular I am unable to trace the flow of funds through the banking system. I can see that the equation for domestic credit takes account of the public sector borrowing requirement. Moreover one can go from that to the effective exchange rate, and from the effective exchange rate into the expenditure side of the model and the price side. Of course, the model in its present form is described very definitely as being within the spirit of international monetarism, but I am surprised that certain other money/credit/expenditure links seem so weak.

My difficulty in interpreting the monetary aspects of the National Institute model was mentioned earlier. They refer to this subject under the heading of money supply, but, to take the case of money endogenous, it is difficult to interpret the equation as a structural one determining money supply. Instead it seems it contains a mixture of what I would think to be demand and supply elements. Again, having got real balances into the model it is difficult to trace what happens to them. They do not enter directly into either the consumption or investment equations and I do not see any indirect entry via interest rates. There are interest rate variables in various of the equations for prices. There are also effects working through the balance of payments and the determination of the rate of exchange. Let me hasten to add that I do not doubt that appropriate connections exist between the monetary and real parts of the model. Without them the simulations that are offered would be impossible. My point is simply that the outsider, anxious to assess the model sympathetically, finds it extremely difficult to make the connection between the fiscal operations of the public sector, the public sector borrowing requirement, changes in M3, and the subsequent behaviour of expenditure, output and the balance of payments. More to the point, insofar as the connections exist, they do appear to be rather more mechanical than behavioural.

The Cambridge model is infinitely easier to follow in this regard. They proceed from world inflation rates and world interest rates to the British rate of interest, thence into the demand for money, treating the British inflation rate and private disposable income as additional independent variables. They are then also able to connect the change in the demand for money and the balance of payments on current account with DCE. The further connection with the public sector borrowing requirement is made via the sale of public sector debt to the private sector and overseas, and the balance of official financing. Thus the flow of funds is reasonably clear. In terms of behaviour one must again mention how this works through the foreign sector of the model; although this model is certainly not an international monetarist one, and therefore does not transmit price effects in the same way as say the London Business School model does. Nonetheless as we have remarked above there is a direct connection between the monetary variables and the income expenditure relationships via interest rate effects and attempts to capture the consequences of credit restrictions. The following quotation is most important: 'we have found some evidence that the ratios of both consumption and investment to private disposable income are positively related to movements in share prices, and have proxied this "wealth effect" with negative coefficients on long term interest rates'.

Conclusion

I am unable to say in conclusion whether I feel that what ought to be emphasised is the extent of what the models have in common or the nature of their differences. This dilemma also arises if I look briefly at their policy proposals.

Thus, in considering demand management from the present until 1981, both Laidler and Ball and Burns recommend that the exchange rate be left to float free. Moreover, they imply a degree of easing of monetary stringency in the coming year followed by a reduction in the rate of monetary expansion subsequently. Professor Laidler gives no precise figures.

I am struck by certain similarities between the projections for this period given by the National Institute and the London Business School. The paths of the consumer price index are extraordinarily close and even the average earnings figures do not differ all that much if one compares Table 4.17 of the National Institute paper with Table 3.8 of the London Business School paper. What is a little surprising is that the National Institute model assumes a more devalued exchange rate but a rather lower increase in average earnings which must offset each other in giving rather similar behaviour of the consumer price indices. However, one should not go too far in pointing out the similarities. There are also plenty of differences, for example, the likely paths of gross domestic product, exports of goods and services, and the percentage change in M3.

The Cambridge projection for the period is altogether different, but one is inclined to believe that this depends very much more on the policy differences than on the model differences. In particular, they maintain competitiveness as the result of a very drastic reduction in the exchange rate. They pay the price in that inflation does not really reach single figures at any time in the period, and pre-tax average earnings actually accelerate up to 1979 and from next year on do not fall below 13 per cent per annum.

The Cambridge model contains within it a very high rate of unemployment for the whole of the period, and so do the London Business School and National Institute models. Professor Laidler has grave doubts about whether his model can be used to project very far forward without taking account of some important structural changes. Nonetheless, he too would not be regarded as all that optimistic about the future level of unemployment. The most he is willing to say is 'that the same early bout of expansionary monetary policy might reduce it somewhat in the first year'.

This leads to one methodological question, namely whether the Cambridge model would give much the same results as the National Institute and London Business School models if it adopted the same policy prescription for the period. I think the answer to the question must be that it would generate the inflation improvement and the improvement in the current balance of payments. Where it would differ would be in its projection of unemployment which by the end of the decade would be very much higher still. I think we need to pursue the question of why this should be so. I also believe, from the policy point of view, we need to focus our attention much more carefully on the unemployment problem. Is there some policy initiative we are now missing which would enable us to get to something corresponding more closely to full employment before 1980? Have there been fundamental shifts in the output employment relationship which simultaneously prevent us doing that and prevent us analysing the problem in this kind of macro model? Does the answer lie in the last set of policy recommendations suggested by the National Institute, namely an exchange rate kept moderately high, a continuous incomes policy, and some strong degree of reflation throughout the period?

8 Fiscal Policy and Crowding Out

by M. J. Artis

Introduction

This paper attempts some analysis of the scope and role of fiscal policy in the four models as reflected in their policy recommendations and, where available, in model simulation results and technical specifications. For these purposes the comparative policy re-runs are of greater interest than the comparative forecasts of the future, and the more detailed information provided on the National Institute and Cambridge models offers more scope for evaluation than is possible for the London Business School or for Professor Laidler's models. These considerations are strongly, but inevitably, reflected in the bias of the appraisal offered here.

Fiscal Stance in the Policy Simulations

The first problem to be considered is that of constructing an indicator of fiscal stance which will enable some comparisons to be made between the alternative policies recommended and between them and the historical period. Estimates of the full employment budget deficit are employed here, but not without some reservations. These are of three main kinds: first, conventional measures of fiscal policy, such as the full employment budget deficit, can be criticised as subject to a systematic expansionary bias in periods of inflation; second, it is clear that the significance of a given full employment budget deficit (even one of given composition) must vary according to the model with which it is associated; third, in practice, their estimation for each of the simulation runs involved a number of crude approximations being made. Reflection suggests that these reservations are not in practice so overwhelming, either alone or in combination, as to disqualify the use of the full employment budget deficit as a comparative indicator of fiscal policy; at any rate, it seems reasonable to rely on the first differences of the series as an indicator of the course of fiscal policy in each simulation, even if direct comparison of their levels across simulations is an exercise which must be attended by greater caution.

We must, however, first consider the reservations mentioned in greater detail before making any such comparisons. There is an argument that, in inflationary conditions, any measure of fiscal policy which, like the full employment budget deficit, is based on the cash flow of government expenditure and revenues is an upward-biased indicator of fiscal stance and will give a misleadingly expansionary impression of policy. The argument is based on the observation that the rising price level implies a fall in the real value of outstanding national debt, an act of confiscation which should be regarded as a special form of tax (an inflation tax), but one which is not reflected in the cash flow definition of tax revenues. Compounding the bias, from this point of view, is the fact that the increased debt service costs associated with the inflation-induced increase in interest rates *will* be reflected in the cash flow definition of government expenditures. The extent of the bias, moreover, may be quite large: for example, recent estimates of the inflation tax by Miller and Temple [9] suggest that it is broadly equivalent in magnitude to the actual deficit incurred in the middle years of the 1970s. It could be argued that these inflation tax 'revenues' should be incorporated in the budget deficit measures. Opposition to this suggestion can be based on one of two principal considerations: first, that the effect on consumption of the inflation tax is, at most, very much less than that of ordinary taxes; second, that however effective this tax it should not be classified to fiscal policy since inflation is not a government policy instrument. Whilst the latter is quite an attractive argument in principle, it depends on an empirical judgement that the government does not intend to use inflation as a substitute for taxation, a judgement which, whilst not seriously in question for Britain in the 1970s, could no doubt be queried for other countries at other times. The former line of argument seems ultimately the more important, for, even though the comparative demand-effect of different types of regular taxation (for example the effect of capital taxes versus that of the income tax) is not used as a criterion to distinguish which revenues should, and which should not, be incorporated in regular budget measures, the extent of the bias imparted to such measures of fiscal policy by the omission of the inflation tax clearly does depend on its demand effect. Moreover, it clearly is important to have an estimate of this effect even if it is decided on *a priori* grounds not to include the inflation tax in the measure of fiscal policy, because it is at least a measure of the deflationary behaviour of the private sector, which *ceteris paribus*, budgetary measures might seek to offset.

Our models differ radically in the extent to which they recognise, in any way, the legitimacy of the demand effect of inflation taxation. The National Institute model, for example, appears to omit any such consideration altogether; the London Business School model, on the other hand, gears private sector savings behaviour to the inflation rate, though not directly, it would appear, to the extent of the erosion of the value of wealth. The Cambridge model is more explicit; the fact that it models the private sector's acquisition of financial claims in nominal terms, together with the notion that there is a constant desired ratio of the stock of such claims to disposable income, is designed to capture the idea of behaviour aimed at preserving the real value of financial assets. In this sense, it would appear that the Cambridge modellers treat the inflation tax on a par with regular taxes, although they do not take the further step of adjusting their full employment budget deficit measures for it.

An important reservation about the comparative use of the full employment budget deficit arises from the consideration that the value of any such indicator must vary with the model employed. This is dramatised by the observation that whereas National Institute practice would justify the attribution of differing demand weights to the different tax and spending components of the budget, and hence would favour a weighted version of the full employment budget deficit, Cambridge practice affords no justification for a weighted measure, and indeed insists that such weighting is mistaken. (This follows directly from their assumptions about the nature of the private sector expenditure functions.) Finally, the full employment budget deficit and similar measures are indefinite about the time lags with which fiscal policy is supposed to be effective, and the models clearly differ in this respect just as much as they do with respect to the value of the long run multipliers embodied in them. For all these reasons, it is clear that considerable caution must be attached to comparisons of full employment deficit levels across simulations.

A final set of reservations arises from the crude estimation methods actually used in the construction of the full employment budget deficit series; that these figures are nevertheless shown in Table 8.1 below only allows the reader to infer that the author would stand by the figures as about the only feasible way of comparing fiscal stance. The full employment budget deficit values were generated by calculating the incremental deficit which would have resulted from closing the gap between the value of GDP in the simulation and full employment GDP, and adding this figure back to the estimate of the public sector deficit already available in the simulation. Full employment GDP was generated as that series of GDP which would approximately have preserved the pressure of demand which prevailed in 1968, as indicated by an inspection of a graph of relevant data on GDP and vacancies. Since vacancies, rather than unemployment, were in fact conservatively taken as the measure of the pressure of demand, the rate of growth of the full employment (high vacancy) GDP series was put at only 2.6 per cent per annum in the second period (1970–5) as opposed to 2.9 per cent in the first. The adjustment factors applied to the full employment gap to derive the incremental deficit, comprising essentially an estimate of the marginal effective rate of taxation and of the income-responsiveness of public expenditures, were those estimated to have been relevant to the actual historical situation, and were based on some recent work by R. W. R. Price [12]. Strictly, the adjustment factors should have been those actually implied, year by year, by the model simulations, but it did not seem feasible to reconstruct these to the required degree of accuracy in all cases. The Cambridge Group produced its own full employment budget deficit measures, using slightly different assumptions about the base level of full employment and its trend, and adopting the convention of assuming that the composition of full employment expenditures would have been such as to generate external balance. For these reasons, and also because the Cambridge figures presumably use the adjustment factors appropriate to the simulation there are inevitable differences between our full employment budget deficit and that of the CEPG (see Table 8.1). Since, however, absolute differences in levels can be heavily discounted in the present instance (an arbitrary difference in the choice of base level, for example, could lead to such discrepancies), it is comforting to note that in the first differences there is virtually total agreement as to sign between the two series and a high degree of consistency in the size of these changes.

The figures shown in Table 8.1 include a full employment budget deficit calculation for the neutral fiscal policy defined by the London Business School base run which is based, broadly, on indexed initial tax rates and trend government spending. By comparison with this standard, both the policies actually followed in the first period (1964–9) and those recommended *ex post facto* appear deflationary in character, whilst the opposite is true, and even more emphatically, of the second period (1970–5). There is general agreement that the conditions of the initial year in each period were inappropriate (though in opposite ways); with somewhat greater diffidence it may be observed that the CEPG and National Institute recommendations appear to be more expansive in character, for both periods, than those

Table 8.1 Fiscal stance: the full employment budget deficit[a] as per cent of GDP

	Recommended NIESR	Recommended CEPG[b]		Recommended LBS	Actual[b]		Neutral[c]
1964	4.7	4.1	(5.0)	2.7	4.0	(5.1)	4.3
1965	2.3	3.8	(4.2)	0.9	3.2	(3.7)	3.6
1966	1.8	4.1	(4.2)	1.1	2.4	(4.0)	4.5
1967	4.4	2.4	(3.8)	1.3	3.6	(5.2)	4.5
1968	3.8	4.2	(3.9)	−0.2	2.8	(3.3)	4.8
1969	1.0	1.4	(0.1)	0.3	−1.4	(−1.3)	5.7
Unweighted total 1964–9	18.0	20.0		6.1	14.6		27.4
Index of policy action[d] 1964–9	0.50	0.42		0.15	0.56		—
1970	−1.6	−2.3	(−2.2)	−1.1	−2.6	(−2.3)	−3.2
1971	3.2	1.8	(1.1)	2.6	−0.4	(−0.7)	−2.4
1972	2.8	3.2	(2.0)	2.3	1.5	(1.4)	−2.8
1973	4.4	2.3	(0.6)	−0.2	4.7	(3.6)	−1.3
1974	9.8	5.3	(3.5)	2.4	5.3	(5.0)	0.7
1975	9.6	8.9	(7.3)	3.2	4.6	(5.2)	−1.0
Unweighted total 1970–5	28.2	19.2		9.2	13.1		−10.0
Index of policy action[d] 1970–5	0.26	0.35		0.45	0.21		—

[a] *Surplus shown by a minus (−) sign.*
[b] *Figures in parentheses are CEPG-calculated FEBDs.*
[c] *LBS base run.*
[d] *Coefficient of variation of the first difference of the series generated by subtracting Neutral from Recommended, normalised for negative signs by adding the largest negative observation to the mean in the denominator.*

associated with the London Business School, consistently with the higher pressure of demand sustained in the two former simulations and their resort – in contrast to the London Business School – to incomes policies and import controls.

There is less sympathy between the fiscal policies of the modellers in the first than in the second period, but all seem to agree in suggesting a rather greater degree of stability in policy in the first period than seems evident in the historical record. In general, the *ex post* policy recommendations seem to avoid the more extreme policy U-turns to be found in the historical record, most notably in the deflationary phase of 1968–9 and again in the rapid U-turn from deflation to reflation in the early 1970s. But the modellers agree that a sharper expansionary response in 1974 would have been appropriate. The desideratum of a stable growth in GDP does not, in such circumstances as those of quadrupled oil prices and world deflation, imply that policies should be stable – rather the opposite; but in more normal circumstances it has become conventional to suppose that the onus is on the fine-tuner to demonstrate that unstable policies have a more favourable outcome than highly stable policies.

The London Business School base run is characterised by trend government spending and indexed tax rates. Aside from the action implicit in the indexing, it thus seems reasonable to describe this policy as a neutral one involving no discretionary action. The first differences of the full employment budget deficit estimate for this run may therefore be used as a benchmark for measuring the activism implied by the actual historical and recommended policies. Specifically, a modified coefficient of variation was estimated for the first difference of the series generated by subtracting the neutral policy full employment budget deficit values from the actual and recommended policy full employment budget deficit values. Thus, a policy which recommended a series of full employment budget deficits different from neutral policy only by a constant amount would generate a coefficient of variation measure of zero; correspondingly, a more activist policy implying considerable changes in full employment budget deficit values compared with those implied by neutral policy would generate a relatively large coefficient of variation. The seeming complexity of this measure (shown in Table 8.1 as the index of policy action) should not disguise the fact that it can only be intended as a heuristic and highly approximate measure of fiscal activism. For what it is worth, comparison of the policy action indices measured in this way for the recommended policies with that estimated for actual policy indicates that whilst all modellers would have favoured greater policy stability in the first period than historically provided, the contrary is the case for the second period. Perhaps the modellers, but not the authorities, have wisely heeded the object lesson provided by those military commanders whose preparation for the next war would only have been appropriate for the previous one!

Effectiveness of Fiscal Policy

It has become fashionable to speculate that fiscal policy can have little or no effect upon output. The reasons why such a speculation might be seriously entertained should be sharply distinguished from one another, however. One possibility is that the expansion of government expenditures or the increase in private spending induced by the tax remission associated with an expansive fiscal action will be offset, more or less completely, by an induced reduction in other spending components. In general terms, this would involve a crowding out of alternative expenditures by fiscally-induced expenditures; the standard, but special, case of this is crowding out caused by the effect of the higher interest rates induced by the fiscal expansion against the background of an unchanged money supply. An alternative possibility is that the leakages from the income-creating process are so great as to mean that the standard multiplier applicable to fiscal policy is relatively low; in particular, in the present context, observers would look to a high marginal propensity to import for an explanation of such a condition.

The Assignment Rule

A further possible consequence of the latter condition is that the solution of the model will show that the ratio of the effect on GDP to the effect on the balance of payments (taken without regard to sign) will be less for a defined fiscal action than it is for an action (like devaluation) which bears on external competitiveness. In these circumstances, if policy adjustment is considered to be a discrete and decentralised process, the appropriate policy assignment rule will be that associated with the New Cambridge economics, that is a pairing of fiscal policy with the external balance and of the exchange rate with internal balance. Such a result is not the peculiar product of the special assumptions of the CEPG model, for whose latest simulation results [4] indicate it is still characteristic since just such a result holds also for a range of fiscal policy options in the Cambridge Growth Project – see Barker [2] – and could just as well hold for a conventional model like the National Institute's. The apparent peculiarity of this assignment rule may rather be put down to the peculiarity of the policy-setting assumptions, a feature which makes the derivation of this rule a rather contrived affair.

Although the relatively high marginal propensity to import may be significant for the assignment rule conclusion, it does not follow that the multiplier for a model which generates such a rule is necessarily low. In fact, the CEPG multiplier is relatively high. This can be seen to be a direct consequence of the expenditure function properties, which provide for a financial asset/nominal income adjustment on the part of the private sector (Cripps *et al.* [6]) such that:

$$FA = \alpha(1 - t)Y \tag{1}$$

where FA is the net stock of financial assets of the private sector – that is its claims on the liabilities of government and overseas sectors, t is tax rate and Y is nominal income. First differencing of (1) yields:

$$NAFA = \alpha(1 - t)Y - \alpha(1 - t)Y_{-1} \tag{2}$$

Since the NAFA of the private sector is identically equal to the surpluses of the government and overseas sectors (with signs reversed), (2) can be rewritten substituting these surpluses and simplifying to provide the multiplier expressions (given the price level):

short run	long run
$1/[\alpha(1 - t) + m + t]$	$1/[m + t]$

These compare with a conventional multiplier of

$$1/[s + m + ct]$$

where m is the marginal propensity to import, c and s the marginal propensities to consume and save and $(1 - \alpha)$ has the character of a marginal propensity to absorb. Simulation results, as already noted, support this implied contrast in multiplier sizes, the conventional National Institute estimate being for a multiplier of around 0.8 as compared with a CEPG figure of nearly 1.5.

Crowding Out

Conventional crowding out depends on the responsiveness of interest rates to changes in the amount of money demanded, and on the responsiveness of expenditures to this induced interest rate response, a response which may be accompanied by wealth effects both in the demand for money and in the expenditure functions. As modelled by the CEPG and the National Institute, however, crowding out of this form is trivial at its most strongly positive and seemingly slightly negative over the longer run. This tendency towards negative crowding out appears to stem from a relatively powerful bond coupon effect as debt is refinanced at the higher interest rates induced by fiscal expansion, and these increased debt service payments feed through into higher personal incomes and consumption. It is not difficult to argue that there is something a little bizarre about the dominance of this effect.

Conventional analysis, see for example [5], suggests that since crowding out depends on the effects of the increase in interest rates induced by expansive fiscal policy when the money supply is held constant, it could be measured as the difference between the value of the fiscal multipliers when the interest rate is held constant and its value when the money supply is held constant, this difference being expressed as a proportion of the former multiplier. Simulations of the National Institute model provide just the measures needed for this calculation, with results as shown in Table 8.2, differentiated according to alternative assumptions about earnings and the exchange rate. This differentiation, however, does not concern us here. It can be seen that there is no evidence of strong crowding out in either case, and indeed some evidence of a tendency towards negative crowding out.

Table 8.2 Crowding out in the NIESR model

Multipliers for a standardised increase in public authorities' current expenditure, calculated against a control solution.

	Exchange rate fixed, Earnings exogenous			Exchange rate flexible, Earnings endogenous		
Quarter	$k(\bar{R}_L)$[a]	$k(\bar{M}_3)$[a]	c(%)[b]	$k(R_L)$[a]	$k(\bar{M}_3)$[a]	c(%)[b]
4	0.84	0.80	4.8	0.96	0.90	6.3
8	0.76	0.76	zero	1.06	1.06	zero
16	0.49	0.48	0.2	0.80	0.89	−11.3
24	0.61	0.61	zero	0.47	0.47	zero
30	0.66	0.71	−7.6	0.28	0.24	−14.3

Source: P. Ormerod, *Structure and Properties of the NIESR Model*, National Institute Discussion Paper No. 4.

[a] $k(\bar{R}_L)$ *and* $k(\bar{M}_3)$ *are the 'constant interest rate' and 'constant money supply' multipliers, respectively.*

[b] c(%) *indicates the percentage of crowding out calculated as the ratio* $[k(\bar{R}_L) - k(\bar{M}_3)]/k\bar{R}_L$.

The National Institute model [11] provides for a demand for money subject to partial adjustment with a positive elasticity in the own (Certificate of Deposit) rate and a negative elasticity in the Consol Rate (R_L) and the customary expected signs on inflation and income variables. This function is inverted to give an equation in $\bar{R}_L$ (CD rate exogenous) for the $\bar{M}_3$ simulation of the model. This procedure may itself be questioned on the grounds that equation inversion is an inadequate way of describing the difference between a demand-determined money supply regime and a supply-determined one, particularly as the partial adjustment characteristic of the function will give rise to rather implausible interest rate over-shooting (see Artis and Lewis [1]), but this can perhaps be regarded merely as a specific instance of the more general case (see Lucas [8]) against macro-economic simulation of alternative policies when adaptive behaviour to the novel policies simulated cannot be allowed for. The term structure of interest rates is preserved elsewhere in the model unchanged as the Consol Rate alters, a significant exception arising only as a result of lags in the adjustment of building society interest rates. The characteristics of the inverted money demand function would *ceteris paribus* make for a relatively high degree of (positive) crowding out, since the interest elasticity is relatively low (in the long run −0.56) and the income elasticity quite high (+2.5) thus indicating a relatively high degree of response of interest rates to expansive fiscal policy.

The evidence of the simulations shows that this is offset – indeed more than offset – by the fact that the conventional negative response of expenditures to increased interest rates is very weak and is combined with the positive bond coupon effect. The negative effects are mediated through cost of capital effects on the price level and via transitory rationing and permanent disincentive effects in the dwelling investment sector. At the same time, however, sector net property income rises as a result of higher interest rates when a more expansive fiscal policy is combined with an unchanged monetary policy (constant money supply): the most obvious interpretation of this is that it is a bond coupon effect arising from the need to refinance maturing debt at increased coupon rates.

(In technical terms, the presence of this effect means that the IS schedule can be pictured as swivelling in a clockwise direction after its initial fiscally-induced shift, becoming more inelastic as the proportion of debt refinanced at high coupons grows. In the limit, the schedule may slope positively. Both the relative ordering of the short and long-run IS schedules in terms of their elasticities and the final slopes suggested are of course unconventional.)

In the case of the CEPG model, it is not absolutely clear that crowding out is negative because appropriate simulations do not exist. But it is clear that positive crowding out is negligible and that the bond coupon effect of higher interest rates has the same qualitative effect as in the National Institute and, incidentally, also in the Cambridge Growth Project model, see [2]. The CEPG model solutions are complicated by the fact that the money supply is taken to be demand-determined at all times (though a supply side variable – advances restriction – does appear in the equation) and is positive in the only interest rate (MLR) entering the function. The Consol Rate, which enters the expenditure function with a negative sign, is determined essentially in the gilt-edged market where, given MLR, it equilibrates flow demand and supply for gilt-edged securities. (Thus, in technical terms, for given parameters of the functions governing exports and imports, government expenditure and taxation, the CEPG system can be pictured as combining a downward sloping LM function (in Consol Rate – income space) with a relatively steep and dynamically clockwise-swivelling IS function.) An increase in public authorities' current expenditure, as described by the simulation result (PAC) shown in Table 8.3 tends to raise income and to lower Consol Rate for given MLR. The conventional multiplier is quite high, leading to a large rise in income and money demanded at constant MLR. The increase in banks' demand for gilts, combined with the induced incremental balance of payments deficit and decline in the balance of official financing, more than offsets the added supply of gilts associated with the rise in the public sector borrowing requirement, so leading to a fall in Consol Rate. When, by contrast, an increase in the volume of world trade is the expansionary factor (VOL in Table 8.3) the improvement in the balance of payments outweighs the combined effect of the reduction in the public sector borrowing rate (arising from higher tax receipts at higher levels of income) and the increase in banks' demand for gilts, to put upward pressure on Consol Rate. An increase in MLR above what it would otherwise be (MLR is determined by a reaction function linking it to overseas rates), leads to a rise in Consol Rate through a simple term structure effect and to some negative effects on GDP which become increasingly trivial as time elapses. This is consistent with the presence in the CEPG model of an explicit debt-interest equation which provides for the refinancing of existing debt at higher coupons. It is apparent that the induced fall in Consol Rate of simulation PAC (Table 8.3) could be cancelled by a modest increase in MLR and that such an increase would have a trivial effect on GDP. Alternatively, the positive money supply effects of simulation PAC could be cancelled by a decrease in MLR, leading to a modest addition to the GDP increase. On this basis, crowding out is negligible to negative; given a longer simulation period it seems possible that the MLR simulation would, after a lapse of time comparable with the National Institute's 30 quarters – or perhaps less – produce a positive effect on GDP.

Table 8.3 CEPG simulation results for changes in defined condition variables[a]

		GDP	M3	PSBR	BoF[c]	RL[d]
Unit value[b]		483.165	523.847	1230.548	1230.548	0.010
				Normalised responses[b]		
PAC	Year 1	0.25	0.20	0.14	−0.11	0.00
	2	0.30	0.25	0.12	−0.16	−0.03
	3	0.30	0.24	0.11	−0.14	−0.03
	4	0.29	0.24	0.11	−0.13	−0.03
VOL	Year 1	0.28	0.28	−0.08	0.20	0.05
	2	0.32	0.31	−0.11	0.23	0.05
	3	0.32	0.27	−0.16	0.29	0.06
	4	0.30	0.25	−0.16	0.31	0.07
MLR	Year 1	−0.14	0.21	0.16	0.41	1.31
	2	−0.10	0.30	0.20	0.37	1.33
	3	−0.04	0.37	0.21	0.30	1.29
	4	−0.01	0.39	0.20	0.28	1.27

Source: CEPG, *Ready Reckoner*, 1977–80, mimeo. 1977.

[a] *The simulations are:*

PAC: a one per cent rise in government current expenditure

VOL: a one per cent increase in world trade volume

MLR: a basis point increase in MLR.

In each case the figures quoted are the difference between the simulation and the control run.

[b] *Responses are normalised in terms of unit values, of which the first year only is shown as an indicator; thus the effect on GDP in Year 1 of the PAC simulation is 120.8/483.2 = 0.25. The M3 figures are however quoted as per cent per annum and (presumably) indicate the difference in annual growth rates between the simulation and control run.*

[c] *The balance of official financing.*

[d] *The Consol Rate.*

Inspection of these models for evidence on the crowding out issue thus produces the possibly surprising result that crowding out is certainly negligible and, over the longer haul, tends to be negative; this result is also confirmed by the simulation of the CEPG model, and seems to be based on a bond coupon-markup effect. Such an effect does not appear in the literature on crowding out: in that literature bonds are assumed to be irredeemable, so the question simply does not arise. The bond coupon effect to which Blinder and Solow [3] drew attention, moreover, was of a different type; it related only to the service costs of added debt and not to the increased service costs of existing debt. It could, nevertheless, be argued that Tobin and Buiter's comments [13] on Blinder and Solow's 'coupon effect' are also applicable here, that is the increase in government expenditure in the simulation should be redefined to be an increase *net* of the added coupon payments (this would imply, then, deducting from the standard stimulus of public authorities' current expenditure, an amount equal to the induced rise in debt-interest payments). But this seems to be something like an evasion of the problem. For, if it is correct to allow for the effect of the increased coupon payments arising as interest rates increase (and after all, why not?) is it not also correct to allow for the effect of the decline of the market value of wealth as interest rates rise and bond prices fall? Is it not, in any event, rather surprising that this bond coupon effect should be powerful enough to offset the negative effects of higher interest rates on expenditures? The first of these problems is related to, though distinct from, that pertaining to the asymmetrical effect of inflation on conventional fiscal policy measures, the problem with which we began our discussion; there, we were concerned with the fact that the inflation-induced coupon effect adds to the expansionary impression of policy while the contradictory effects of the fall in the real value of debt are omitted; the difference is that here the coupon and valuation effects are related to interest rate changes by non-inflationary factors.

References

[1] Artis, M. J. and Lewis, M. K., 'The demand for money in the United Kingdom, 1963–73', *Journal of the Manchester School*, September 1976.

[2] Barker, T. S. (ed.), *Economic Structure and Policy*, Chapman and Hall, London, 1976.

[3] Blinder, A. S. and Solow, R. M., 'Does fiscal policy matter?', *Journal of Public Economics*, November 1973.

[4] Cambridge Economic Policy Group, *Ready Reckoner: 1977–80*, mimeo, 1977.

[5] Carlson, K. M. and Spencer, R. W., 'Crowding out and its critics', *Federal Reserve Bank of St Louis Review*, December 1975.

[6] Cripps, F., Fetherston, M. and Godley, W., 'What is left of "New Cambridge"?', *Economic Policy Review*, March 1976.

[7] Fetherston, M. J., *Technical Manual of the CEPG Model*, Cambridge Economic Policy Group, 2nd edition, mimeo, May 1977.

[8] Lucas, R. E., 'Econometric policy evaluation: a critique' in Brunner, K. and Meltzer, A. H. (eds.), *The Phillips Curve and Labour Markets*, North Holland, 1976.

[9] Miller, M. H. and Temple, P. A., 'Estimates of inflation taxation in the UK', mimeo, March 1977.

[10] National Institute of Economic and Social Research, *National Institute Model III, May 1977 Review*, mimeo, 1977.

[11] Ormerod, P., *The Structure and Properties of the National Institute Model*, National Institute of Economic and Social Research, Discussion Paper No. 4, 1977.

[12] Price, R. W. R., 'Fiscal policy', in Blackaby, F. T. (ed.), *British Economic Policy, 1960–74*, Cambridge University Press (forthcoming).

[13] Tobin, J. and Buiter, W., 'Long-run effects of fiscal and monetary policy on aggregate demand', in Stein, J. L. (ed.), *Monetarism*, North Holland, 1976.

9 Monetary Policy

by C. A. E. Goodhart

Introduction

This paper considers the way monetary policy instruments are used in the papers in Part I and examines their role in determining the path of the economy.

Model Structure and the Role of Money

On the first page of the London Business School paper, the authors suggest that 'differences in conclusions may be arrived at as a consequence of the structure rather than a manipulation of the models employed. This may lead to the view that conclusions drawn from a given model tell one more about the behaviour of the model rather than the behaviour of economic reality.' Having read the four first-round papers, I have come to wonder whether the reason for differing conclusions lies instead in the various authors' fundamental perceptions of the nature of the economy rather than in minor details of structure.

Economics is largely concerned with the working of markets; the major division lies between those who believe that markets can work relatively efficiently with prices varying flexibly and smoothly to remove excess demand or supply and those who believe that various frictions, socio-political constraints, power imbalances within the market, poor information, and so on cause markets, or at least certain key markets, to work relatively poorly, so that price movements do not suffice to clear them. Included in the first group are those described as monetarist, though I have come to regard the term 'market optimist' as both a more neutral and a more descriptive term, while among the second group of 'market pessimists' are those who believe, for example, that large-scale state intervention in the market process is both desirable and necessary for the achievement of satisfactory economic outturns. Measured on this scale Laidler and the London Business School appear to be among the ranks of the market optimists, while the Cambridge Group and the National Institute are market pessimists.

In this respect the crucial market is the labour market. The CEPG and the National Institute generally treat wages as pegged independently of the level of demand. The CEPG state that 'the level of money wage settlements is assumed to be set, under conditions of free collective bargaining, by attempts to achieve a particular real disposable wage at the settlement date': this target real wage appears to be exogenously, indeed arbitrarily, determined. Although the National Institute model includes a Phillips curve, they have little faith in it, and frequently seek to override it by the use – assumed to be successful – of incomes policy. Accordingly with wages pegged, by incomes policy (National Institute) or union demands for a rise in living standards (CEPG), there is no loss whatsoever, in terms of a trade off of unemployment against inflation, in expanding the economy at full steam ahead. Indeed there is some gain because the increase in productivity will hold down nominal costs, until the pressure of domestic demand becomes so large that it puts downwards pressure on the exchange rate. Once that should occur inflationary pressures would rise sharply because, according to all the models, increases in import prices, following a devaluation, appear to pass through virtually completely and quite rapidly onto wages: this latter econometric finding would seem to raise questions about the policy of seeking to hold the exchange rate at levels that would maintain competitiveness.

In any case, with wages thus pegged, the basic objective of stabilisation policy, for the National Institute and CEPG, is to stabilise the level (and growth) of real output at the full employment, highest feasible level. For this purpose monetary policy is just one possible instrument for operating on the level of real demand.

Laidler and the London Business School, however, deny that it is possible to achieve a preferred level of real output by demand management. In Laidler's case this is because he adopts an expectations augmented Phillips curve, with a coefficient of unity on the expected rate of inflation (which implies the existence of a natural rate of unemployment). The London Business School, however, start with a broadly similar wage equation to the CEPG, that is an equation unaffected by the pressure of demand, not because they doubt whether such pressures could affect the market but because they have not found them in the past to be significant. With a labour market equation of this kind, the crucial constraint on output (and therefore for demand management) is the balance of payments; and devaluation, for the reasons noted above, is little help. The London Business School also, rather summarily, eschews import controls. With both devaluation and import controls eliminated as a means of relaxing the balance of payments constraint, the growth of real output is fairly tightly constrained by real factors such as productivity and the propensity to import, largely outside the influence of demand management. Although following a different chain of analysis from Laidler, the London Business School has also come to doubt if full employment policy can be achieved by demand management.

Once, however, it should be accepted, as Laidler and the London Business School accept, that in the longer run the level of real output, unemployment and growth cannot be controlled by demand management, then the main purpose of stabilisation policy must be to stabilise financial developments. The London Business School conclude that 'stabilisation policy can create the appropriate financial framework for this growth to operate within but an exaggerated belief in our capacity to create full employment through fiscal and monetary means is only likely to destroy financial stability in much the same way as we have experienced in the last ten years.' Given this latter perception of the economic system and of the purpose of stabilisation policies monetary policy becomes not a subsidiary instrument of demand management but a main focus of concern.

The Transmission Mechanism

With monetary policy mainly working via a market process of changing relative prices, for example, of existing assets relative to their costs of production (in contrast to fiscal policy, where calculations of direct and multiplier effects abstract from market processes) there could be some presumption that 'market pessimists' would expect to find a lesser role for monetary variables to affect expenditure decisions than would market optimists. There is some sign of this in the first-round papers with the London Business School finding more and larger channels of monetary influence than the National Institute or CEPG, the latter being remarkably consistent in its findings of low price elasticities virtually everywhere.

Nevertheless the main routes for charting the direct effect of monetary variables on real expenditures are common to most models. The building society housing expenditure nexus, with both interest rates and mortgage rationing affecting housing demand, has been clearly observed. With persons facing imperfect credit markets, hire purchase conditions and bank lending to persons are generally found to affect consumption. A more important development in recent years has been that some variant of 'real balance', or liquid assets, or financial wealth variable now appears significant in several consumption functions, and helps to explain the unexpected rise in the savings ratio in the 1970s.

It has usually been harder to find significant or important effects of financial variables on company expenditures, when using the standard explanatory equations, for example an accelerator equation to model fixed investment. It has always remained a puzzle to me that whereas the effects of financial developments on consumption, housing and external flows seem quite well determined, the major concern of the authorities about the effects of monetary policy on the economy has more often been with its effect on investment, where the importance of such effects is rather poorly determined.

Both the CEPG and the National Institute include interest rate effects and credit flows subject to rationing in their expenditure functions. They have not yet included (or found to be significant?) any real balance, or wealth, effects, for example as an influence on consumption, but I would assume that they would not object in principle to doing so. The London Business School provide a rather richer, but essentially standard, menu for monetary effects, with a liquid assets variable entering both the durable and non-durable consumption equation.

The only innovation in this area among the papers presented is provided by Laidler who, building on work largely pioneered by P. Jonson of the Reserve Bank of Australia, has included an estimate of disequilibrium money holdings in his expenditure functions. Laidler's attempt to replicate this aspect of Jonson's model for Britain did not succeed (a result which Laidler attributes to the fixed exchange rate regime allowing any such disequilibrium to be rapidly eliminated). Moreover Laidler simplifies by assuming a zero interest elasticity of demand. Once that assumption is dropped (as it should be), it is not possible to estimate the interest elasticity without fitting a demand function, but one should not fit a demand function to periods off the demand curve, so one has to use some prior indicators of excess supply periods, which is possible but messy.

External Effects

Even with a real balance, or wealth, effect entering into the consumption function, these models all show that monetary variables have little direct effect on expenditures. This is indeed what I would expect in any economy as open as Britain. The main impact of monetary policy in such an open economy would come through its effect on external developments, the exchange rate and the balance of payments. Of course when the exchange rate is pegged, the direction of causation runs the other way: the major influence on money policy actions, interest rate variation, ceilings on bank lending and so on, becomes the need to protect the exchange rate and to establish foreign exchange reserves commensurate with that need. Under these circumstances external developments largely determine money developments and these have the limited results on the economy already noted.

All four models presented here have essentially been developed to fit such a fixed exchange rate regime. A freely floating rate regime would be quite different. In such a regime monetary developments, including importantly the rate of growth of the monetary aggregates, would directly influence the exchange rate, largely through capital flows, strongly influenced by expectations, but also perhaps through the current account; and by this route would have further, and in my view much more powerful, effects on the real economy beyond the limited direct effect on expenditure functions.

A major difficulty for modelling purposes is that since 1972 Britain has neither been on a clearly fixed nor a clearly floating regime, but has followed a complex and changing set of objectives externally. This causes considerable havoc to several of the models. Laidler fits his model to an early period, 1954–70, specifically to be able to remain throughout within a fixed exchange rate regime. Once beyond 1970, however, simulation of the model produces nonsense results, one important reason for this being that the proper specification of the model changes with the change in the exchange rate regime; but formulating and testing that revised specification remains unfinished business.

That is also true for the London Business School, but they have done more work towards this. At the moment their work, though most interesting, lacks internal consistency. They estimate a quasi-reduced form equation(s) for the exchange rate, in which the trend value of the exchange rate depends on relative monetary growth and/or purchasing power parity, with the actual value adjusting to the trend with a lag but moderated by oil money flows and the cumulative current account. So relative monetary growth directly influences the exchange rate. But to do so, it must presumably affect actual transactions passing through the market. But in their model capital flows (*a fortiori* current account flows) are *not* influenced by relative monetary growth – indeed in several extant models the current account position is a main influence on capital flows, which with a J-curve implies extreme instability. Thus if Britain, say with North Sea oil, should have a combination of current account surplus plus faster monetary growth, the London Business School would appear to model a falling exchange rate coexistent with a large balance of payments surplus. Is that combination likely?

The National Institute avoid the difficulties of modelling the capital account altogether by estimating an alternative quasi-reduced form equation for the exchange rate in which the divergence of the rate from purchasing power parity depends, apart from a complicated lag adjustment, on past trends in the trade balance and on the United Kingdom/United States Treasury bill rate differential, with British rates normally assumed to be exogenously set. In view of the feedbacks via the J-curve from the exchange rate to the trade balance, I should be interested in the stability properties of this system. Is this equation supposed to hold under free floating conditions? If so, what is the implicit equation for the capital account? Or does the equation represent in part an authorities' reaction function, showing what will determine their intervention? The behavioural status of this equation is distinctly murky.

In contrast to the National Institute the Cambridge Group appear to treat the economy as having been – and going to remain – on a pegged, but adjustable, exchange rate. They estimate capital flow equations and thence a residual balance for official financing. Interest rate differentials enter, without great power, in the determination of short-term flows, and British short-term rates are assumed to be related through a reaction function to world interest rates and the rate of domestic inflation. Thus with pegged exchange rates, relatively small interest rate effects on capital flows, and interest rates determined by factors other than the growth in the money stock itself, the potential impact of domestic monetary policy upon external developments is effectively weakened. I believe that this view was indeed realistic until 1972, but I wonder whether so little has really changed since then.

This whole subject, the determination of capital flows and exchange rates and the influence of monetary variables on these, seems to me to represent the main problem, and agenda for research, for model builders. It is also without doubt the most difficult area for research, in part because the nature of the authorities' own actions and reactions has been variable.

Policy Proposals

If the papers in Part I were meant to provide an instructive guide for the illustration of past errors, I found them in the main to be disappointing. Monetary policy has little role to play anyhow in the

CEPG and National Institute models, with a relatively small – and no doubt, they would add, unpredictable – effect either on domestic expenditures, inflation or external developments. The one policy recommendation that they make – common to all the papers – was not to have unleashed the change to Competition and Credit Control in 1971–2. That the change over to the new system was in the event accompanied by certain undesirable and unfortunate side effects within the monetary sphere is undeniable. But it should be remembered that much of this should be ascribed to the pent-up rush which inevitably, but to an incalculable extent, followed the relaxation of severe, prolonged direct controls, which themselves were causing inefficiency and diversions of credit channels. In some large part the difficulties of 1972–3 should be laid at the door of the previous period of credit ceilings, rather than with the move to liberalisation in 1971–2.

Apart from this the only policy-related analysis within the monetary field in these two sets of papers calling for much comment is to be found in the National Institute's attempt to estimate the extent of crowding out [1]. They find virtually no crowding out. However, I believe that certain aspects of the form and use of their model, which bring about this conclusion, are incorrect.

They begin with a demand for money function of a fairly standard form, using my notation,

$$\log \frac{M3}{P} = a + b_1 \log Y_{-2} - b_2 \log \text{cons}_{-2} + b_3 \log CD_{-2}$$
$$- b_4 \log \dot{P} + b_5 \log \left(\frac{M3}{P}\right)_{-1},$$

where y is real output, cons the Consol rate, CD the Certificate of Deposit rate, $\dot{P}$ the rate of inflation, subscript -1 a quarterly lag, b_1, b_2, b_3, b_4, b_5 all >0 and significant. This is a straightforward demand for money (M3) equation; I should, however, note that similar equations which we have run in the Bank have exhibited instability in the coefficients when run over different time periods, and poor *ex post* forecasting ability.

To deal with circumstances in which money is assumed to be exogenously determined, this equation is simply reversed thereby appearing to show that the current consol rate is determined by the money stock in the *future* two quarters. This must be nonsense: I doubt whether it is sensible and useful to analyse the effect of the adoption of monetary targets by running a demand-for-money function backwards although this is commonly done; indeed I must confess to having done so on occasions myself. Having done that, the National Institute assume the Certificate of Deposit rate to be exogenously fixed, irrespective of movements in other interest rates. There is no justification for this, except possibly during periods of corset control. In fact bank deposit rates rise with interest rates generally, and the CEPG calculation that a rising own rate will raise M3 when rates rise generally, may be nearer to the truth, at least over a limited range of values. So the rise in consol rates necessary to control M3 is greatly understated. Next the National Institute assume that both short and long rates vary by the same amount, whereas in the first instance short rates usually vary twice as much as long rates. All told they underestimate by a large multiple, the movements of interest rates necessary to control M3.

Compared with other modellers the National Institute have found only a relatively weak effect of interest rates directly on real expenditures and external flows, but do unusually – in an interesting variation of their own – have interest rates directly affecting costs and prices. This latter effect is apparently powerful enough in their model to offset entirely the strengthening effect on the exchange rate of a weaker level of real output and higher interest rates, so the exchange rate falls *more* after a fiscal stimulation with M3 controlled (than with interest rates held constant) and nominal GDP and *inflation is faster*. We all have our fundamental perceptions of the economy, and in my view if that is what the National Institute model produces, then the model is wrong.

I have little to say about Laidler's policy proposals. His model only fits properly over the first of the historical episodes and here he follows the general recommendation of a much earlier devaluation allowing for steadier policy thereafter, without the severe stop of 1969–70. Thereafter Laidler's policy proposals derive not so much from a formal model but from the theoretical precepts of a monetarist viewpoint. These have been discussed widely and Laidler's paper does not provide more specific, or quantified, policy guidance than is already available, for example in some influential newspapers and journals.

The London Business School approach to the exercise of policy simulation was the most ambitious and aimed at the most rigour. I doubt, however, if it fully succeeded. The attempt to construct first a policy neutral path was so counterfactual in itself, that seeking to build from such an artificial base a suitable contra-cyclical path for policy seemed to this reader to drown in a sea of data without providing much illumination. Moreover I remain unclear whether their preferred approach of adopting a target exchange rate and adjusting monetary and fiscal policy to that end was really their view of the optimal policy approach, or whether it was partly imposed on them by their inability to model a floating rate system. Having adopted a target exchange rate (and how would that be chosen?) this must then presumably allow unforeseen variations in world inflation to feed through on to British inflation. If, as the London Business School, suggests, we have no medium-term control over unemployment and output, why not then at least control what the model suggests that we could control, which is our own rate of price inflation by controlling the rate of growth of the monetary aggregates and allowing the exchange rate to float? While I found the London Business School paper, and model, the most stimulating of the four, I did feel that they were currently in some confusion on both structure and policy over the relationship between external and internal financial developments.

In one respect, partly determined by the manner in which the exercise was set up, I did feel that all the paper writers were excessively harsh about the conduct of policy in both the historical episodes. In the years 1963–6 and 1971–3 governments, egged on by many commentators, were quite consciously taking some risks with stabilisation policy in the interests of growth. Admittedly the gambles failed and currently belief in government's ability to raise growth has faded (perhaps rightly so), but it was neither an ignoble nor, I would suggest, a self-evidently stupid pursuit.

What comes out of all this, I fear, is that models cannot give much help to policy makers. Looking at exactly the same economy, and even using on occasions very similar structural equations, different modellers come to totally different policy conclusions because of their fundamental perceptions about the working of the economy. Econometrics has not, at least so far, provided any alternative for basic judgement, only some quantitative dressing and support for such judgements.

Monetary Operations

To conclude on a more technical note, the modellers showed considerable diversity in their appreciation of how the monetary authorities operated. Laidler, for example, treated domestic credit expansion as exogenously fixed (1954–70). Although this assumption is commonly used by monetarists, its application to Britain except perhaps in 1969–70 (under the aegis of the IMF) is incorrect and the use of this invalid assumption will bias the results.

During this period the authorities were actually controlling short-term interest rates and also credit ceilings, but such control variables should not generally be modelled as exogenous since interest rates were varied, and credit ceilings imposed or removed, in response to prior developments, particularly external developments. Because of their on/off characteristics, *inter alia*, it will be hard to take account of the endogeneity of such phenomena as bank lending ceilings and the 'corset', and these virtually have to be entered as special dummy variables. On the other hand controlled money-market rates could usefully be entered in reaction-function form, as has been done by both CEPG and the London Business School. CEPG includes world interest rates and British inflation in its reaction function, the London Business School the current account balance, Britain's inflation and the movement in the effective exchange rate. My own view is that modellers should not treat such reaction functions as stable behavioural equations, but feel free to posit (and test) for example whether variations in the rate of growth of M3 from its desired level might have influenced the relationship from, say, the early 1970s onwards. Policy objectives do change and that should be reflected in reaction functions.

Besides fixing MLR through this reaction function, the Cambridge Group have a rather confusing relationship whereby the volume of government bonds necessary for the non-bank public to take up, if the demand for money function is to be satisfied, is achieved by variations in the slope of the yield curve, that is with long rates rising relative to short when such bond sales need to become larger. This formulation has occurred in several places (including an earlier version of the London Business School model), but I am not happy with it. The slope of the yield curve is determined much more by market factors such as expectations than by the authorities' debt management operations. However, finding *any* reasonable statistical fits to explain the past path of either gilt sales or bank lending remains very difficult.

Although the Cambridge Group thus suggest that bond sales to the non-bank public respond to (or cause) shifts in the yield curve, their demand for money function has only MLR as an argument, with a positive sign (proxy for own rate). Accordingly they appear to be suggesting that there is no way, except by direct controls, ceilings, corsets, etc., in which the authorities could control M3, if the demand for money should rise with a growing economy – an important result for the conduct of monetary policy, but one which the authors do not press. Although interest rate effects (on M3) are not actually perverse in the London Business School model, they are so weak that the London Business School regard variations in the public sector borrowing requirement as the main method of controlling domestic credit expansion and M3. The London Business School, therefore, have a hierarchy of instruments whereby the main macroeconomic function of fiscal policy is to set the public sector borrowing requirement at the right level to control DCE/M3, and the main function of monetary policy is to set DCE/M3 at the right level to control the exchange rate.

Reference

[1] Ormerod, P., *The Structure and Properties of the National Institute Model*, National Institute of Economic and Social Research, Discussion Paper No. 4, 1977.

10 Counter-Inflationary Policies

by Ralph Turvey

Introduction

The National Institute, CEPG and the London Business School all seem to agree that incomes policies would be useful if they worked but each is more sceptical than the one before about how reasonable it is to assume that they will work and will go on working. These different judgements appear to reflect the general wisdom of their authors rather than to constitute computable consequences of their models. As regards price policies, none of the authors appear to want them; they are scarcely mentioned.

The belief that incomes and prices policies would be useful if they worked does not interest Laidler, as far as I can tell, presumably because he finds it difficult to believe that they could work for long. If they had never been invented before, and so had no history of disillusion, he might conceivably have welcomed them as temporary devices for changing expectations.

The Wage – Price Spiral

The reason why an incomes policy that worked would be useful in the eyes of the first three groups of authors deserves consideration. Take the National Institute model first. In it, consumer prices are 'essentially determined by labour costs per employee and import prices, although indirect tax rates, interest rates, productivity and the pressure of demand all have some influence'. Furthermore, 'the most important determinant of average earnings is past changes in prices'. If we leave everything out of their price and wage change equations except prices and wages, that is, hold hours, demand pressure, import prices, productivity and so on, constant, there is thus a pure wage-price spiral mechanism as follows:

$$\dot{W}_t = 0.392\dot{P}_{t-1} + 0.524\dot{W}_{t-1}$$
$$\dot{P} = 0.152(\dot{W}_{t-1} + \dot{W}_{t-2} + \dot{W}_{t-3} + \dot{W}_{t-4})$$

If a steady-state is destroyed by an exogenous 10 per cent increase in wages then, according to these equations, wages will be 25.9 per cent above the steady-state level four quarters later and prices will be 10.3 per cent up. Ultimately they will rise by a total of 51 per cent and 28.9 per cent respectively, raising real wages by 17 per cent. Similarly, an exogenous 10 per cent rise in prices will raise wages and prices by 8.6 per cent and 12.9 per cent after four quarters and 17.8 per cent and 21.6 per cent ultimately so that real wages fall by 3.1 per cent.

One could regard the first of these two equations as a Koyck transformation: wage-change depending upon price-change with a distributed lag. But in this case it seems equally reasonable to think of some wages reacting to other wages. Hence an initial 10 per cent increase in the wage level consists, say, of a 20 per cent increase for 50 per cent of wage earners and this triggers off increases for other groups. The statement that a 10 per cent wage increase would ultimately raise wages by 51 per cent is therefore rather misleading; the arithmetic could equally well indicate that a 50 per cent increase for 20 per cent of wage earners will ultimately raise average wages by 51 per cent.

Although the equations thus appear to capture the wage-wage spiral as well as the wage-price and price-wage spiral, there remains the difficulty that regressing variables upon variables which include their own lagged values usually gives very good fits so that in any particular case a good fit may not mean much. Furthermore, if we accept the lagged wage-term as reflecting the wage-wage spiral, then 0.392 seems implausibly low as the coefficient of $\dot{P}$.

In the Cambridge model, if lags are disregarded, wages in the business sector rise in proportion to consumer prices (given constant direct tax rates) while, *ceteris paribus*, as in the National Institute model these prices rise as much as wages multiplied by the share of wages in costs. Hence there is no wage-wage spiral but, with a long-run coefficient of $\dot{W}$ on $\dot{P}$ of unity, the wage-price price-wage spiral will produce a bigger ultimate wage and price increase following an exogenous increase than in the National Institute model where the long-run coefficient is less than unity.

The lag structure of the Cambridge model is more complicated than that of the National Institute because of the useful distinction between wage settlements (whose frequency increases when prices rise faster) and actual average wages, which reflect past settlements. In pressing for the adoption of the twelve-month rule, the Government appears to attach considerable importance to this distinction. If the rule is successfully applied, then even if the Cambridge model correctly describes the past, it may cease to hold in the future. Expectations do not enter the model because changes in the rate of inflation lead to changes in the time between settlements, but fixing the latter at twelve months may force the unions to formulate price expectations.

So far, I have considered only the pure wage-price price-wage spiral in both models. In both it is a major part of the inflationary mechanism, suggesting that an incomes policy which reduced wage settlements below what they otherwise would be or which merely postponed some of them would reduce or slow down inflation. A similar conclusion follows from the alternative wage-price models reviewed by the London Business School [1].

When it comes to the pressure of demand, the Cambridge model excludes, and the National Institute include, a dampening effect of high unemployment upon wage increases. On price increases, the National Institute model gives some role to the pressure of demand while the Cambridge model does not. On the other hand, a cyclical change in labour productivity does not affect prices in the Cambridge model (where they are set in relation to normal rather than actual costs) but does affect them in the National Institute model. Thus a fall in output and a (proportionately smaller) fall in employment have two opposing lagged effects in the latter model. On the one hand they have a depressing demand effect upon prices and wages, and on the other the fall in productivity has a cost-increasing effect upon prices. How much difference would it make if both sets of reactions were omitted?

To sum up so far, both models include a pure wage-price price-wage spiral. The National Institute model can be interpreted either as implicitly including a wage-wage spiral, in which case its wage-wage spiral is weak, or as having a long-run coefficient of $\dot{W}$ on $\dot{P}$ of implicitly including a wage-wage spiral, in which case its price-wage spiral is weak, or as having a long-run coefficient of $\dot{W}$ on $\dot{P}$ of 0.82[$0.392 \div (1 - 0.524) = 0.82$] which, as they note, might have been replaced by imposing one of unity as in the Cambridge model. It is interesting to note that, using quarterly data of four-quarter percentage changes for the period 1964 II to 1975 IV, replacing the level of unemployment with the change in employment gives a long-run coefficient of average earnings (wages and salaries combined) upon prices of unity. The Cambridge distinction between wage settlements and actual wages is obviously a good idea in principle. But I still do not know the relative importance of: (i) other wage increases, (ii) past price increases and (iii) the pressure of demand in determining settlements and the intervals between them and hence in determining average actual wages. Nor can I see much hope of ascertaining the relative importance of (i) other wage increases and (ii) past price increases, either econometrically or by studying the genesis of wage claims. After all, a high wage settlement on the part of one group may both cause another group to want one themselves and/or make them think that they are likely to succeed in getting one.

Unfortunately, the distinction is an important one for incomes policy. To the extent that wage increases are demanded primarily to compensate for price increases, an incomes policy which limits such compensation will store up demands for the future. But to the extent that it is relative wages that matter this is not so generally likely. It is true that an incomes policy may create anomalies in relativities, but much of the discontent with anomalies relates to those which existed upon the introduction of the policy and which were frozen by it. Once the policy ends, the resulting stored-up demands to rectify these anomalies will immediately be manifested in wage claims. These, however, will be made on behalf of those workers who resent the anomalies, a fraction of all workers, whereas claims to restore real wage reductions will be more general.

In discussing wages it is important to remember that, according to the employment figures in the Blue-book, central government and local authority employees constituted 15.7 per cent of the working population in employment in 1965 and 21.1 per cent in 1975. Their wages and salaries help determine public authorities' expenditure rather than the costs of marketable output, so that they are relevant to a wage-wage spiral if there is one, rather than to the wage-price, price-wage spiral. The Cambridge model assumes that they bear a fixed relationship to wages in the business sector. Another point about this model is that settlements involve collective bargaining while there are of course many workers who are not covered by collective agreements. Hence the question arises of whether their wages keep up with those of workers whose wages are negotiated collectively.

Collective Agreements

Some information can be got from the New Earnings Surveys. Firstly, using data for the gross weekly earnings of adult male workers whose pay was not affected by absence, taking those national collective agreements under which earnings are reported both in the 1971 and 1976 Surveys and weighting these by the sample numbers in the 1971 Survey I have calculated the following percentage increases in earnings affected by major collective wage agreements: private sector 119; central and local government and NHS 125; public enterprise, excluding coal 135; public enterprise, including coal 143; business sector, excluding coal 125; public sector, excluding coal 129. Over this five-year period as a whole, therefore, there has been a roughly constant relationship between adult male earnings affected by major collective agreements in the business and non-business sectors. Public-sector earnings (where wage bargaining is most centralised) rose faster than private sector earnings, even if coalmining is excluded, but in previous periods which were ones of expansion the opposite was probably true.

A comparison of increases in average gross hourly earnings excluding overtime of full-time men (not, as above, of weekly earnings) between those affected by one of the listed major collective agreements and those not affected has been made from year to year using the New Earnings Survey matched samples, as follows:

Percentage increase	*1972–3*	*1973–4*	*1974–5*	*1975–6*
Affected	+14.2	+15.0	+32.2	+22.0
Not-affected	+13.5	+14.3	+28.0	+19.5

It appears that non-union earnings *have* lagged behind union earnings over this four-year period. (Remember that some of the earnings not affected by one of the major collective agreements will have been affected by minor collective agreements.)

Economists who believe that labour markets behave in textbook fashion argue that, while unions generate higher wages for their members, this is a once and for all phenomenon so that union pushfulness cannot explain a process of rising wages unless union power is continually growing. Perhaps it has been growing, but nonetheless the above comparison does suggest to me that unions play a major part in the wage-wage or price-wage spiral. The textbook approach is of course consistent with the rapid rise in coalmining wages and with the maintenance of the relativities between the market and non-market sectors, but does not seem necessary to explain them.

Social Justice and Relativities

Various attempts have been made to explain the wages explosion of recent years in terms of feelings about social justice concerning relativities. It is conceivable that an extension of the area over which people make comparisons between their own wages and other people's wages could have increased discontent and led to greater and sometimes mutually inconsistent attempts on the part of unions to raise the relative wages of their members. Some recent writings have, however, made me doubt the importance of any such autonomous mechanism as the cause of *accelerated* inflation. Burton [2] has pointed out that, rather like psychoanalysis, the 'relative deprivation hypothesis' can explain almost anything, so that though it may be true it is not useful. Daniel [3] in summarising PEP's 1975 national survey found (page eighteen) 'that between 1962 and 1975 nothing measurable had changed, with regard to the extent that people felt relatively badly off or the groups against whom they spontaneously compared their own position'. In the same paper, (page 23) he summarised part of another study as showing that 'where the comparability of the earnings or increases of some other group of workers had played a part in the negotiations, the group or groups of workers used for purposes of comparison had been those doing similar types of job locally'. These findings seem to me to rule out the notion of an autonomous wage-wage spiral as the root of our troubles but do not destroy, indeed they reinforce, the notion that rises in the cost of living and comparability are the factors which cause wages to rise by much the same amount in different parts of the economy.

The fundamental difficulty is that wage increases *do* make their beneficiaries better off (or prevent them from becoming worse off) even though they do not make everybody better off. This appears to be widely recognised. A recent sample survey reported in the press showed a majority of respondents to believe that an incomes policy would be good for the country and a minority to believe that one would be good for them personally. The public, in short, is sensible.

The use of the term social contract was thus an appropriate recognition of the nature of the problem. So long as a wage increase in excess of productivity growth in any collective agreement either deprives third parties of real income and transfers some of it to the employees or avoids a transfer of real income from them towards third parties, those employees will want and frequently obtain such an excessive wage increase. It is no use telling them that rapid wage increases lead to unemployment, even when it is true, if it is other people who become unemployed.

Implications for Policy

When there are externalities, as there are here, they ought to be internalised or removed. There seem to be three logical possibilities. One is the social contract method. A second is to increase the elasticities of demand for their products facing employers and hence increase their derived elasticities of demand for labour and to make the heights of these demand curves independent of the wage level. A social contract internalises the externalities, while stabilising MV, appreciating the currency in line with world prices, removing trade barriers and encouraging competition diminishes or removes them. Finally, the economic system can be changed!

A social contract which properly internalised the externalities would have to be as complex as the labour market and this, I suppose, means that it is totally impracticable. The only kind of agreement that can be negotiated on a tripartite basis, whether it be given the name of Statement of Intent or Social Contract, is one that is simple. And a simple agreement which interferes with or supersedes the complex network of local and shop-floor collective bargaining cannot endure for more than a year or two, as we now know very well. Consequently, the most that can be hoped for from any agreement is that it temporarily dampens the wage-wage and price-wage spiral during a period of major disturbance.

Therefore, I agree with the idea that in 1965–9 an incomes policy should have been introduced to make (an earlier) devaluation effective, instead of being used in the hope of avoiding devaluation as in fact happened. In 1970–5 I would have again introduced an incomes policy following the oil-price increase or (if I had been clever enough) in response to the commodity boom. In both cases, the policy would have aimed at preventing the rise in import prices from serving as justification for wage and salary increases and would have included measures to protect the low-paid and social security recipients. The argument would have been that a need to change the terms of trade or to accept a change in them makes us poorer, that real earnings must therefore fall or rise only slowly and that, as the burden of this ought to be assumed only by those able to bear it, a package of redistributive measures to protect the poor was a necessary part of the policy. Thus I would have sought agreement that, firstly, that part of the rise in the cost of living due to import price increases did not justify wage or salary increases and, secondly, that tax increases on most people were necessary to make tax reductions or benefit increases possible for the 'poor'. The decomposition of the cost of living index into an external and a domestic component would have provided the necessary statistical background for this.

Apart from the timing and justification of incomes policy, this approach would have differed from the one actually followed in that it would not have included any attempt to improve the relative wages of the low-paid. Such an improvement may be desirable, but my approach would have taken care of the poor by working on the disposable incomes of poor *families* rather than on the pre-tax earnings attached to low paid *jobs*. An attempt to raise the relative pay of the latter is unlikely to command the assent of those higher up the earnings ladder. Any narrowing of differentials can only come from long-term structural changes in the labour market and requires correspondingly long-term policies.

If incomes policies had been adopted in order to weaken the inflationary spiral in response to import price increases, it would seem only realistic to refrain from having them in other circumstances. They would thus constitute an occasional salutary recognition that the rest of the world does not owe the United Kingdom a living but would do nothing for purely domestic inflation.

Let us now turn to the second of the three logical possibilities listed above. This might look rather like a return to free trade and the gold standard, extending far beyond my terms of reference in any case. All I shall discuss here therefore, having raised the basic question about whether and how demand elasticities can be raised, is the kind of prices and incomes policy which operates entirely upon the demand side of the market by preventing firms from paying more than an approved increase in their wage and salary bills.

The main advantage of such a policy is that it does not supersede local and shop-floor bargaining or perpetuate within-firm anomalies existing upon the introduction of the policy. This is because it fixes the average wage increase rather than setting a norm which becomes universal. The main problem of such a policy is the choice of sanction, where one possibility is price control and the other is to impose a fine or tax on excess wage increases. In either case there must be detailed and regular investigation of firms' accounts. With price control the authorities would have to make detailed decisions about the details of price structures and check that domestic sales were not treated as export sales. Presumarly this sort of thing is what the Price Commission has been doing and it horrifies me. Our NBPI investigations, being one-off, were conducted flexibly and produced useful suggestions for structural change, but even so they distracted management attention from the job of managing. While some such inquisitions are a necessary evil in order to secure adherence to rules of competitive behaviour, the routine and rigidity of a Price Code seems to me to be unavoidably detrimental to enterprise. The only counter-advantage is that the stricter and more continuous surveillance of large firms does something to restore the balance between them and smaller firms, but this is a very negative point.

The possibility of levying a tax or fine on excessive wage increases (and of simply prohibiting them in the case of public enterprises) is thus the less unattractive of the two. In either case, the allowable wage-bill would have to vary proportionately with the number of employees or, preferably, with the number of employee-hours worked. If overtime were included in the latter the British disease of excessive overtime would be exacerbated, while if it were excluded useful overtime would be discouraged. There would be an incentive to employ more low-paid workers (and part-time workers if numbers rather than hours worked formed the base), there would (on the same assumption) be a tendency to reduce the fragmentation of negotiations, so that the side-effects would not all be unfavourable. Nevertheless, as a permanent system of checking inflation, it is not an attractive one.

A prices policy is normally demanded by the TUC as a complement to an incomes policy. One reason for this is that if prices are restrained as much as wages, the wages restraint does not hurt. But if the purpose of an incomes policy is to replace a 20 per cent price rise and a 17 per cent wage rise with a 3 per cent price rise and no wage increase (that is to accept a fall in real incomes imposed by the cupidity of foreigners or the vagaries of nature without undergoing an inflationary spiral) one cannot expect prices to be restrained as much as wages. Hence the only acceptable reason for demanding a prices policy to match the incomes policy is the feeling that non-wage non-salary incomes should share the burden. If this can be achieved by dividend restraint and by taxation instead, the case for a prices policy seems weak.

References

[1] Ball, R. J., Burns, T. and Laury, J. S. E., 'The role of exchange rate changes in balance of payments adjustment: the United Kingdom case', *The Economic Journal*, No. 345, Vol. 87, March 1977.

[2] Burton, J., 'A critique of the relative deprivation hypothesis of wage inflation', *Scottish Journal of Political Economy*, Vol. 24, No. 1, February 1977.

[3] Daniel, W. W., *The Next Stage of Incomes Policy*, PEP, Vol. XLII, No. 568, December 1976.

11 The Balance of Payments

by John Williamson

Introduction

A question of fundamental importance in shaping attitudes to demand management policy is that of the nature of the effective constraint on the level of output. The London Business School takes the view that this constraint is provided by the balance of payments. The CEPG view is similar insofar as the authors refuse to fatalistically accept the external constraint, and are hence led to place great stress on the importance of securing adequate expenditure switching. David Laidler takes the contrary view: that the level of output is essentially constrained by the inflationary pressures generated by too high a level of demand, rather than by any medium-term difficulties in inducing sufficient expenditure switching to reconcile a payments target with an 'internal balance' target. The National Institute paper does not seem to contain any constraint on demand expansion. It is true that their model has an expectations-augmented Phillips curve (albeit one in which the authors have 'little faith') while expenditure switching is rather easy. This might lead one to suppose they concur with Laidler – until one solves their equation for the Phillips curve and finds that the natural rate of unemployment is almost 11 per cent, vastly in excess of the level that their preferred policies are designed to produce. The explanation of this paradox is that whenever expectations get uncomfortably augmented the equation is shut off by introduction of an incomes policy. The conjunction of easy expenditure switching with an absence of any effective demand pressures on the wage-price level leaves me at a loss to understand why the authors are apparently content with unemployment as high as 1.8 per cent.

Balance of Payments Constraint

My own view has long been that it is unnecessary, and therefore irrational, to allow output in the medium term to be constrained by the balance of payments. Reflection on the London Business School and Cambridge models has, however, led me to conclude that the alternative view contains an important if limited element of truth. I shall therefore commence by examining the alternative view as presented with particular force by the London Business School.

Consider their theorem previously articulated in Ball, Burns and Laury [1], which asserts that devaluation will produce no medium-run expenditure switching since the price level will rise in proportion to the devaluation and the system will return to its original position. Presumably the fundamental belief underlying this assertion is that the income distribution achieved in a country reflects some form of optimisation process subject to constraints, and is free of money illusion as reflected in rigid-wage assumptions or the theoretically-discredited $\dot{w} - \ldots\ldots + \alpha\dot{p}$, $\alpha < 1$, type of wage equation. How, it is then implicitly asked, can a change in a nominal variable like the exchange rate be expected to alter the outcome of a rational optimisation process? It is an important question, but one with an important answer: devaluation will alter the outcome of the optimisation process *if the constraints subject to which optimisation takes place include the pressure of demand*, unless fiscal policy is inflation-neutral and the money supply is elastic. To see this, consider a model in which wage changes are determined by a Phillips curve. The initial effects of devaluation include both the generation of price inflation and a stimulus to exports through increased competitiveness. If the inflation curtails real absorption, either through the fiscal drag emphasised by the London Business School or the monetary deflation emphasised by monetarists (or both; or by discretionary policy), then the new equilibrium must be a point at which net exports have risen; for restoration of equilibrium requires that unemployment revert to the natural rate. Devaluation therefore causes medium-term expenditure switching. (The error that Ball, Burns and Laury made when they considered demand-pressure effects [1, p. 7] was to fail to note that at the point they treat as the new equilibrium absorption is lower than before while relative prices are the same, so that unemployment must exceed the natural rate.)

The question of whether there is some form of trade-off between unemployment and inflation is therefore as central to the theory of payments adjustment as it has long been recognised to be to the theory of inflation. The papers in Part I take very different attitudes to this issue as well. Laidler has a highly significant trade-off explicit in his equation (2); neither the London Business School nor the Cambridge Group has any trade-off, despite the fact that at least the former has searched for one; while the National Institute has a trade-off in which it does not believe. Other authors have reached similarly conflicting conclusions, so that if one had to rely on econometric evidence for the British economy one would indeed be in a difficult situation. There is, however, no reason to take such a narrow view of the class of legitimate evidence. One might, for example, look at the econometric evidence from other economies, which is predominantly favourable to the existence of a trade-off; from this standpoint British experience might be regarded as the observation in the 5 per cent tail of the frequency distribution of international experience. Or one might recall that plausible asymptotic properties of macro models depend critically upon the existence of a trade-off in some form. Or one might ask why Kenyans do not have 'real wage targets' as high as Swedes, and conclude that the answer is that they prefer living in employed poverty to starving while demanding wages at which no one can afford to employ them. Or one might examine in detail some of the British evidence against a trade-off, such as that contained in the influential Henry, Sawyer and Smith paper [3], and note that their preferred theory (that of Sargan) was originally formulated with an unemployment term and that this remained significant until 1966. This was the year before the opportunity cost of being unemployed was first substantially reduced – an event that was not reflected in the estimating equation and whose absence robs the finding of the subsequent insignificance of unemployment of any persuasiveness. In short, my own view remains that there is an overwhelming presumption that raising the pressure of demand tends to exacerbate inflation.

However, the evidence that this does not work through a simple (including expectations-augmented) Phillips curve is now fairly strong. The alternative formulation that must now be regarded as the front-runner is that of Sargan [5], in which workers form a target real wage (as in the Cambridge model) which is dependent upon the level of unemployment (unlike the Cambridge model, where real wage targets are exogenous and emphatically free of market influence – a circumstance that first brought the Kenyan conundrum noted above to my mind). Incorporating this hypothesis into the standard type of general equilibrium model used by most economists for balance of payments theorising leads to some interesting conclusions.

First, consider starting from the typical postwar British position of internal balance and external deficit and ask what sort of demand management policy is needed to accompany a devaluation designed to remedy the external deficit. The answer is that it is one involving deflation not just sufficiently large to release resources for the balance of payments (as we have long taught), but one that will produce enough unemployment to induce workers to accept the lower real wage target consistent with the release of resources from internal absorption. This story seems more consistent with British experience following the 1967 devaluation than do those implied by previous theories. The same conclusion follows from Ball, Burns and Laury [1] in the version where a Phillips curve with a unitary coefficient on the price term is introduced. A very important question raised by the theoretical demonstration that adjustment of a deficit requires transitory unemployment is the extent to which that transitory unemployment can be reduced by accompanying deflation by devaluation. It is a question that the large models should be able to answer.

Second, consider the problem of designing a policy to achieve full employment, starting off from a position of unemployment and external balance where a country has been treating its demand policies as payments-constrained. With a conventional Phillips curve the necessary policy of demand expansion must be inflationary, because it will both depreciate the exchange rate and add to the pressure for wage increases. With the Sargan hypothesis there is also a third effect at work: the additional output produced by reflation helps satisfy wage demands and thus acts as a counter-inflationary force. It would seem to follow that once a deflation has gone sufficiently far to reduce real wage demands to the levels that can be financed out of existing production plus the additional output that could be produced by reflation, it may be possible to eliminate the residue of inflation while reflating. Whether Britain has now reached this happy state seems to me the critical question determining whether reflation is now economically responsible; and the considerable remaining doubt on this issue perhaps provides the intellectual case for delaying significant reflation until the outcome of the wage round is evident.

The best available evidence therefore seems to lead to a model where expenditure switching is possible (unlike the London Business School model), but where it is distinctly more difficult and painful than implied in the National Institute or Laidler models. This position is closest to that taken by Cambridge, who are thereby led to emphasise the importance of securing sufficient expenditure switching to sustain adequate levels of demand. It is therefore natural to examine briefly their further view that devaluation is an inferior instrument to import controls for securing the necessary degree of expenditure switching.

Devaluation or Import Controls

In part the Cambridge Group preference for import controls seems to stem from a new version of an older reason for doubting the efficacy of devaluation; elasticity pessimism. The actual price elasticities assumed, 2.5 for exports and 0.5 for imports, can certainly not be criticised as unreasonably low. Nevertheless, their model appears to deliver a low improvement in the balance of trade per unit twist to the inflationary spiral and loss to the terms of trade because it is assumed that only 30 per cent of a gain in relative costs is reflected in reduced export prices. The residual 70 per cent increases export profitability but this does not seem to have any supply-side effect on the volume of exports [2, p. 36].

Another important base for the heterodox Cambridge Group preference would seem to be the supposed differences between the two strategies in their impact on inflation and income distribution. There is no question that devaluation is inflationary, nor that insofar as it succeeds in securing expenditure switching it redistributes income from wages to profits: the question is whether import controls are very different in these respects. The view that they are rests on the strict cost-plus equation that is used [2, p. 38]. I am no believer in the 'law of one price', but the presumption that there is *some* arbitrage effect on domestic prices is too strong to be completely dissipated by their negative finding on this issue. Even if there is some residual advantage in these respects to the protectionist strategy, it is one that could be rather easily offset through fiscal policy if profits were in fact regarded as in danger of taking too large a share of national income.

In my view the strongest claim that can be made for the protectionist strategy is that it might be significantly faster acting than a devaluation strategy. Against this one has to weigh the argument that protectionism would inevitably distort output and investment incentives away from the firms and sectors that have competed successfully on world markets towards those that have failed to compete with imports. So long as the Cambridge Group refuse to acknowledge this point (let alone answer it, though that is of course impossible) they will not have even started to establish their case for a 'lets follow Uruguay's example' strategy.

The Level of Competitiveness

The earlier discussion suggested that achieving and maintaining a level of competitiveness adequate to permit operation of the economy at the natural rate should be an over-riding objective of policy. Deviating from this objective in order to hold a particular exchange rate (1964–7), or allowing appreciation so as to terminate inflation quickly, or embarking on a free float because one cannot make up one's mind on the appropriate target for competitiveness, mortgages the future. This conclusion obviously raises the question: how much do the various teams claim to know about the appropriate target for competitiveness, and do their views agree? With a view to answering this question Table 11.1 shows the principal indicator of export competitiveness employed in each of the four papers for the period 1964–76, together with a similar series for the indicator that I have customarily used and a simple average of the preceding five measures.

Table 11.1 Export competitiveness, 1964–76 (1970 = 100)[a]

	NIESR	CEPG	LBS	DEWL	JHW	Average
1964	103.7	106.3	103.6	111.7	102.6	105.6
1965	105.1	106.8	105.9	113.9	103.5	107.0
1966	107.1	108.3	108.1	114.2	105.4	108.6
1967	105.6	106.9	107.9	112.9	104.4	107.5
1968	99.3	97.3	96.7	98.8	98.9	98.2
1969	97.8	99.1	98.6	99.5	101.1	99.2
1970	100	100	100	100	100	100
1971	100.0	106.6	105.3	104.5	100.9	103.5
1972	97.1	109.8	105.0	105.8	102.7	104.1
1973	90.4	101.5	96.7	99.6	95.5	96.7
1974	87.5	93.8	97.8	99.1	94.4	94.5
1975	91.7	97.6	104.4	104.9	97.3	99.2
1976	91.7	92.3	97.5	n.a.	95.7	(94.3)
'Equilibrium'[b]	—	99.2	103.8	105.0	—	—

[a] *A higher number indicates lower competitiveness. The sources are as follows:*

NIESR: *relative price of exports of manufactures.*
CEPG: *export competitiveness, Table 1.2.*
LBS: *EER/PPP1, Table 3.5.*
DEWL: *consumer prices/world prices × exchange rate, Table 2.4.*
JHW: *unit value of UK exports of manufactures/unit value of exports of manufactures of all countries, from* National Institute Economic Review.

[b] *Equilibrium levels of competitiveness are expressed in terms of the average measures shown in the final column. The sources for these estimates are as follows:*

CEPG: *the reference to maintaining 1969 competitiveness.*
LBS: *the reference to a 'correct' rate in 1971–2.*
DEWL: *the reference to an equilibrium rate having been re-established by mid-1972 (before the pound was unpegged and promptly floated down!).*

The first thing to note is the embarrassing extent to which these alternative measures of essentially the same thing diverge. In one case, indeed, a systematic difference is built into construction of the series: both the London Business School and Laidler indices are based on comparisons of consumer prices, but the former specifically assume that maintenance of constant competitiveness requires that United Kingdom consumer prices rise 1.2 per cent per annum less than those in competitor countries. The rationale is the smaller gap between productivity growth in the traded-good and non-traded-good sectors in slow-growing Britain, and is correct if the comparison has to be made in terms of consumer prices – though I do not know why anyone should choose to make this comparison in terms of a measure so remote from export competitiveness. Even discounting Laidler's index on that ground, however, the differences are quite sharp: for example, between 1973 and 1974 competitiveness improved by some 7.5 per cent on the Cambridge measure while it deteriorated by one per cent on the London Business School. It is time some serious work was done with a view to comparing alternative measures of export competitiveness and deciding which one performs best; until that is done any policy of managing the exchange rate with a view to preserving an appropriate level of competitiveness is bound to be something of a gamble. Such work on this subject as I am aware of points to export prices even though this means using unit value indices [4]; hence my own choice. To be neutral, however, I conduct further discussion in terms of the average measure shown in the final column of Table 11.1.

Three of the four teams provide fairly explicit answers as to the level of export competitiveness that they believe would have reconciled external balance with whatever sort of internal target or balance the model incorporates in the middle of the period under review. The Cambridge concept for the internal target is a normative full employment concept; the Laidler concept is the natural rate; while the London Business School concept is the unemployment rate that exists when income has just risen to the point where imports match the exports that can be sold at the exogenous real wage, given the pressure of demand in the rest of the world. The National Institute is exceptional in revealing no awareness that this might be an interesting issue, but since their preferred solution involved a 15 per cent devaluation in 1965 one may assume that they would tend to agree with the Cambridge Group. The answers provided also display significant divergences. It is interesting to examine whether these can be explained by different policy targets. So far as the external target is concerned, although none of the papers are very explicit there is no evidence of any dissent from the pre-oil price increase consensus that a modest current surplus approaching £500 million per annum was appropriate. There is more divergence on internal targets. The Cambridge Group mention approvingly that their preferred strategy would have reduced unemployment 'below half a million' (2.2 per cent), so I interpret their target as perhaps 1.8 per cent. Laidler's estimate of the natural rate is 2.8 per cent; and the London Business School preferred strategy seems to yield an average unemployment rate of about 2.3 per cent over 1970–4 (inferred from Table 3.7). I exclude 1975 from the calculation because I agree with the London Business School that the practically-achievable level of output is heavily influenced by the world conjuncture. (This leads me to regard the counter-factual dreams of British booms in 1967 and 1975 indulged in by the National Institute and Laidler respectively as implausible.) These targets are at least ordinally consistent with the variations in equilibrium competitiveness shown in Table 11.1. My own back-of-the-envelope calculation as to whether they can explain the whole difference goes as follows:

(i) 1 per cent unemployment is roughly equivalent to 2 per cent of output;
(ii) which implies a deterioration of perhaps 0.8 per cent of GNP in the current balance (holding competitiveness constant);
(iii) which was equal to £440 million in 1972;
(iv) which, using Cambridge figures [2, p. 36] for the response of trade to changes in competitiveness, would have required a real depreciation of some 3.5 per cent to neutralise a cut of 1 per cent in unemployment.

My calculation therefore suggests that differences in targets explain most, though not all, of the different views about the desirable level of competitiveness. However it would be interesting to learn what the large models imply about this issue of the unemployment/competitiveness trade-off holding the external balance constant.

Laidler's estimate of the natural rate is in fact the only guide we have as to an appropriate internal target, given that neither the National Institute nor the Cambridge Group seriously look for asymptotic constraints while the London Business School look for a wrong (external) one. I would therefore conclude that, even giving the benefit of the residual doubts to Cambridge and allowing for somewhat less export pessimism, one would get an estimate of the equilibrium rate in the early 1970s of around 102. This is substantially above any figure recorded since sterling started to float in 1972. The persistence of deficits since that date raises the question as to whether the Cambridge Group are not correct in their belief that there are 'persistent adverse trends in United Kingdom producers' share of world and home markets' at a given level of competitiveness. I should like to argue that some such trend may well exist, but that Cambridge seem to exaggerate its strength; that a target of holding competitiveness at something like 95–8 during the years of oil abundance, using the oil funds to provide assurance of the continuity of sustained but moderate expansion rather than to underwrite a consumer boom, would seem justified; and that the crawling peg would be the best exchange-rate system to reconcile pursuit of a competitiveness target with adequate control of the money supply. Laidler shares the usual monetarist belief that payments imbalances can never be sterilised for long. While often true, the one case where it is clearly false is when the payments' surplus stems from oil royalty payments direct to the government. All the government need do is buy foreign assets rather than spend. However space permits neither an adequate treatment of the strategy that should guide policy in the coming years, nor a post-mortem on the comparative recommendations for the two previous historical episodes called for by the terms of reference. The exploration of some of the basis issues that need resolving before a more literal pursuit of my terms of reference could prove fruitful, and which I have sought to provide will, I hope, make it fairly evident where I would have come out on many of the specific questions.

References

[1] Ball, R. J., Burns, T. and Laury, J. S. E., 'The role of exchange rate changes in balance of payments adjustment – the United Kingdom case', *Economic Journal*, March 1977.

[2] *Economic Policy Review*, March 1977.

[3] Henry, S. G. B., Sawyer, M. C. and Smith, P., 'Models of inflation in the United Kingdom: an evaluation', *National Institute Economic Review*, August 1976.

[4] Junz, H. B. and Rhomberg, R. R., 'Prices and export performance of industrial countries, 1953–63', IMF, *Staff Papers*, July 1965.

[5] Sargan, J. D., 'Wages and prices in the United Kingdom: a study in econometric methodology', in Hart, P. E., Mills, G. and Whitaker, J. K. (eds.), *Econometric Analysis for National Economic Planning*, Butterworth, London, 1964.

PART III

Report of the Discussion

12 The Search for Common Ground

by M. V. Posner

Introduction

Some thirty-five economists whose names are in the back of this book spent two days just before Christmas 1977, under the chairmanship of Robin Matthews, arguing in detail about the issues raised in the papers printed in Parts I and II. I offer in what follows an editor's version of the main themes of this discussion, in a way designed to be read independently of the papers themselves, although the discussion itself made frequent reference to those papers.

There were two issues which were not explicitly down for discussion, but nevertheless rumbled along in the background throughout, and are here brought briefly to the foreground. Their exposure will I trust give some of the flavour of the discussion, and at the same time describe both its scope and its limitations.

The first of these background issues concerns the extent to which 'common ground' should in fact be sought in this sort of discussion. Laidler and the London Business School team, despite the very clear and doctrinally pure line presented in their main papers, showed themselves prepared in discussion to move a long way on such issues as the efficacy of monetary policy and the appropriateness of exchange rate manipulation. But they were notably less forthcoming on the question of incomes policies. The Cambridge Economic Policy Group were not minded to fudge the issues, as they saw them, in any way: in their closing contribution they specifically dissociated themselves from any flavour of monetarist doctrine, and were inclined to assert throughout the importance of a clear and quantitatively-based approach to the major issues discussed. The merit of the Cambridge approach was that it inhibited the editor of these proceedings from searching out a sort of lowest common denominator of policy prescriptions or theoretical perceptions, and brought to the conference a productive toughness of analysis, albeit presented in a velvet glove. The virtue of the more exploratory and tentative approach favoured by other contributors was chiefly that it enabled new perceptions and understandings to be established, at least in the minds of some of us.

This dialectic appeared also on another plane, that of the relevance of the models presented in the first-round papers. Most of the conference participants were not model proprietors, nor have we ever worked in a model team ourselves, and this will also be true of most readers of this volume. I am myself one of this large majority, and I assert bluntly that this is nothing to be ashamed of. But nor is it a form of ignorance, or more properly a lack of experience, of which we should be particularly proud. One of the main purposes of the conference was to bring the knowledge, experience and above all the discipline of the model builders to bear upon policy issues in a manner designed to be accessible to the ordinary political economist. In my view, although we did not succeed completely in this aim, and the Cambridge team in particular felt we could have been more rigorous in our determination to use the model analyses to direct our discussion, we did go a very long way.

The London Business School also have developed a very rigorous approach to the modelling of economic behaviour, and readers of their paper in this volume and their other recent writings will be aware of the ways in which they have dramatically changed their approach to policy simultaneously with changes in the way they have chosen to model the economic system. The argosy of the London Business School's development from their bad old days when they shared the consensus view of the Treasury and National Institute modellers to their homecoming as 'international monetarists' was reasonably well known before the conference began; but it was fascinating to watch the team set sail again towards the new goal – that of 'international Keynesianism'. This continued interaction between modelling and policy recommendations is one way in which models can be used.

The Cambridge Group's model also develops (we heard, for instance, how research was proceeding on the modelling of wage settlements) and we were all brought to understand the determination of the Cambridge team to reflect in their model and in their prescriptions the empirical facts as they understood them, irrespective of theoretical argumentation. Indeed the Cambridge team were the strongest exponents of the importance of modelling, and the essential discipline of analysing policy prescriptions from the different teams on a common analytical base. As I make clear at the relevant place in the record, it is hoped that the confrontation between the main model building teams will continue outside the conference, and outside the pages of this book.

A more tentative and pragmatic approach to the importance of models was demonstrated by the National Institute team, and probably by most of those conference participants who had been responsible for policy advice in Whitehall over the last decade. For them, model building was a useful tool, and whatever enlightenment could be coaxed from the intransigent data would be welcome. But on most crucial issues the data turn out to be either Delphic in the way they speak, or even plain silent. Blackaby told us that all attempts to model wage behaviour at the National Institute had failed to a greater or lesser degree, and he made explicit the conclusion he drew from this, namely that successful political intervention in the wage-fixing process was possible. The model, according to this approach, was a way of organising our ignorance in the most helpful way, and of making various assumptions mutually consistent and exposed to view: but to ask more than that of it was to ask the impossible. Even as a forecasting tool the model could not be allowed to operate on its own; and its role in policy analysis was again the subsidiary one of exhibiting, in simulation mode, the possible implications of certain policy measures on certain assumptions.

For Laidler, the model had started as a purely expositional device, and he had of course neither the resources nor the background necessary to build the large and complex model of the other three teams. But in fairness to Laidler, it has to be said that, as he explains, his model and its estimation had led him to come to some rather different conclusions on crucial points from those which his theoretical presuppositions would have led him to expect.

On this second background issue, the use of models, the conference reached no more unanimity of purpose than on the first. Goodhart had asserted in his paper, 'Econometrics has not, at least so far, provided any alternative for basic judgement, only some quantitative dressing and support for such judgement', while Turvey on the last day's discussion concluded bluntly 'econometrics was an infant science'. However, I think that many of us carried an impression from the conference nearer that of Peston, who felt that the contribution to be made by large models to the understanding of Britain's political economy had not by any means been exhausted, and that more resources should be put into their development and discussion.

The Underlying Economic Issues

In this session of the discussion, we concentrated on four main groups of topics raised by the treatment in the papers.

Wages, Prices and the Exchange Rate

All four first-round authors expressed views on this issue, and the papers by Peston, Goodhart, Turvey and Williamson all refer to it as well. A summary of the doctrines put forward in the first-round papers would read as follows. The Cambridge Group hold that the wage bargain is about real wages; that cost-push forces are set up by any changes which compress real wages below their target level; that depreciation of the real exchange rate depresses real wage incomes at least temporarily unless offsetting changes in taxation can be made; and that as a matter of fact the income and price elasticities for traded goods are such that quite large changes in manufacturers wage costs are necessary if the exchange rate is to be used as an instrument for materially increasing output levels over what would otherwise have occurred. It follows that real depreciation on the scale required is likely to be very inflationary, and therefore difficult or impossible to achieve and maintain. (In discussion at the conference it was suggested that this impossibility *could* be overcome if the government ran large deficits to maintain real consumption and these deficits were accommodated by unusually large financial surpluses in the private sector. However this possibility is not countenanced by the Cambridge Group.) If incomes policies were to be used to moderate inflation under these circumstances, the strain on those policies would be very great. It would be even greater than over the last couple of years because the compression of real wages that has occurred in the period 1975–7 has been largely the mirror image of the big boost to real wage incomes given by the acceleration of the inflationary process in 1973–5.

The National Institute go about things in a rather different way. They set the exchange rate so as to preserve export competitiveness, forecast money incomes, prices, savings, government expenditure, taxation and net exports in the normal way. This yields a good balance of payments and some spare productive capacity, which to some extent the Institute are prepared to use up by expansionary fiscal policy. It is this reasoning which gives rise to their tax cut policy, not a cunning play of a desired path for real wage incomes, and a net saving in the company sector which would act as a sort of 'free variable' enabling the Institute to achieve its real wage target without adding to aggregate effective demand.

The outcome for real wages is then whatever it turns out to be – and the Institute will say that the results recorded in their tables for real wage incomes are within the bounds of plausibility and not such, on the basis of their understanding of the data, as would be likely to stimulate extra cost push pressures in the wage market. The pattern of accumulation of financial assets by the various home sectors of the economy is a matter of interest for them, but not of crucial importance. If they were asked to be much more pessimistic about the international trade elasticities, particularly about income propensities to import, an issue pressed hard by Peston in discussion, they would become more worried about implications for real wage incomes and cost push pressures.

Nevertheless it was suggested that the National Institute results do contain an implausible pattern of tax cuts and large financial surpluses in the private sector. One plain man explanation of how this mechanism might work, not I think acceptable for differing reasons to either of the protagonists, would go as follows. The government would cut direct taxes on wage earners, thus increasing post-tax real incomes while keeping real wage costs to manufacturers at whatever level would otherwise have been reached. These extra real incomes will be spent, and the cash will go to swell company profits. But the companies will not spend their extra cash flows, and therefore company sector acquisition of financial assets will increase to the size necessary roughly to accommodate the increase in the public sector deficit. In any case, the National Institute respond to this suggestion by referring us to Table 4.16 on page 122, in which they show that any abnormal increase in private sector net savings occurs in the *personal* sector, quite otherwise than I have just suggested, and that in any case this increase in real terms is less than one-quarter over the five-year period, say, 1977–81.

Laidler believes that it is possible to have the wrong exchange rate, as a result of past history or past mistakes, and he allows a small depreciation in his simulation of the 1964 episode. But he believes it is possible to determine the path of both money wage and price movements at home by combining an appropriate rate of growth of the money supply, without any need to invoke special incomes policies, which he believes to have been positively damaging in their effects in the past. Although he was not entirely explicit on this point either in his paper or in discussion, it seems that his view about 1977 onwards is that it will, alas, be very difficult for Britain to pursue a sound monetary policy consistent with price stability at home and full employment. Laidler saw this issue as one aspect of the general problem of resource allocation. But one way of explaining this type of problem in the North Sea oil context seems to me, as editor, as follows. The two aims of price stability and full employment could be made consistent only if there were both an easement of regulation and an increase in the entrepreneurial will to investment overseas, thus dissipating the balance of payments surplus in a benign way. Real consumption can rise as a result of North Sea oil, without raising the domestic price level at all, through an improvement in the commodity terms of trade associated with an appreciation of the exchange rate. However, to be consistent with continued full employment, it would require a moderation in the rate of increase in money wages, and this Laidler acknowledges may not be immediately realistic; hence the pessimism. But if, instead of concentrating on the terms of trade (which need not change at all, save for statistical problems) we consider the increase in available resources, we can then envisage the economy merely substituting out of oil imports into imports of brandy and foreign holidays and more Japanese tape recorders per head than would otherwise be owned. However, if this is to be the route by which North Sea goodies are spread around, some easement of fiscal policy will possibly be required (along the Cambridge or National Institute lines) and little or no appreciation of the exchange rate.

The London Business School approach to this topic, in its most rigid and rigorous form, takes competitiveness, by some test, as a constant, which may be subject to stochastic influence, but cannot in principle diverge from its equilibrium value. This extreme position, however, the London Business School explained in discussion, was not the one they wished to defend. There would always be circumstances – the aftermath of a war, a once-for-all disturbance of the price level (perhaps like Spain since the death of Franco or France in 1968), cataclysmic events of one sort or another – which would lead to disequilibria that it was sensible to accommodate through once-for-all increases in the domestic money supply and once-for-all changes in the exchange rate. Equally, although this point was not much pursued in discussion, it was recognised that structural economic or technological disturbances could also change trading patterns in such a way that previously established relative real exchange rates were inappropriate. At this point there was a feeling that the London Business School doctrine was perhaps not grossly dissimilar to some versions of the Bretton Woods adjustable peg system to which some of the more senior members of the conference had adhered in the past. A useful helping hand to those seeking to understand the place of purchasing power parity theory in the London Business School doctrine was offered by Burns, who pointed out that in principle their model could include a favourable response of exports to the increase in profits which would occur when the exchange rate fell, but the world price in world currency of home exports was maintained unchanged. The London Business School had been unable to find such an effect statistically; they did not believe that it could be very large; and in the long run even this effect would wash out as prices rose. But at least there was no dispute about the analysis.

There was much discussion of the relationship between import prices, the general price level, and the wage level, and the alleged property of the British economy that in the recent past the coefficient of wages on prices had been close to unity after a short time-lag, implying that real wage incomes could not be permanently depressed by a change in the exchange rate. This result was described in a shorthand way during the discussion as the absence of money illusion; and MacDougall, followed by several other speakers, suggested that the speed of adjustment of wages and prices was now much faster than, say, after the 1949 devaluation, and the efficacy of exchange rate manipulation was also now much less. Two special points were however stressed by the modellers here. First, the Cambridge Group pointed out that it was money wage *incomes* that could be expected to respond in this way, and not money wage *costs*: and post-tax wage incomes (real take home pay) could of course be influenced by government tax policy as well as by the level of money wage settlements and the price level. The argument here refers back to the Cambridge Group argument about the behaviour of the government budget in exchange rate simulations; but other speakers drew the implication that, in periods when the exchange rate was being deliberately forced down by government, it might become particularly important to lower both taxation and government expenditure – extra pounds in the ordinary man's pocket might be of more value in inducing wage restraint than a continuation of public expenditure at its previously determined level.

Secondly the National Institute argued that even if we assumed that there did exist an expectations augmented Phillips curve, and a coefficient of wages on prices which eventually approximated to unity, it did not follow that exchange rate changes were ineffective. The wage-price relationship took time to work through, and the time-lags on that relationships were greater than the time-lags of the response of net export volumes to exchange rate changes. Several speakers pointed out that the implication of this approach was that one original disequilibrium might have to be corrected by a whole sequence of depreciations, one following another as the wage-price relationship eventually worked itself out. This analytical point was not resisted, but several speakers comforted themselves that there would eventually be dynamic effects (export-led growth?) which would make it unnecessary to depreciate further. As editor, I am bound to say, first, that this optimism can apply logically equally as well to the Cambridge Group's chosen weapon of import restrictions; and secondly, that while these dynamic effects may well have characterised German and Japanese experience, and more relevantly French experience after the two devaluations of President de Gaulle, I have yet to meet a benign dynamic effect walking down Whitehall.

There was not much argument about the Cambridge 'real wage resistance' approach. Flemming asked pointedly what forces determined the level or rate of increase of desired or expected real wages, the implication being that, like the Keynesian rate of interest or the pre-war Oxford 'mark up' theory of pricing, the desired real wage rate was left hanging by its own boot straps. There was a general disposition to accept that real wage resistance was an important factor, but perhaps not a willingness to believe that any target was entirely immutable. The Cambridge Group stressed that the level of the target is not determined by economic factors and trends alone, but may be strongly influenced by incomes policies or the political situation; and therefore wage inflation cannot be modelled as a purely endogenous phenomenon as all versions of Phillips curve theory purport to do. However the way in which previous price and tax changes influence negotiations and the way this in turn feeds through into earnings can be modelled; this is what the Cambridge Group analysis attempts to do.

Laidler interjected three points. First, he reminded us that in his analysis it was not the wage-price relationship which was crucial, but the relationship between the target for unemployment that the authorities chose, and the level of unemployment to which the economy would itself tend at any, property anticipated, steady state rate of inflation. If the target and the 'natural' level of unemployment were identical, any chosen rate of inflation could be reached after suitable time-lags. If the target and natural rates diverged, then the rate of inflation was out of control. But secondly, he admitted that expectations had become extremely volatile in the last few years (perhaps a richer and more accurate statement than the earlier agreement about the decay of money illusion), and that this fact presented grave difficulties to those responsible for the administration of policy. At least this second point of Laidler's received general assent.

Thirdly, he reminded us of the unresolved question of the relationship between wage controls and the exchange rate. On one doctrine, with a given rate of increase in the money supply, wage controls which constrained the rate of increase of money wages below the path they would otherwise have followed, would tend to maintain the exchange rate above what would otherwise have been its path. On the other doctrine, these wage controls would lead to excess money supply which would stimulate outward capital flows, helping to bring the exchange rate down. He reported that of course he had a disposition to believe the second of these doctrines, that the empirical evidence as he understood it did not provide the criterion for choosing between them, but that it was necessary in fact to decide which theory was right for practical policy purposes. (This issue bears upon the question of *whether* exchange rate manipulation might be achieved for example, I myself prefer the second doctrine, if I must choose one or the other.)

Most of our discussion was based on the implicit assumption that an exchange rate change required a change in the terms of trade for it to become effective; this change in the terms of trade was likely to depress real wage costs per unit of output to the manufacturer in absolute terms, and relatively to real profits per unit of output. Both Matthews and to some extent Peston challenged these assumptions – they reminded us that an exchange rate change could alter the relative attractiveness of activity in, respectively, the tradeable and non-tradeable sectors of the economy. This sort of change need not effect the international terms of trade at all.

An example (not offered at the conference) may be useful here. Comparing two equilibrium conditions, with a zero balance on trading account in both cases, it might be possible to run an Oxford college either with a large number of college servants who would clean manually, or instead with a number of imported items of automatic cleaning equipment, operated by the undergraduates themselves: in the second case, displaced college servants could obtain employment in the Morris motor works (those were the days), leading to increased exports of British cars to pay for increased imports of electric vacuum cleaners. No change in the relative real wages of British and foreign workers in manufacturing industry would be involved, and no change in the government's fiscal stance. What would be required, presumably, is some appropriate price stimulus to induce workers to shift from one line of activity to another and it is this stimulus which is provided by a movement in the exchange rate: but it is not the class of wage earners who lose, merely the class of those employed in or employing factors of production in the non-traded goods sector.

Indeed, in the traditional literature on the exchange rate it has always been recognised that a small country, a price taker in both the market in which it buys and the market in which it sells, can have no control over its terms of trade at all. But exchange rate changes might still, for a country of this sort, influence the degree to which it was integrated with the world economy.

I cannot pretend that this particular aspect of the exchange rate controversy was fully aired at the conference. I think it is a property of all the models presented to us that, for them, the exchange rate is a way of varying the terms of trade, and hence real wage costs per unit of output, although of course some contributors believe that in practice it is extremely difficult to influence the real wage in this way. It may be that even those most sceptical about exchange rate manipulation as a way of influencing real wages would be prepared to envisage a 'Matthews' type use of the exchange rate instrument to increase the scope of the traded sector of a home economy. But this must be analysed elsewhere.

In this debate, parts of which took place at different stages during the two days of the conference, there did seem to be some considerable meeting of minds on the analysis of the inflation/wage rate/exchange rate nexus. Much does depend on the quantities: the size of the exchange rate adjustment required; the speed of the reaction of wage settlements; the effect of higher levels of employment on the personal tax rates consistent with any target balance of payments; the extent to which parts of the private sector might be prepared to accumulate financial assets more rapidly than normal; the degree of universality of purchasing power parity relationships; and so on. A newly appointed Chancellor, with five years ahead of him and no immediate crisis, might well feel that the arguments provided at least the raw material for the construction of a decent policy paper on this group of topics. (I fear this boastful claim may be read as irony. It is not so intended.)

The Balance of Payments Constraint and how it might be Eased

Those who lacked absolute faith in the exchange rate as an instrument for balance of payments adjustment (and few of us had overriding confidence in the availability or efficacy of the exchange rate weapon) were prepared to join in some limited argument about the extent to which balance of payments difficulties really constrained the domestic performance of the economy, and the extent to which that constraint might be lifted by import restrictions. There was general agreement that the balance of payments operates as a constraint on government *policy*, and some agreement also that, for a complex mixture of historical reasons, the constraint was more binding for Britain than others of her trading partners with similar ratios of imports to GDP. There was some dispute about whether very large countries like the United States were subject to any policy constraints at all from external causes, with the London Business School asserting that even the United States could not ignore the eventual effect on its exchange rate and therefore its domestic price level of domestic policy measures; but this point was not much pursued. More difficult was the traditional Board of Trade argument that, policy aside, what constrained British *performance* was not the mysteries of the balance of payments but merely the straightforward inadequacy of its economic agents. There was sharp disagreement about the importance of these 'supply constraints' – an issue to which we return in the next section.

On the question of the policy constraints imposed by the balance of payments, there was a widespread gloomy consensus, no doubt owing much to the public discussions mounted recently by the London Business School and the Cambridge Group arising from the high marginal income propensity to import. When Ball suggested, half humourously, that he preferred to be described as an international *Keynesian* than as an international *monetarist*, some of those present recalled the controversies of the 1930s, when similar questions, about the degree to which an increment in home demand would overspill into foreign trade, were used to argue against simple Keynesian remedies in one country.

Some discussion ensued about the relative political acceptability internationally of import controls and exchange rate manipulation as ways of escaping from these constraints, and of limiting the 'openness' of the economy; and it was pointed out that a government which simultaneously expended its home economy but limited the extent to which this action would suck in manufactured imports could hardly be accused of a net dose of beggar my neighbour tactics. (The same argument could be applied in favour of dirty floating designed to obtain an exchange rate advantage.)

If imports were restricted, how would this affect the domestic price level, and the distribution of real purchasing power between wage earners, the domestic company sector and foreign suppliers? This is a crucial question underlying part of the controversy between the devaluers and the import controllers. One group would wish to argue that any apparent gain in the terms of trade from having quantitative restrictions instead of a lower exchange rate will be dissipated, because a queue for imports means higher import prices, the contrast with the devaluation case being the secondary one as to whether the gain goes to one part of the company sector or another. The alternative point of view, which was argued vigorously at the conference, is that the determination of the prices of manufactures owes very little to the pressure of demand: this doctrine is, it was argued, one of the best empirically supported propositions in British descriptive economics. But as one opponent of this view pointed out, these empirical results refer precisely to a period in which there were no artificial shortages, and circumstances alter cases – a good example of the sort of tension between theories, statistics and models which characterises a lot of this controversy.

The other major element in the alleged contrast between the modus operandi of quantitative restrictions and devaluation refers to the extent to which it might be possible for the government to offset (for instance through lower personal taxes) the required fall in real wage costs per unit of output associated with the assumed worsening of the factoral terms of trade in the devaluation case. As reported in the previous section, it had been pointed out that if higher levels of activity could be afforded, the actual government deficit could be lower, consistently with any desired balance of payments even if tax rates were themselves smaller; and this would mean that real wage costs to the employer could fall, as theoretically required, while real wage incomes were maintained. An associated point is that productivity increases as the degree of capacity working itself increases, and this effect provides another way of separating the necessary paths of real wage costs and real wage incomes. It seems to me however that these forces apply irrespective of how the increase in activity and employment is brought about – whether by quantitative restrictions or devaluation; and therefore these mechanisms cannot be called in aid to help decide the controversy between the schools of thought on this question.

If indeed quantitative restrictions do succeed in maintaining the terms of trade at a better level than would be brought about by an exchange rate depreciation which had the same effect on employment, output and so on, then there is no doubt that the path of real wage incomes would be better in the quantitative restrictions case. But if this putative relative gain in the terms of trade could not be obtained or would not last, then there would not in general be any better performance of real wage incomes. There was a suggestion, later in the discussion, of a further degree of sophistication in this argument. It could be true that the level of profits in manufacturing industry would be necessarily higher in the devaluation case than in the quantitative restrictions case, and therefore the distribution of the real domestic product might need to be less favourable to real wage incomes. But this point was not explicitly discussed, and I mention it here only to warn the readers of the point, not to express editorial blessing of it.

Is the Economy Supply Constrained?

It is a commonplace of much economic commentary that the British economy, particularly its manufacturing sector, has difficulty in supplying goods even when 'statistical' unemployment and spare capacity are very high. One aspect of this complaint is the often described inability of manufacturers to produce the types of goods required to compete with foreign products – and indeed this is one of the facts which is generally thought to underlie the lack of enthusiasm with which exchange rate induced cost competitiveness is viewed by many observers. Nevertheless, the Cambridge Group were concerned explicitly to deny supply constraint as a continuing characteristic of an underemployed manufacturing sector, not just because it conflicted with their policy recommendations, but because it was directly contradicted by the evidence as they read it. This was another illustration of the relationship between empirical evidence, modelling and policy recommendations – quite contrary to the intentionally provocative remark in Goodhart's paper (page 188). The National Institute hold similar views, but did not choose to press them so hard. This was another good example of the contrast between the logical clarity pursued *jusque'au bout* by the Cambridge Group and the equally strong determination of the National Institute not to press points harder than their judgement thought appropriate.

Laidler, because of his theoretical inclination to give some attention to the notion of a natural rate of unemployment, was prepared to incorporate in his framework of thought and policy recommendations the notion that productive potential was more limited than the standard calculations suggest.

The London Business School concept of a supply constraint is not a physical one, such as that adduced by myself below. Instead of this crude practical notion, they advance a more subtle idea, based on economic relationships, suggesting that at the margin profits will not expand enough in the long run permanently to sustain high levels of employment caused by the initial expansion of demand.

Nobody was asserting that in 1977 the British economy in particular or the OECD as a whole was producing at capacity output. The question at issue was the likely division of an increase in aggregate demand in money terms between quantity increases and price increases and, more generally, the extent to which the overspill of increased home demand into imports suggest that policy should be directed more to the supply side than to the demand side. An implication of the London Business School view on this question was that the standard models might well misrepresent demand relationships, because the model specifications provided no way in which supply constraints might be captured, and therefore a mis-estimation of demand response coefficients would necessarily occur. Not only, as was widely recognised, could these demand type models not be used to answer questions about supply constraints (such as occurred by common agreement in the first few months of 1974), but even their estimates of demand responses might be mistaken.

The traditional Keynesian response to this sort of argument is that it is only by bearing up against supply constraints with increasing demand that proper incentives are given to economic agents to break these constraints. The Cambridge team, following this tradition, stressed that capital investment tends to be higher with higher pressure of demand – an empirical result; that profits were higher when the pressure of demand was higher; and that it was hard to find from the statistics any evidence of supply constraints, not only in the exceptional conditions of 1977, but also during some of the earlier periods. At this point the Cambridge Group reported one aspect of some calculations in which they had been engaged, simulating on their model some of the policies or results of the other teams. In particular, it seemed that the Cambridge Group had a higher trend of productive potential than the London Business School and the National Institute: for instance, on the Cambridge analysis National Institute policies, which that team had believed might produce unemployment of about one million in 1981, would lead to unemployment of about 1.9 million; and London Business School policies, which that team had believed would lead to unemployment of about 1.5 million in 1981, would lead to 2.3 million unemployed. Clearly there was at work not only a difference of view about how the economy might respond to variations in demand in the short run, but also differences of opinion about the trend of supply factors through time. These longer term questions were not further discussed at the conference, but will be the subject of later work.

Posner argued that any close inspection of any industry, either today or over the last two decades, would have shown many cases in which, in particular industrial plants, certain aspects of supply were constrained even though there was plenty of 'statistical' spare capacity or unused labour. But this sort of standardised fact was difficult to fit in with theoretical arguments.

Monetary and Fiscal Policy; is there an Endogenous Cycle in the British Economy?

In the last few years economists have expressed very diverse views on three associated questions. First, given that the industrial world is subject to cyclical influences, is there anything which the authorities ought to do to insulate the home economy from these influences? Secondly, quite apart from the world cycle, is there an endogenous British cycle against which policy should be set? And thirdly, given that it is agreed that *some* counter cyclical effort should be exercised by the authorities, what is the relevant weight to be given to fiscal and monetary instruments?

No one disputed the commonsense proposition that Britain's economic activity was positively correlated with deviations of world trade from its normal path. There was some disagreement with the London Business School view that the current account of the balance of payments was negatively correlated with world trade. This point was not much pursued, but doubtless arises from the different empirical results obtained by different teams to the question of the relative weight of the cyclical effect of higher commodity prices (bad for British import costs) and booming trade in industrial products (good for the volume of British exports). The London Business School and Cambridge seemed to share some agreement on the proposition that there was not much in the way of an endogenous British cycle to offset, but they differed on their policy recommendations to deal with the world cycle: the London Business School, to the surprise of some speakers, would wish the British authorities to offset the world cycle in so far as this was possible; the Cambridge team, except in so far as import controls were in place, believed that this was not possible. The National Institute found some evidence of an endogenous cycle, and were in general somewhat more activist in their approach than the other teams.

On the question of the choice of policy weapons, Laidler reported that it was common ground among all the first-round authors that there were identifiable effects of fiscal policy on British economic activity, but that the multipliers were rather small (and the remarks on this subject in Artis's paper were not disputed). He also agreed that the long-run crowding out effects in his model were imposed and therefore the fiscal effects which he discovered were all transitory. At a later stage of discussion there was some argument about the effects of interest rate charges on investment, and although Laidler suggested that the difficulty of finding such an effect might be due to aggregation problems, there was no dissent from Dicks-Mireaux's general proposition that it proved impossible to find interest rate effects in practice. Laidler reminded us of some theoretical propositions about long-run crowding out, and how difficult it was to fit in strong fiscal effects with propositions that all economic agents concentrated on permanent rather than transient incomes. But the general results that he had reported in his paper passed unchallenged.

On monetary policy, Goodhart reminded us of the importance of distinguishing the cases of flexible and fixed exchange rates, and the conference noted Miller's generalisation of Laidler's results – an essay which showed Laidler was really very fiscalist in his approach, his difference with some of the other first-round authors being purely on the matter of the efficacy of monetary policy.

There was only one extended discussion of monetarist hypotheses as such – about the transmission mechanism as it worked in the second historical episode. This is reported in its proper place below. Several participants spoke in monetarist language, and there were extended discussions in which terms like the 'rate of growth of the money stock' were used in ways in which Keynesians would wish to translate as 'rate of growth of effective demand in money terms'. It was left to the Cambridge Group alone to dissociate themselves from this type of language, but several participants felt that it was perhaps not necessary to make so sharp an issue of what was in many ways merely a matter of taste in the use of language.

The Historical Episodes

Episode 1: 1964–9

All four first-round authors agreed that the initial fiscal stance was too loose, and this view was not seriously disputed by any of the discussants (although it was emphasised that the political realities associated with the election, on a hair line majority, at the top of the boom, of a government committed to expansion made fiscal restrictions difficult to justify). The sticky performance of some of the main indicators in the first part of 1964 was emphasised, despite the relatively comforting conformity between the 'foresight' and 'hindsight' charts in Boreham's paper (page 143). Godley suggested that the unemployment figures should have provided sufficient indication of over-heating, and Surrey emphasised that policy should have been based on forecasts rather than the recent past; but others felt the signs had been hard to read and attention to any one series was undesirable.

Considerable attention was given to the question of whether the 1967 devaluation was a failure and to the associated question of whether an earlier devaluation would have been a very much better thing. The conference did not find it easy to accept the stereotype criticism of the 1964–9 record reported on page 129. Goodhart and Godley both suggested that what had gone wrong in 1968–9 was wages, not primarily monetary policy, with the failure to hold the public sector wage front in the last year or two of the period leading to the excessively rapid erosion of the competitive advantage achieved in 1967. Some speakers repeated the conventional argument that whereas a small movement in the exchange rate would have been sufficient in 1964 or 1965, by 1967 it had become necessary to overshoot on the exchange rate in order to restore international financial confidence, and to overshoot on fiscal policy at home in order to ensure that the turn around on the balance of payments was sufficiently large and rapid. A smaller movement in 1964 would have avoided some of these difficulties. But the projections in the first-round papers do not show so markedly superior results with an earlier exchange rate movement as to support fully this diagnosis, unless benefit is taken for avoiding the built up of wage pressure at the beginning of the next episode.

The London Business School defended their policy for this period. They pointed out that the results which they predicted were far from miraculous, and defended their policies on the twin grounds that they did not require the politically troublesome exchange rate movement, and that they left the economy in a state of better health than the historical record provides. They also offered their interpretation of monetary events in 1969, emphasising the way in which a slack monetary policy – in particular a failure to allow interest rates to rise so as to finance a sufficient portion of the government's cash needs in the gilt-edged market – had encouraged both excessive price movements and excesses in real spending at home. The failure of the balance of payments to come round more rapidly or more fully was associated with these monetary excesses in a way rather familiar (to some round the table) from the comments of scholars in the IMF research department at the time. Shonfield emphasised the importance of the background of world trade against which these events were played, and the attitude of the international financial community to exchange rate movements in 1964 and 1967.

Episode 2: 1970–5

Discussion of this episode followed roughly along the lines of pp. 132–5 above. The first question was what went wrong with the fiscal stance in 1970 itself. Some contemporary commentators had seen that the fashionable doctrine of the winter of 1969–70 – that the budget was tuned about right, and should not be arbitrarily interfered with for electoral reasons – was critically wrong, by amounts up to two per cent of GDP. It was a fine example of the errors into which a prejudice against fine tuning can lead an excessively wary government. Those forecasting teams who had made better judgements at the time (particularly the National Institute) were the first to stress that any group of forecasters, official or private, must take into account the strong probability that it will get things badly wrong every now and then. What seems to have happened in 1970 is that by the time the official forecasters had cottoned on to what was happening there was a change of government, and fiscal sternness, increasingly reinforced by a predilection for a Phillips curve approach to wages, had become the ruling philosophy. This is a good example of a systematic intermixing of minor technical errors in assessing the path of the pressure of demand and changes in the strategy, or choice of intermediate targets, for economic policy generally.

A similar switch of intermediate policy targets seems to have occurred in 1971–2, as unemployment replaced inflation as the chief cause of worry in policy makers minds. The 1972 budget, on the tax side, might have been tolerable on its own, but its accompaniment of permissiveness on public expenditure led in practice to a doubling of that fiscal stimulus which would have been judged appropriate by most observers at the time. It was this underlying increase in public expenditure that left the fiscal stance in the summer of 1973, before the oil price increase, markedly too expansionary. This too was not properly recognised at the time by all observers, although the Cambridge Group saw it clearly. Ironically enough, what the National Institute and the Cambridge Group with the benefit of hindsight, would now regard as the 'optimal strategy' for the winter of 1973–4 would have been to leave things as they were: a fiscal policy that was excessively expansionary before the oil price increase caused a contraction in home and overseas demand became roughly appropriate once the oil price increase had happened.

The device of Competition and Credit Control, probably appropriate for the narrow interests of the clearing banks, had not made things any easier for the control of demand in the summer of 1973. Some speakers thought that the blame must lie on the government for failing to understand that, in agreeing to the new devices of monetary policy, it had implicitly agreed that interest rates might have to rise sharply. Other speakers thought that the rise in interest rates which had been permitted had not been unreasonably small, and that the responsibility lay on the shoulders of those who had failed to understand that in unleashing the clearing banks they had also unleashed a whole string of secondary and tertiary banks and permitted the debacle of City speculative activity just at the time when it was least opportune.

The Cambridge Group which had been prominent amongst those drawing attention at the time to the excessively expansionary practices of 1972–3 argued that it should have been possible, by putting together indicators of tax and public expenditure movements, to see that both the level and the rate of increase in demand for output was too high during 1972–3. The OECD world as a whole was moving at this time into the simultaneous boom, unique in post-war experience, that led inevitably to the sharp increase in commodity prices and domestic inflationary pressure in many industrial countries. It might well have been better for Britain to have chosen to restrain home demand in 1972–3, either through a more restrictive fiscal policy (Cambridge) or through a more restrictive monetary policy, which would have held back the depreciation of sterling, limited the expansion of British exports, and held back the domestic price increase (London Business School). (Readers will note that although these two approaches are put in different languages and seem to rely on different economic relationships, they are not grossly dissimilar: for instance, a restrictive fiscal policy would have allowed a more restrictive monetary policy without more upwards pressure on interest rates, and hence have led down the London Business School route.)

But all countries cannot simultaneously go against the international fashion – otherwise the international fashion itself changes. Williamson concluded from this simple point of logic that the Cambridge Group's recommendation for caution in 1972–3 could not be part of a general law about economic policy. Others quite happily agreed with this point, but drew quite opposite conclusions: there was no need whatsoever, they implied, for our policy recommendations to the British authorities to be part of a general recommendation to OECD as a whole.

Discussion developed on the different ways of measuring and arguing about the 'capacity ceiling' in 1972–3. Goodhart thought that the relationship between unemployment, vacancies and capacity utilisation had changed early in the 1970s, and it might have been better if the implied policy targets to which Ministers were adhering had been reassessed at this time. The argument here referred back to an earlier point of Livesey's, who had suggested that making policy targets explicit and debating them publicly, would be one way of improving the conduct of economic policy. Several speakers emphasised that what might have been going wrong at that time was the speed of approach to the ceiling not the level of capacity utilisation to which the authorities were aiming. Cripps suggested that in the 1971 recession there had been a greater than usual degree of dishoarding of labour, which meant that 'statistical' unemployment was higher, relative to the degree of capacity utilisation, than in the past. When the increase in demand eventually took place, the typical firm was short of labour and therefore could not respond as quickly as had been possible in earlier periods, and this phenomenon in the labour market was associated with speculative stock building for intermediate goods. The rapid fall in unemployment in 1973 was the natural lagged response to the labour shortages experienced by many firms in 1972, and it should have been possible at that time to have taken restrictive policy in the early part of 1973: and it was recalled that this had been the actual approach of the Cambridge Group at the time.

There was an argument about the transmission mechanism of monetary policy at this point. Those of a monetarist persuasion were reasonably clear that they had identified the transmission mechanism by which, in this period, increases in the money supply had led to increases in prices. In simple terms, under a system of floating rates, an increase in the money supply led to a fall in the exchange rate, which led in turn to a rise in import prices, which led to an increase in both wage demands and 'market clearing' levels of money wages, which led in turn to an increase in manufacturers costs. The key part played by the fall in the exchange rate in this story induced in some other speakers familiar doubts. Was it really plausible to suggest that monetary changes were more productive of price increases in a floating rate regime than in a regime with fixed rates? Presumably, under fixed rates, the authorities had large stocks of financial assets (exchange reserves) with which they could satisfy excess demand for resources at home; and provided speculators had much smaller stocks of relevant financial assets (so that they could not protect themselves by speculation against official action) this official use of stocks could stave off price rises. Such a combination of conditions under fixed exchange rates had been described in Hicks' analysis of 'fixprice' markets in an open economy.

But if changes in the money stock had little effect on prices when exchange rates were pegged, or at least a very delayed effect on prices, did it follow that there could be larger increases in the volume of output, provided there was spare capacity at the beginning of the story? If this were so, then it seemed, at least to some participants of only moderately anti-monetarist views, as if the monetarists had yielded too much: a transmission mechanism which works only under floating rates is not the construct of general equilibrium theory which they had been led to expect. At least one of those present reflected that he understood at this point the deep significance of the London Business School suggestion that they were international *Keynesians* rather than international monetarists: because in a world system floating rates could not explain simultaneous inflation in all countries, and therefore changes in the world money supply could not be allocated the causal role which some commentators had claimed.

Burns implicitly corrected this line of reasoning by stressing the well known proposition that inflation had been spread through the OECD world in 1972–3, perhaps with the help of flexible exchange rates (because countries which would in earlier cycles have put on the domestic brakes fairly early in the interests of protecting their exchange reserves, in this boom had been tempted to escape the consequences of their actions by letting the exchange rate go) but mainly because raw material prices were forced up by high growth of monetary demand.

Two final sceptical remarks by monetary experts were received in respectful silence. Goodhart pointed out that the concept of the money supply was seldom clear enough for policy purposes, and reminded us that, for instance, in 1972 there had been no significant correlation at all between movements in M1 and M3 on a quarterly bases. Which horse should be watched by an enthusiastic punter? And Laidler thought that the excessive popular attention paid to month by month movements in monetary indicators was absurd on the grounds that only broad year by year movements were of real importance.

The conference then turned from an interpretation of history, to a discussion of policies. Attention was paid particularly, following a useful intervention by Cripps, to the analysis of 1974–5 and of the contractionary shock given, simultaneously with the boost to traded prices, by the OPEC price increase. Would it have been possible, the modellers had asked themselves, so to tailor policy as to avoid both these consequences? In the National Institute simulation, a moderately expansionary fiscal policy together with a firm incomes policy would have avoided the worst of the recession and the run away in wages, although no doubt it might have been very hard to achieve a revision of the threshold agreement. The London Business School seemed to proceed by getting the rate of price increases down to a very low level by the end of 1973, and hence to recommend policies which would have led to an appreciation of the exchange rate in 1974–5, thus preventing the increase in world prices from penetrating the British market. This appreciation of sterling had been recommended at the time, it was recalled, by one or two voices in the wilderness, who had been criticised for proposing the impossible. In their present simulation the London Business School had avoided this accusation, because their policy for the earlier part of episode 2 had got the economy into a position by 1973–4 where domestic wage and prices increases were already very low. To follow German policies while starting from the inflationary base in which history had actually placed us in 1974 might have been rather difficult. To follow the same policies after a preparatory period of low monetary growth might have been far easier; but the conference were reminded that the cost of these London Business School prescriptions was a performance of output during episode 2 that was poor relatively to the results claimed by the other teams, though still better than the historical record.

The Cambridge team, to get their policy prescription to work, had to have an increase in output. They had started from a recognition that in practice the loss of GDP in 1974–5 had been greater than the loss on the terms of trade alone, because this fall in real disposable national income at full employment had been compounded by a large fall in activity. Therefore the key to their policy recommendations was action which would make it possible to increase output without infringing the balance of payments constraint, and hence to avoid some of the inflationary penalties by protecting the path of real wage incomes per head.

Surrey pointed out that it would be wrong to exaggerate the weight carried by incomes policies in the National Institute simulations. Their cut of 2½ per cent in indirect taxation restrained the first-round increase in prices (thus avoiding some of the triggers under the threshold agreement) and also provided the required expansionary pull on the economy. They would have run a rather larger deficit on the balance of payments, because, as shown by the historical record, there was no shortage of capital account finance for the United Kingdom during 1974–5. The role of incomes policy was to be seen as building a protection against the fears of both the domestic financial markets and the international financial community that these sensible measures would lead to an acceleration in wage inflation. But the Institute were not merely saying that it would have been nice to have had more incomes policy, but were showing how a relatively small and adjusted dose of that policy, if introduced in a timely fashion, would have done arguably more good than all the subsequent effort of 1975–6.

Episode 3: 1977–81

This session started with Laidler asserting, without dispute from others, that the characteristic of this period that made it peculiarly difficult was the fact that we were not endowed with certain knowledge of the future: indeed this episode was the only one which reproduced at all generally the normal uncertainties and fears of those who advised on policy measures. None of the modellers were prepared to predict any easy return to full employment, and indeed by the standards of the past most of them, even if their chosen policies were to be followed, predict the continuation of high unemployment into the future. Turvey explained the arguments of those who blamed the deficiency of investment demand on high real wages, to which it was retorted that this must be erroneous in a closed economy; and in an open economy, the question of whether it was possible to use the exchange rate to maintain higher demand was once again central. Williamson led the argument into the difficult terrain of discussion of the time-lags involved. Even supposing that the London Business School and Laidler were right about the long-run asymptotic qualities of the system, how did they know that it would take four years for the effect of slow monetary growth to feed through into wage fixing in all the many parts of the labour market? And if it did take only four years, where was it written down on tablets of stone that we should abstain from any amelioratory action for four whole years?

Laidler here suggested, and the point appeared also in discussion of episode 2, that the speed of reaction of prices in a system of floating exchanges was too great for it to be sensible to engage in expansionary policy while the process of adjustment had not been fully worked out. On this point, Burns was cautious, more prepared to compromise on a slightly faster increase in the money supply and a slightly lower exchange rate. Oppenheimer rebelled at the notion that monetary changes operated only through international mechanisms, drawing attention to the markets for physical assets in Britain in the period covered by episode 2.

There was considerable discussion of the likely performance of exports, measured in terms of Britain's share of world exports; and of the likely performance of imports (in terms of Britain's marginal propensity to import at any given exchange rate in the absence of quantitative restrictions). There seemed more than usual disagreement between forecasters on this question, but the difference did not seem unduly correlated with difference in theoretical perceptions.

The overwhelming impression created by this leg of the discussion was of preoccupation of all the modellers with the problem of embedded inflationary expectations and what needed to be done to remove or modify them; and of the extent to which this preoccupation necessarily limited the attention that could be paid to the other targets of policy. The Chairman put this point, half jocularly, by suggesting that in face of this dilemma each team 'cheated' at a different place in the story. The Cambridge Group introduced import controls, to get increases in output at less cost to the terms of trade than with exchange rate depreciation. The National Institute cheated by introducing a successful incomes policy. The London Business School cheated by having wage earners who watched the index of changes in M3 and adjusted their wage demands accordingly. And Laidler cheated by assuming, in some of his arguments at least, that we lived in an asymptotic world. This complaint was received in good part by the participants, but perhaps they did too little to answer it.

Lessons from the Three Episodes

Artis was asked by the Chairman to sum up. He stressed the continuing uncertainty about model specification and econometric estimation, and indeed about the underlying economic structure that was being analysed. There were elements of convergence, but he feared that some of these were spurious, in the sense that they were not 'bolted down' to common agreement on behaviour equations or relationships. Examples were consumer expenditure equations and wage equations – specifications offered in the first-round papers spanned the whole gamut of doctrines advanced by economists over the last three decades. There was, more gratifyingly, a general inclination to search (more pejoratively, to 'mine') the data to find some effect of monetary upon real variables, and although there continued to be difficulties in arriving at estimates these were not too strongly correlated with philosophical standpoints.

The policy recommendations for the historical periods were notably different from stereotype in two respects. First, it was now not *so* clear as some of us had thought that the 1967 devaluation would have been far better if it had come earlier. And while Competition and Credit Control may have been unfortunately timed, it had not been shown to be a prime villain of the piece.

All first-round authors seemed to agree that a measure of fiscal relaxation was appropriate 'now' – December 1977 – and this at least provided an element of common ground.

List of Participants

ECONOMIC POLICY CONFERENCES
CONFERENCE ON DEMAND MANAGEMENT

Birkbeck College, 19 and 20 December 1977

Professor M. J. Artis
F. J. Atkinson
Professor R. J. Ball
Sir Kenneth Berrill
F. T. Blackaby
A. J. Boreham
T. Burns
Sir Alec Cairncross
J. Callaghan
T. F. Cripps
L. Dicks-Mireaux
M. J. Fetherston
J. S. Flemming
Hon W. A. H. Godley
C. A. E. Goodhart
Professor D. Laidler
J. S. E. Laury
D. Livesey
R. C. O. Matthews (*Chairman*)
Professor M. Miller
Sir Donald MacDougall
Professor R. R. Neild
P. Oppenheimer
P. A. Ormerod
Professor M. H. Peston
M. V. Posner
D. Robinson
T. M. Rybczynski
D. Savage
A. Shonfield
G. Smith
D. K. Stout
M. J. C. Surrey
Mrs W. Thompson
R. Turvey
Professor J. Williamson
G. D. N. Worswick

Index

The letter 'E' indicates the episode involved where appropriate, E1 being 1964–69, E2 1970–75 and E3 1977–81 (projected).

The abbreviations CEPG (Cambridge Economic Policy Group), LBS (London Business School) and NIESR (National Institute of Economic and Social Research) have been used.

Artis, M. J., 167–79, 226, 234
Artis and Lewis (1976), 52, 176

Balance of payments:
 and inflation target rate, (E3) 85
 and Public Sector Deficit, 68
 CEPG views on, 10
 function of, in UK model (1954–70), 44–51
 in 1964, 9, 10
 models contrasted about, 200–208
 Monetarists' prescription for, (E1) 52–5, (E2) 55–9, (E3) 60–63
 monetarist views of, 42–4
 monetary policy and, 184
 1964 deficit, 105–7
 1975 deterioration in, 116
 1981 projection for, 118–19
 search for common ground on constraints in, 220–23
 statistician's view of, (E1) 142, (E2) 147
 surplus anticipated, (E3) 96
 Williamson on, 200–208
 competitiveness level, 204–8
 constraint, 200–203
 devaluation or import controls, 204
Ball, R. J., 68, 221
Ball and Burns, 36, 52, 66–100
Ball, Burns and Laury (1976), 67, 201, 203
Banking sector in NIESR model, 103–4
Bargaining, Free Collective, 68
Barker, T. S. (1976), 173
Beckerman, W., 105, 129
Blackaby, F., 66, 213
Blinder and Solow (1973), 179
Bond Coupon Effect (Blinder and Solow), 178–9
Boreham, A. J., 139–50, 227
Bretton Woods, 3, 52, 53, 55, 216
 see also Keynesianism
Budd and Burns (1977), 70
Burns, T., 216, 231, 234
 see also Ball and Burns
Burns and Warburton (1976), 87
Burton, J. (1977), 196

CAP, UK acceptance of, 16
Capacity utilization in NIESR model, 102
Cash balances, getting rid of excess, 39
CEPG model and policies:
 alternative strategies, (E3) 13–14
 balance of payments aspects, 200–208
 compared with others, 151–66
 conventional policies (E3) views on, 14
 devaluation effects, (E3) 14
 devaluation or import controls, 204
 export competitiveness, 204–8
 in agreement with LBS on exchange rates, 130
 in counter-inflationary policies, 191–9
 in monetary policy, 180–90
 Keynesian influence on, 155–6
 review of past policies, 15–18
 simulations, 9–34, 131:
  fiscal policy in past, 16
  incomes policy, 18
  monetary policy in past, 17
  policy assessments of 3 episodes, 9–15
  policy simulations, 15–34
  political constraints, 16
  residuals, treatment of, 15
  time periods, specification of, 15–16
  (*see also* Common ground, search for)
Certificate of Deposit Rate, 175, 187
CES production functions, 103

Collective agreements, 194–5
Collective bargaining, 68
Commodities, price rise in (1973), 111, 114–15, 116–17
Common Ground, search for, 4–5, 211–35:
  economic issues, 213–26:
    balance of payments constraints, 220–23
    Endogenous cycle element, 225–6
    exchange rate, 214–20
    fiscal policy, 225–6
    monetary policy, 225–6
    prices, 214–20
    supply constraint problem, 223–5
    wages, 214–20
  episodes, the three compared, 226–35:
    (E1) 226–8, (E2) 228–33, (E3) 233–4
Competition and Credit Control (Bank of England's) (1971), 13, 28, 92–4, 112, 133, 229, 235
Competitiveness in exports, 204–8
Conservative government, (E2) 11–13, 111, 132
Consol Rate, 175–7
Consumer expenditure:
  in NIESR model, 102
  (1975–78), 69, 72, 80, 82, 84, 96
  statistician's view of, (E2) 145–6
Consumption function, model comparison of, 152–3
Corporation Tax, introduction of (1966), 108
Cost push impulses (1970), 56
Costs, statistician's view of, (E1) 142, (E2) 146
Counter-inflationary policies, 191–9
  collective agreements, 194–5
  implications, 196–9
  Social Justice and relativities, 195–6
  wage-price spiral, 191–4
Cripps, T. F., 9–34, 230, 232
Cripps *et al.* (1976), 174
Cross and Laidler (1976), 46
Crowding out, 174–9

Deflation, reducing imports by, (E2) 116
Demand for money function, 45–51
De-policisation, 2
Devaluation:
  1949, 217
  1965, (E1) 18–21
  and trade performance, (E1) 10–11
  and wages, (E2) 12
  effective date was really 1965, 105
  failure to make in 1964, 53–4
  (1967) in demand management, 104
  or import controls, which?, 204
  (1967), search for common ground on, 227
Dicks-Mireaux, L., 226
Domestic Credit Expansion (DCE), 40–44, 48, 52–4, 60, 84, 89, 96, 98–9, 188–90

Econometric models compared, 151–66:
  limitations, 154–5
  money, 162–4
  size, 151–4:
    consumption, 152–3
    employment, 153–4
    exports, 153
    prices, 153, 159–61
  study's conclusions, 165–6
  theory involved, 155–9
  wages, 161–2
Economic assessment, statistician's, (E1) 140–44, (E2) 145–7
Economic policy, CEPG's annual assessments of, 9–15
Economy:
  is it supply constrained?, 223–5
  monetarists' analysis of open, 37–44
Employment, *see* Unemployment
Endogenous Cycle element, is there common ground on?, 225–6
Episodes, definition of the three, 1
E1:
  CEPG policy assessments, 10–11
    policy simulations, 18–25
  LBS, 75–9, 89–91
  main issues of demand management model, 129–32
  monetarist viewpoint, 52–5
  NIESR simulations, 104–10
  search for common ground, 226–8
  statistician's view, *see* Statistician
E2:
  CEPG policy assessments, 11–13
    policy simulations, 25–30
  LBS, 79–81, 91–4
  main issues of demand management, 129–32
  monetarist viewpoint, 55–9
  NIESR simulations, 111–18
  search for common ground, 228–33
  statistician's view, *see* Statistician
E3:
  CEPG policy assessments, 13–15
    policy simulations, 30–34

E3:—*continued*
LBS, 81–4, 94–6
main issues of demand management model, 135–8
monetarist viewpoint, 60–63
NIESR simulations, 118–24
search for common ground, 234–5
Eurodollar Interest Rates, 17
Exchange Rate:
and export competitiveness, (E1) 18
and price stability, (E2) 55–9
CEPG and LBS in agreement over, 130
competitiveness and changes in, (E2) 25
crowding out and, 175
economy when fixed, 38, 40, 42
effect of floating, (E2) 12
fixed and stabilization policy, 68, 85–9, 96
flexible, 38–41
floating conditions and stabilization policy, 70–3
seen as a main issue, 132
future policy over, (E3) 118
in NIESR model, 103
monetary policy and, 184
policy, Posner on, (E2) 134–5, (E3) 136
search for common ground over, 214–20
Expenditure function in UK model (1954–70), 45–51
Export competitiveness, 204–8
Exports:
function, model comparison of, 153
in NIESR model, 102
prices and continuous depreciation, 71
External Capital Inflows, (E1) 25

Fetherston, M. J., 9–34
Fiscal policy:
adjustments to variable in, (E1), 20–21, (E2) 27
Artis on, 167–79:
assignment role, 173–4
crowding out, 174–9
effectiveness, 173
stance in policy simulations, 167–72
CEPG's review of past, 15–17
monetarists' view of, 40–44
NIESR on, 110, 115, 123
Posner on, (E2) 131, 133
search for common ground over, 225–6
Fixed investment in NIESR model, 102
'Fixprice' markets, 231
Flemming, J. S., 218
Full employment, *see* Unemployment

Godley, W. A. H., 9–34, 227
Goodhart, C. A. E., 180–90, 213, 214, 223, 226, 227, 230, 231
Gradualist principle, 37

Henry, Sawyer and Smith (1976), 202
Hindsight discussed, 3

IMF:
and causes for recession, (E3), 13–14
Letter of Intent, 14
on fine tuning debate, 98–9
Import growth, 1978 projected, 96
Imports:
in NIESR model, 102
reduction of, by deflation, (E2) 116
restrictions:
and stabilization policy, 75, 85
for, (E3) 14
LBS and, 181–2
or devaluation, which?, 204
Incomes policy:
adjustments to variables, (E1), 20–21, (E2) 27
a main issue, 131
CEPG's review of past, 18
Conservative (1970), 3, (E1) 10–11
in stabilization policy, 75, 86
LBS, 86
NIESR on, 111, 115–20, 124–5
Posner on, (E2) 132–3, (E3) 135–8 (*see also* under Wages)
Indirect taxation, 79, 115 (*see also* Taxation)
Industrial Relations Bill (1971), 3
Inflation:
and incomes policy, (E1) 10–11
and stabilization policy, 68–70, 84–5
and wages spiral, (E2) 12
determined by world conditions, 68
determining the policy of anti-, (E3) 118
expectations (UK model 1954–70), 45–51
expected reduction of, 96
monetarists' prescription for, (E1) 52–5, (E2) 55–9, (E3) 60–63
monetarists' view of, 39–40
Posner on, (E3) 136
search for common ground over, 214

Inflation:—*continued*
statistician's view of, (E1) 140, (E2) 145
taxation, 168–9
trade-off with unemployment, 201–2
see also Counter-inflationary policies; Inflation Rate
Interest rate:
CEPG's simulations on past, 17
LBS on, 72–3, 78, 81
International trade, 1964 effects of, 129–30
Inventory cycle, (E3) 85
Investment, fixed in NIESR model, 102
IS schedules, 176–7

J-curve, 184–5
Jonson (1976), 48, 183
Jonson, Moses and Wymer (1976), 36

Keynesianism:
Peston on, 155–9
Posner on, 212, 220, 224

Labour Parliamentary Majority (1964), effect of small, 105
Laidler, David, 35–63, 135, 137 (*see also* Laidler model)
Laidler model:
and counter-inflation policies, 191–9
balance of payments aspects, 200–208
compared with the others, 151–66
export competitiveness, 204–8
in monetary policy context, 180–90
UK 1954–70, details of, 44–51 (*see also* Common ground, search for)
LBS model and stabilization policy:
(general references), 36, 66–9
balance of payments, 200–208
compared with the others, 151–66
exchange rate, (E2) 135
agreement over, with CEPG, 130
export competitiveness, 204–8
in counter-inflationary policies, 191–9
in monetary policy context, 180–90
recommended policies, 84–96
simulation analysis 67–73 (*see also* Common ground, search for)
Livesey, D., 230
Lucas, R. E. (1976), 176

MacDougall, Sir Donald, 217
McKinnon, R. I. (1969), 87
Matthews, Robin C. O., 211, 219, 220, 234
Mayer, Thomas (1977), 37
Miller, M., 226
Miller and Temple (1977), 168
MLR:
crowding out, 177–8
demand management, 112
monetary policy, 189
stabilization policy, 75–6
Models:
assessment of builders of, *see*:
Artis on, *under* Fiscal policy; Counter-inflationary policies; Econometric models compared; Goodhart *under* Monetary policy; Statistician's view; Williamson *under* Balance of payments
balance of payments element contrasted in, 200–208
comparison of, *see* Econometric models compared
export competitiveness element in, 204–8
monetary policy element in, 180–90
productive potential of, 9
Reserve Bank of Australia RBA 76, 36, 183
review of, and counter-inflationary policies, 191–9
Scandinavian, of Price Formation, 67–8
Trade Performance, 9
see also CEPG; Laidler; LBS; NIESR
Monetarist viewpoint, 35–63:
monetarism a macroeconomic doctrine, 35–7
open economy analysis, 37–44
policy problems, (E1) 51–5, (E2) 55–9, (E3) 60–3
UK model 1954–70, 44–51
(*see also* Laidler, David; Laidler Model)
Monetary expansion, simulations rate of, (E1) 55, (E2) 55
Monetary policy:
adjustments to variables in, (E1) 20–21, (E2) 27
CEPG's review of past, 17–18
Goodhart on, 180–90:
external effects, 183–5
model structure and role of money, 180–82
monetary operations, 188–90
policy proposals, 185–8
transmission mechanism, 182–3
Posner on, (E2) 132, (E3) 135
search for common ground over, 225–6

Money:
effects of excess, 39
function of, and model comparison, 162–4
role of, and model structure, 180–82
supply of, and demand for, discussed, 37–8
wages, monetarists' view of, 41
Mortgage market in Stabilization policy, 69–70

National Plan (1965), 105, 129
New Earnings Survey, 194–5
Nield, R. R., 220, 222, 230
NIESR model and demand management policy:
balance of payments, 200–208
compared with others, 151–6
conventional nature of, 101, (E1) 104–10, (E2) 111–18, (E3) 118–24
counter-inflationary policies aspects, 191–9
export competitiveness, 204–8
fiscal policy changes, summary of, (E1) 110, (E2) 115, (E3) 123
incomes policy, 131
monetary policy aspect, 180–90
NIESR model, 102–4
policy simulations:
balance of payments (E1) 108, (E2) 113, (E3) 120
GDP at factor cost, (E1) 106, (E2) 112, (E3) 121
gross fixed investment, (E1) 107, (E2) 113, (E3) 122
net acquisition of financial assets, (E1) 108, (E2) 114, (E3) 122
other indicators, (E1) 109, (E2) 115, (E3) 123
the study's conclusions, 124–5
three major objectives of, 123
Neutral policies:
incomes, 18
monetary, 16–17, 24
trade, 18
North Sea oil:
how to be used in demand management, (E3) 118
monetarist view of, (E3) 60–63
not capable of generating abnormal growth, 96
Posner on, (E3) 135–6
search for common ground about, 215–16
used up with debt repayment?, 119

OECD countries:
boom in (1973 – E2), 132, 229, 231
capacity output lacking in, 224
Oil price rise (1973), *see* OPEC
OPEC price rise (1973):
monetarist view, 60–61
NIESR on, 111, 116–17
Posner on, 3, 132
search for common ground, 232
Oppenheimer, P., 234
Ormerod, P. A., 101–25

Pay Board, (E2) 132
Peston, M. H., 151–66, 213, 214, 219
Phillips curve:
balance of payments, 202–3
common ground discussion, 217, 218, 228
demand management, 103
issues of demand management models, 137
monetarist viewpoint, 39, 57, 62
monetary policy, 181
stabilization policy, 67–8
'Political practicality' discussed, 3
Political restraints, review of past, 16
Posner, M. V., 1–5, 129–38, 211–35
Price, R. W. R. (forthcoming), 170
Price formation function in UK 1954–70 model, 44–51
Price rise in oil, *see* OPEC
Prices and Incomes Board, (E2) 132
Prices, search for common ground on, 214–20
Prices function, comparison of models on, 153, 159–61
Prices-wages spiral, 191–4
Public expenditure, possible changes required in, (E3) 94–6
Public Sector Borrowing Requirement:
fiscal effect on, 40–41
in demand management, 116–17
Posner on, 137

Reflation policy, 111, 118–21, 124
Renton, G. A., 67, 71
Reserves:
low level of (1964), 105
simulation of level of, (E1) 55, (E2) 59

Sargan, J. D. (1964), 202–3
Savings ratio, 68–9, 85–6, 123
School-leavers, 142, 147

Selective Employment Tax, 28, 91, 108
Shonfield, A., 228
Simulations:
  analysis of, 67–73
  and crowding out, 177–9
  CEPG's model, *see under* CEPG
  counter-factual (1969), 54, 57–9
  fiscal policy in demand management, 167–72
  inflation rate, (E1) 55, (E2) 59
  NIESR, *see under* NIESR model
Smithsonian Agreement (Dec. 1971), 12, 132
Social justice, 195–6
  study's conclusion on, 97–100
Statistician's view (Boreham), 139–50
Sterling, undervaluation of, (E1) 52
Stockbuilding, effects of company, 69, 72, 98
Stop–go policy, monetarist view of, 42–4, 60
Surrey, M. J. C., 101–25, 227, 233

Taxation:
  and stabilization policy, 72–9, 82, 91–2, 96
  earnings rate post, (E1) 23–4
  past policies, 17
  proposed cuts in personal, 119
  proposed indexing of personal (from 1979), 118
  used to control inflation, 168–9
  see also Indirect taxation: Selective Employment Tax
Threshold (wage) agreements, (E2) 115, 132, 133–4
Time-lags when policy changed, 130
Tobin and Buiter (1976), 178
Trade performance and devaluation, (E1) 10
Trade-off, unemployment and inflation, 201–2
Trade policy:
  adjustments to variables in, (E1) 20–21, (E2) 27
  CEPG's review of past, 18
Turvey, Ralph, 191–9, 213, 214, 233

Uncertainty, discussion on problem of, 4
Unemployment and employment:
  Full Employment:
    and balance of payments theory, 203
    and fiscal policy, 167–71
    balances, table of, (E1) 23, (E2) 30
  People in employment:
    function, comparison of, in the models, 153–4
    in NIESR model, 102–3
  Unemployment:
    and demand management, 107–9, 121–2
    and stabilization policy, (E3) 82
    natural rate of, 38, 41, 56, 68
    1977 macro-policy instruments on, 61–2
    1981 projection for, 121, 122
    problem, (E1) 11, (E2) 13
    simulations of percentage of, (E1) 55, (E2) 59
    statistician's view of, (E1) 141, (E2) 145
    trade-off with inflation, 201–2
    two million by 1981?, 14

Wage-price spiral, 191–4
Wage rates in NIESR model, 103
Wages:
  function, comparison of, for the four models, 161–2
  index-linking of, 117
  policy discussed, 196–9
  search for common ground over, 214–20
Williamson, John, 200–208, 214, 230, 233
Wymer, Dr Clifford, 49